Billy and Olive Dixon
The Plainsman and His Lady

By
Bill O'Neal

EAKIN PRESS ✪ Fort Worth, Texas
www.EakinPress.com

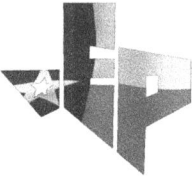

Copyright © 2019
By Bill O'Neal
Published By Eakin Press
An Imprint of Wild Horse Media Group
P.O. Box 331779
Fort Worth, Texas 76163
1-817-344-7036
www.EakinPress.com
ALL RIGHTS RESERVED
1 2 3 4 5 6 7 8 9
ISBN-10: 1-68179-145-5
ISBN-13: 978-1-68179-145-6

Dedication

Dedicated to three members of the Panola College M.P. Baker Library Staff who have helped me immensely with my book projects — always efficiently and with good cheer.

Cristie Ferguson, Director of Library Services who arranged my exotic interlibrary loan requests for years and who graciously has made time on the library schedule for public events featuring programs and signings of my books.

Sherri Baker, Reference Librarian who has embraced my projects with the soul of a sleuth. No interlibrary loan request has been too obscure to elude her, and for this project she conducted an exhaustive on-line search which produced information I never expected to acquire.

Shay Joines, newest member of the library staff and a technological wizard. She has aided with my last three book projects, producing manuscripts and working her magic on the hundreds of digital images that have brought life to these books.

Contents

Acknowledgments

In July 2015 I was a participant in the Annual Roundup of the Wild West Historical Association. Our meetings take place from Wednesday through Saturday, with a field trip on Fridays. The 2015 Roundup headquartered in Amarillo, while the field trip took us on four buses to Adobe Walls, site of two battles: an 1864 clash between 1,300 warriors and an outnumbered U.S. Army column led by Col. Kit Carson, and an 1874 fight between twenty-eight buffalo hunters and a war party of six hundred or more braves.

The 1874 battle featured an epic shot made by Billy Dixon at a distance of nearly one mile. I was asked to address the crowd of two hundred about Billy Dixon, while the other speakers were Brett Cruse of the Texas Historical Commission and Alvin Lynn, an expert on the 1864 battle. Brett, Alvin, and I were on a panel together the next day, and both of these highly knowledgeable men freely shared their insights with me. To be in the presence of Brett and Alvin at Adobe Walls was an inspirational as well as a highly informative experience for me, and it was their example that animated me to begin the development of this book.

I soon enlisted the aid of Sherri Baker, reference librarian at Panola College and an interlibrary loan specialist. Sherri has the tenacious temperament of a detective, and she has helped me with numerous book projects in the past. She has never been more helpful than in tracking down information about Billy and Olive Dixon, and I am deeply grateful for her invaluable assistance. The newest member of the college library staff, Shay Joines, possesses impressive technological skills. She masterfully worked with the hundreds of images I collected, assembling the best of them as a major component of the story of Billy and Olive Dixon.

Early in the project my sister and brother-in-law, Judy and John Smith of Lampasas, helped me to explore the mysterious background of Billy Dixon. John is a resourceful amateur genealogist, and he located completely unexpected information. John and Judy also found family facts about Olive, the ancestors of Billy and Olive, and the Dixon children and grandchildren. I am indebted to Judy and John for locating these key facts.

Cathy Smith, archivist of the Haley Memorial Library in Midland, responded to my petition for help from her rich resources by promptly finding four excellent images and a collection of most useful documents. It is the second book project in a row in which Cathy has come to my aid, and I am fortunate indeed that she can so readily access the meticulous files of her institution.

Chuck Parsons, a noted author of western history, informed me of an article he had written in a 1985 edition of *The Prairie Scout*, the publication of the Kansas Corral of the Westerners. Chuck's article, "Buffalo Hunters or Lincoln County Warriors?," is about a photograph of six people. The only one who has been positively identified is Billy Dixon, but it is my contention that the young lady standing behind Billy is Olive Dixon. Chuck's analysis of the image only strengthens my belief, and I am grateful to him for sharing this article with me.

I owe a similar debt of appreciation to Chris Penn of England. Chris heard from our mutual friend, acclaimed western writer Jack DeMattos, that I was working on a biography of Billy and Olive Dixon. Chris previously had performed serious research on Billy, and he contacted me from England mentioning that he had a copy of Dixon's 1898 deposition in a federal damages case related to Adobe Walls. Chris offered to send me photocopies of the deposition, which amounts to twelve pages and which I was delighted to incorporate into the book.

I had the invaluable opportunity and privilege to visit Billy and Olive Dixon's lovely granddaughter, Virginia Irwin Maynard, at her home in Amarillo. Virginia and I talked at length about her grandparents, and she made available to me family photos, artifacts, and a scrapbook compiled by her mother, Edna Dixon Irwin. I owe Virginia an enormous debt of gratitude.

At the popular Frontier Texas! museum in Abilene, visitor services manager Rebecca Kinnison directed me to displays pertinent to my subject, and invited me back for a program and book signing. In Snyder, at the Scurry County Historical Museum, I was welcomed by the staff, even though the museum was closed to the public on a Monday. Administrative assistant Brenda Tovar assured me it would be all right to investigate the exhibits on a Monday, and curator Laurel Lamb brought me to the basement to examine weapons not on display. Laurel also opened an exhibit case so that I would have a better photo angle. Through the years I have delivered a number of programs at the Scurry County Museum, and office manager Ericka Jayne Christian urged me to return when the book is published.

At the Southwest Collection on the campus of Texas Tech University, archivist Monte Monroe and his assistant Robert Weaver collected numerous documents and newspapers from their massive holdings for my examination. Librarian Tai Kreidler, executive director of the West Texas Historical Association, obtained my schedule for the rest of the week and began calling and emailing numerous friends to alert them of my research needs and of my pending arrival.

Warren Stricker, Director of the Panhandle-Plains Historical Society Research Center in Canyon, heard from Tai and responded to my scheduling needs. Although the Research Center does not open until one o'clock on weekday afternoons, Warren graciously allowed me to come in at mid-morning. He assembled a vast array of sources, and research assistant Millie Williams cheerfully helped me with photocopying and other tasks throughout the day. I am indebted to Warren and Millie for aiding me in collecting a treasure trove of materials from their immense holdings.

At the Polk Street Methodist Church, where Olive Dixon worshiped for more than a quarter of a century, I was ably assisted in searching for membership details by Financial Secretary Natalie Chappell and administrative assistant Carol Moreno. Staff members of the Downtown Public Library of Amarillo also were of great help to me in accessing their excellent local reference files.

Lynn Hopkins, administrator of the Hutchinson County Museum in Borger, was alerted by Tai Kreidler of my visit. She graciously ushered me into her office and began showing me various treasures held by the museum, including a rare recording made by Olive Dixon — the first time I had heard her voice. Lynn shared numerous materials with me, and I am grateful for her generosity to a stranger.

The widowed Olive Dixon moved her family to Miami for more than a dozen years. At the Roberts County Museum I was shown one artifact after another by Emma Bowers, who has served as curator for fifteen years. I am grateful to Emma for directing me to the museum's resources with such a sure hand. County Judge Rick Tennant very kindly toured me through the handsome Roberts County Courthouse, which opened only a few years before Olive moved to town.

Ada Lester, a native of Mobeetie and a dedicated local historian, was told of my coming by Tai Kreidler. Ada contacted me by telephone and urged me to call Weldon Walser, a rancher who owns the site where Fort Elliott stood. For years Billy Dixon operated as an army scout out of Fort Elliott. On previous trips to Mobeetie I had read the historical markers near the fort site, but now Weldon Walser generously offered to conduct me across the property. For nearly two hours he pointed out where various buildings had stood and he showed me photos he had collected of troopers on the parade ground. I am deeply appreciative of the time Weldon took from a busy day (an irrigation pump had just broken) to acquaint me first-hand with the now-vanished outpost.

Following this exciting tour I found Ada Lester and Suzanne Lohberger at the Mobeetie Museum Research Center, housed in a 1923 elementary school. A grant provided a $500,000 renovation which transformed the former school into a superb museum, complete with commodious exhibit rooms and excellent library space. For the remainder of the day Ada and Suzanne pulled out newspaper files, typed transcriptions, photographs, and documents, many of which I photocopied. I am most grateful to Ada and Suzanne for a delightful and productive day in Old Mobeetie.

When this project began to materialize, I approached Billy Huckaby, owner of the Wild Horse Media Group of Fort Worth. Billy has acquired Eakin Press in recent years, and under the Eakin banner he has published my two most recent biographies, *Sam Houston, A Study in Leadership* (2016) and *John Chisum, Frontier Cattle King* (2018). It has been a privilege to work with Billy, who has produced my books in timely and competent fashion. I was elated when he agreed to publish my effort on Billy and Olive Dixon, and I am grateful to him and his staff for another fine volume, as well as for their aggressive marketing efforts.

My daughter, Dr. Berri O'Neal Gormley of Colleyville, is a college administrator who has a lifelong interest in history. For the past two years Berri has been of invaluable aid in publishing my State Historian blog (lonestarhistorian2), and she willingly agreed to produce a manuscript worthy of publication submission from my handwritten pencil scrawl. It was a pleasure to work with Berri on this project, and I hope she knows that she has my love as well as my gratitude for her efforts on my behalf.

Bill O'Neal

Chapter One

A Panhandle Wedding

I was in love with the West . . .

Olive King

The bridegroom and preacher were late. It was Thursday afternoon, October 18, 1894 — the wedding day of Billy Dixon and Olive King. He was famous as a hero of Adobe Walls and a Medal of Honor winner for action in the Panhandle. She was an adventurous young schoolmarm who had come from Virginia to the Texas Panhandle to visit a cowboy brother. In the sparsely settled Panhandle cow country Billy and Olive found each other.

Olive King arrived in Texas in the spring of 1893. She was met at Canadian by her older brother, Archie King, a cowboy for the Bar CC Ranch. Archie had a wife and a baby boy whom Olive had never met, and he had invited his sister for a get-acquainted stay in a striking remnant of the Old West. Olive promptly fell in love with the Panhandle Plains. "Never had I seen such tall grass and such expanse of clouds and sky." The scenery "was gorgeous, rich, fresh and clean . . ." The impact was immediate and permanent: "I loved the country from the first. Everyone was friendly and all were equal."[1]

Olive responded warmly to the people of the Panhandle: cowboys, ranchers, ranch wives, her new sister-in-law Sena, and her little nephew, Woods King, named after her deceased father. There were camping and fishing trips with neighbors, a Fourth of July dance, a Thanksgiving dinner.

Despite Olive's deep enjoyment of the Panhandle and its people, Sena became pregnant again and Olive began to feel that she should leave the sod home of her brother and his growing family. Reluctantly she contemplated returning to Virginia. But she was offered a teaching position at a tiny rural school located just south of the Canadian River. With an unexpected opportunity to stay in the Panhandle, Olive found lodgings just two-and-one half miles south of the little school with a family named Lewis. Late in November 1893 she met Billy Dixon, who lived just five miles away at Adobe Walls.[2]

Mrs. Lewis eagerly assumed the role of matchmaker. Although Billy was

Billy Dixon had striking good looks, with a sweeping moustache and the shoulder-length hair of a plainsman. *Through permission from Virginia Irwin Maynard, Billy's granddaughter.*

painfully shy around women, he soon adored the pretty young schoolmarm. Billy proposed to Olive in July 1894, and he wrote a letter to her mother, formally requesting Olive's hand in marriage.[3]

By the time Mrs. King's reply arrived a month later, wedding plans were well advanced by Olive and Mrs. Lewis. Since there were no churches in the area, Dixon suggested a civil ceremony by the nearest county judge or justice of the peace — an idea that was immediately vetoed by the ladies. Olive insisted on being married by a minister, and Mrs. Lewis offered her home for the ceremony and a wedding supper.

Dixon thought of Rev. C.V. Bailey, a Methodist circuit rider who headquartered in Mobeetie. Methodists had sent missionaries from the United States to Texas immediately following news of the Texan triumph at San Jacinto in 1836. Methodists

Olive King at eighteen, two years before she came to Texas and three years before her wedding. *Through permission from Virginia Irwin Maynard, Olive's granddaughter.*

industriously founded churches in Texas, organized circuits, and formed Sunday schools. During the 1880s, as railroads extended into northwest Texas, Methodists opened new churches in new communities and sent circuit riders into the Panhandle. On Sundays these traveling preachers customarily held services at two or three locations. Mobeetie was seventy-five miles from the Lewis home, but Reverend Bailey agreed to make the journey.[4]

Olive had sewn a light blue dress for the July Fourth celebration the previous year, and she and Mrs. Lewis began to convert it to a wedding gown with lace and ribbons and bows. The two women created a bridal trousseau, featuring the customary "second day dress." Plans were made for the wedding supper, and for room and furniture arrangements. The Lewis home was a three-room picket structure, and the wedding would be held in the largest room.

On the day of the wedding Reverend Bailey drove up in a buggy, intending to head to Adobe Walls and bring the groom back in time for the four o'clock ceremony. During the afternoon Olive dressed and preparations were made for the wedding supper. Archie and Sena and their two small children arrived, and so did several neighbors.

But four o'clock came and went, and it was a long wait until twilight before the bridegroom and the preacher finally arrived. Reverend Bailey cheerfully assumed blame for the tardiness, admitting that he had insisted on a personal tour of the Adobe Walls battlefield and on visiting with Turkey Track cowboys who made an untimely stop at Billy Dixon's store.

Billy, attired in a blue suit and black tie, and Olive in her wedding dress, at last took their positions before the preacher, who stood in front of a carefully decorated fireplace and mantle. Vows were exchanged and hearty congratulations were delivered. The wedding supper was a success, and a social hour followed. Soon the bridegroom suggested that it was time to head home, and as the newlyweds climbed into the buckboard they were the recipients of enthusiastic good wishes.[5]

The five-mile trail to Adobe Walls was quickly traversed. Billy carried Mrs. Dixon through the front door of her new home, unharnessed and fed his team, then joined his bride inside.

Billy was forty-five when he married; Olive was twenty-one. Despite their age difference, Billy and Olive proved to be soulmates. Billy was fit and handsome and strong. In early middle age he had fallen deeply in love; his passion and affection for Olive overcame his lifelong, crippling bashfulness around members of the opposite sex. Billy was a noted Panhandle pioneer of buffalo hunting days of the 1870s, as well as a renowned hero of Indian combat in the region.

Olive did not reach the Panhandle until the 1890s. There no longer was danger from Indian attack, but hardships remained part of everyday life. The population still was small and scattered. Although living conditions remained primitive with few amenities, "I was in love with the West and was ready and willing to meet any emergency in order to be able to stay in Texas." During her first year she experienced storms, stampedes, and prairie fires, and during her first Thanksgiving a ferocious

Marriage license of William Dixon and Olive King. The signature of Rev. C.V. Bailey is toward the bottom. Bailey filed the license in Roberts County, where he lived. *Courtesy Panhandle-Plains Historical Museum, Canyon, Texas.*

storm battered everyone with "hail, wind, rain, thunder and fierce lightning." Stock animals were killed on the range, and a baby's highchair was found miles down a creek lodged in the fork of a tree. Blizzards were a part of every Panhandle winter. "Many men and much stock were frozen to death every winter," Olive reminisced matter-of-factly.[6]

Undeterred, Olive made her home in the Panhandle for the rest of her life. "For almost three years," she frequently pointed out, "I was the only woman living in Hutchinson County." Billy was proud that "my wife for a period of three years was the only woman who actually lived in Hutchinson County. She may have grown a bit lonesome," he added, "but if she did she never said anything about it."

Although created in 1876, Hutchinson County was so thinly settled that it was not organized until 1901, seven years after Billy and Olive married. Olive seemed proud of her "only woman" identity, because it lent credibility to her status as a Panhandle pioneer. And Billy liked to joke that early in their marriage he could say, "Without making any other men angry, that I had the best looking woman in the County."[7]

Olive and Billy both were natives of Virginia. Her family was proud of its colonial roots in the first American colony. Olive's great-great grandfather, Gen. Andrew Lewis, was a military hero of colonial Indian conflicts and of the American Revolution, and her father had served in the Confederate Army. Now, as a young woman, she had married a hero of the Panhandle Indian Wars and she was creating a home under pioneering conditions. "There were months when I did not see any living soul except my husband and the cowboys who rode the range."[8]

In an interview given when she was seventy-three, Olive posed a rhetorical question: "Did I get lonesome and long for my Virginia home? Not at all. From the beginning I seemed to have fitted into this new life that was as foreign to the old life as day is to night. Never have I regretted that I came. I am proud of my native state, Virginia, and the part my forefathers played in the history of Virginia, but prouder still that I have been allowed to have a small part in the development of the state that has been my home for [more than] half a century."[9]

Olive gave birth to eight children, each without the attendance of a doctor. She had lost her own father when she was seven, so perhaps Billy Dixon provided a bit of a father figure. But her admiration and adoration for this legendary frontiersman were unbridled. Olive persuaded her reticent husband to tell her stories from his frontier days, and she somehow found time to record his adventures. After Billy's death she finished raising their children under difficult circumstances. But she also produced a book about his life, and she continued to write about Billy and other Panhandle pioneers for area newspapers.

As the Panhandle grew and matured early in the twentieth century, Olive worked to perpetuate her husband's fame, securing monuments at Adobe Walls and at Buffalo Wallow, where he earned a Medal of Honor. Olive became a charter member of the Panhandle-Plains Historical Society and, through unrelenting effort, a force for Panhandle history. Finally settling in Amarillo, an urban center of the High Plains, she produced historical pieces about the Panhandle for the rest of her life, while attending and helping to stage historical events. It was a great satisfaction to Olive King Dixon that her children and grandchildren were "raised on history."[10]

So two Virginia-born adventure-seekers found each other in the Texas Panhandle of the 1890s. They found marriage and a rich family life. Olive found a man worthy of deep esteem as well as of love and lifelong devotion. And Billy, a Panhandle icon of heroism, overcame his fear of females and found a sweetheart who would commemorate his remarkable deeds to future generations.

Chapter Two

The Mysterious Background of Billy Dixon

Go West, young man, and grow up with the country.

Horace Greeley
New York Tribune

The standard source for the early years of Billy Dixon's life is the brief account of his origins which he related to his wife while she recorded his recollections. Billy always was known as taciturn, but he was especially close-mouthed about his childhood. In *Life and Adventures of "Billy" Dixon*, published by Olive a year after his death, all she was able to record about his origins was the following:

> I was born in Ohio County, Virginia, September 25, 1850, the oldest of three children. My mother died when her third child was born . . . When I was twelve years old my father died, and with my sister I went to live with my uncle, Thomas Dixon, who lived in Ray County, Missouri. In those days travel was difficult, and Missouri seemed a long way from our home in West Virginia. We had been with our uncle only a few months when my sister was stricken with typhoid fever and died after an illness of about two weeks. This left me alone in the world. My uncle was kind and good to me, but I stayed with him only a year.[1]

Billy failed to mention the names of his father, mother, or the sister who supposedly died of typhoid fever. Indeed, his brief description of his boyhood is a collection of untruths. Census records reveal that he was the third child — not the first — born to William R. and Nancy Privett Dixon, and he was named after his father. Four more children subsequently were born to the couple, for a total of seven — four boys and three girls. William and Nancy were married in 1844, when he was twenty-four and she was sixteen. Their first child, Albert, was born the next year.

Census records reveal that the Dixon children were Andrew (born in 1845), Sarah (1846), William R. "Billy" (1850), Melance (1855), Delilah (1857), Andrew (1859), and Henry (1862). Nancy was thirty-four when her last child was born.[2]

The senior William R. Dixon was born in 1820 at Jefferson in northeastern Ohio. He was the oldest of ten children, including seven boys and three girls. At some point after the 1825 birth of twins Nathan and Albert — children numbers four and five — the family left Ohio, moving first to Warren County, Indiana, then relocating several years later to Missouri. Child number nine, John T., was born in Barton, Missouri, in 1839. Among William R. Dixon's six brothers, John T. — through the names and initials that have come down to us — seems the most likely to have been Billy's "Uncle Tom." Of course, John T. Dixon was only eleven years older than his nephew Billy.[3] According to Billy's account, he was orphaned at twelve, in 1862, when John T. (Uncle Tom?) was twenty-three.

But Billy was not orphaned in 1862. William and Nancy Dixon had their seventh child in 1862. William lived until 1880, dying at the age of sixty in Jefferson City, Missouri, while Nancy seems to have lived into her eighties. None of their seven children died in childhood of typhoid fever or anything else. William and Nancy started their family in Ohio County, Virginia, but during the 1850s relocated to Missouri.

There seems to be no way to reconcile with reality the fanciful tale spun by Billy to his wife decades after his boyhood. Billy was not the oldest of three children — he was the third of seven. Neither of his parents died when he was a boy, and none of his sisters died during childhood. His family moved from Virginia to Missouri when Billy was no more than nine.

What to make, then, of the fabrications Billy told about his boyhood? Perhaps there is partial truth. Perhaps Billy had a row with his father, or perhaps Uncle Tom needed help at his Ray County place. William R. Dixon had resettled his family near Jefferson City near the center of Missouri, and Ray County was only fifty-odd miles to the northwest, not far from Kansas City and the Missouri River. If, for some reason, it was decided that young Billy should move in with his Uncle Tom, it would have been much easier to arrange than the five-hundred-mile journey from Ohio County, Virginia, to Ray County that Billy described to Olive.

Considering the adventurous course of Billy Dixon's life, his account of events begins to carry the ring of truth when he describes living with his uncle. Nearby Kansas City, at the confluence of the Missouri and Kansas rivers, long had been a jumping-off site for the Oregon Trail and the Santa Fe Trail. The area abounded with teamsters, hunters, trappers, steamboat men — rugged characters who had been to the West and who enjoyed telling tales of their frontier adventures, especially to wide-eyed boys who hung on their words.

"While at my uncle's home I had often met men who had been to the far west, and their marvelous tales of adventure fired my imagination, and filled me with eagerness to do what they had done." reminisced Billy. "My dreams were filled with beautiful pictures of that dim region that lay toward the Rocky Mountains."[4]

The legendary mountain man Jim Bridger owned a farm near Kansas City. As a boy he lost both parents and his little brother. Alone in the world, the teenaged orphan worked on riverboats and served a four-year apprenticeship with a blacksmith. At eighteen he enlisted in an epic hunting and trapping expedition up the Missouri, launching his spectacular career as a trapper, scout, and explorer.

Another frontier legend, Kit Carson, was apprenticed to a Missouri saddle shop. He was enthralled by the tales told by customers who were mountain men and teamsters, and when he was sixteen he ran away from the shop and joined a Santa Fe caravan headed by Charles Bent.[5]

Jim Bridger and Kit Carson were the kind of men Billy Dixon admired, and he seemed to adapt elements from their young lives to his own back story. In boyhood, like Bridger and Carson, his imagination was fired by the great West and by the men who dared to venture into the frontier wilds. Perhaps, like young Bridger and Carson, Billy had some type of commitment to work for his uncle, who had no children big enough to be of help. And like Bridger and Carson, the lure of the West was too strong for Billy to resist.

Billy reported becoming friends with an older boy, Dan Keller, who had left home and who also lusted to go west. "My uncle would have been greatly opposed to our enterprise had we told him of it," remarked Billy, "so I went away without telling him goodbye."[6]

According to his account, Billy was about thirteen when he and Dan Keller struck out on their own. Neither boy had a horse or gun, "only courage and our chubby fists." In a sack Billy carried his only extra shirt and a photograph of his mother which "I treasured beyond all my other possessions."[7] He had no photograph of his father — perhaps Billy had hard feelings over being farmed out to an uncle.

As the years passed Billy did not talk about his family in Missouri, not even mentioning the names of his parents. When pressed by his wife for his life story when he was in his early sixties, Billy still did not divulge any names except that of "Uncle Tom" Dixon. Billy referred to himself as the oldest child, he mentioned a younger sister who died of typhoid fever and of the death of his mother in childbirth, followed by the demise of his father a couple of years later. He did not mention that he was one of seven brothers and sisters, nor that the family moved to Missouri during his boyhood.

From boyhood on Billy enjoyed listening to men of the frontier tell about their adventures. Billy and Dan Keller found themselves welcomed at the camps of wood choppers along the Missouri River. "Around the campfires at night the wood choppers told of their exploits in the west — of how they had hunted the grizzly bear, the buffalo, the panther, the deer and the antelope, of how they had been caught in the howling blizzards, of their narrow escapes from drowning in swollen rivers, and of the battles they had fought with hostile Indians." Billy was awestruck by these campfire sessions. "Many times we sat and listened until midnight, . . . and then after we had gone to bed we lay looking at the stars and wondering if it would ever be possible for us to lead such a delightful life."[8]

Of course, with a couple of wide-eyed boys hanging on their words, the old-timers must have "stretched the blanket" a bit.

Frontiersmen were famous for indulging in "windies;" blizzards became colder, grizzly bears more ferocious, rivers more
swollen, Indian warriors more dangerous, escapes from death
more narrow. Eventually Billy became aware of how tall the
tales were, but he never lost his taste for enjoying the windies of fellow frontiersmen. He was in his early forties, for example, when he was courting Miss Olive Dixon in the Lewis
homestead. But on many evenings after supper, "Billy Dixon
would be sitting by the fire listening to the talk of the two Lewis
[brothers], swapping stories with them," while Mrs. Lewis and
Olive eavesdropped during sewing sessions in the next room.[9]

Two decades later, after a lifetime of listening to windies
and adding a few of his own, Billy apparently inserted melo-
dramatic twists — windy style — when Olive asked him for
recollections about his younger years. The brief story he spun
included elements from the young lives of Kit Carson and Jim
Bridger. Then having said everything he intended to about his
childhood, he moved on to a more detailed and perceptive —
and believable — account of his early years on the frontier.

When Billy Dixon and Dan Keller hiked off to the west, they
did not have far to go to the Missouri River. One of three major
river systems in the West (Missouri, Colorado, and Columbia),
the Missouri was busy with steamboat traffic. Large steamboats
used up to four cords of wood an hour. A cord is a stack eight
feet long, four feet wide, and four feet tall. A great deal of wood
was needed to fuel steamboat traffic. Wood cutters set up camps
along the river banks, and Billy and Dan soon wandered into
these encampments.

"The men were rough but generous and hospitable," described Billy, "and we were welcomed at their camps, many of
which we reached at nightfall. We hunted and trapped up and
down the river for several months, often staying in one camp
for a couple of weeks."[10] Probably they helped with the work of
cutting and stacking firewood.

Billy and Dan arrived in Westport, Missouri — which would
eventually become part of Kansas City — on Sunday, October
23, 1864. On that date Missouri's largest battle of the Civil War
was fought at Westport. Amid the roar of cannon and the smoke

of combat, Confederates under Gen. Sterling Price held off two numerically superior Union forces. The two youngsters were filled with excitement.

"Dan and I would have enlisted on the spot had we not been too young," remembered Billy. "But the smoke of battle got into our nostrils, and we were more determined than ever to reach the far west and fight Indians."[11]

Billy and Dan wandered a short distance to the little town of Wyandotte, Kansas, where the surrounding countryside teemed with small game. The two lads hired out to a farmer for a couple of months, before drifting northwest about twenty miles to Leavenworth City. Leavenworth and the nearby fort which gave the town its name, comprised a major jumping-off place for freighting trains to the West.

"Such acres of wagons!" exclaimed Horace Greeley of the *New York Tribune*. "Such pyramids of extra axletrees! such herds of oxen! such regiments of drivers and other employees! No one who has not seen can realize how vast a business this is, nor how immense are it outlays as well as it income."[12]

At Leavenworth, Billy and Dan encountered a veteran teamster named Tom Hare, who was a bullwhacker for a government ox train. Hare bought breakfast for the hungry, footsore youngsters. The bull train was parked about four miles outside town, waiting for winter to break while trying to fill out a crew. With the Civil War still raging, manpower was at a premium. Hare introduced Billy and Dan to the bull train boss, who hired the youngsters for fifty dollars a month (double the pre-Civil War wage) with everything provided, including firearms and ammunition.

"I was only fourteen years old," recalled Billy, "but delighted with the prospect that at last I should begin the journey across the Plains."[13]

The bull train (all of the cattle were steers, but called bulls, and the men who drove them were "bullwhackers" who used "bullwhips") pulled out in mid-April for Fort Scott, Kansas, about one hundred and ten miles due south. Each wagon was drawn by six pairs of oxen. President Lincoln was assassinated on April 14, 1865, and during the trek south the teamsters no-

Fort Leavenworth, where young Billy Dixon began working as a bullwhacker. *Courtesy National Archives.*

ticed black drapery of mourning on doorways throughout the trip. At Fort Scott the bull train went into camp for about two weeks before heading north back to Leavenworth. The high-wheeled freight wagons had no driver's seat, so bullwhackers walked alongside the team and wagon, cracking a long raw-hide whip. First thing each morning the bullwhacker yoked his oxen, then greased the wheels of the wagon. Billy was eager, and he quickly learned rudiments of the job, including how to handle a whip.

"By this time I had begun feeling that I was an old hand," said Billy. "When I was first employed I found it difficult to yoke my oxen, but my small size appealed to the men, and there was always somebody willing to help me. I was now able to yoke my own oxen."[14]

When the war ended, the federal government sold the bull train at Fort Leavenworth. All twenty-five freight wagons and three hundred oxen were bought by a man named Kirkendall, who had served as master of transportation at Fort Leaven-worth. Kirkendall also hired the wagonmaster, who immedi-ately employed all of the men who wanted to keep working. Half of the men quit to do something else, but a full crew finally was recruited. Word soon came that the train would journey west to Fort Collins, Colorado, loaded with military provisions. Each of the twenty-five wagons would be loaded with about seven thousand pounds of freight, including flour, bacon, coffee, sugar, ammunition and other items. In addition to twenty-five bullwhackers and the wagonmaster, the crew was completed with an assistant wagonmaster, a night herder, and an extra bullwhacker.

Excited at the prospect of finally traveling to the West of his lively imagination, Billy outfitted himself in suitable frontier attire. After receiving the pay from his first round trip as a bullwhacker, "I had more money than I had ever dreamed I would possess at one time." He bought "a big sombrero, a Colt's revolver, a butcher knife, a belt, and a bull whip." Dan also invested in similar gear. Looking back, Billy seemed to laugh at the figure he must have cut half a century earlier. "I am sure that the older men must have smiled at the two youngsters, each buried beneath his big hat and leaning to one side under the weight of his 'shooting irons.'"[15]

The bull train set out from Fort Leavenworth, angling northwestward along major trails. Billy Dixon's first trip to the West proved to be difficult almost from the start. Winter rains and frosts had reduced many of the roads to quagmires. In the Salt Creek Valley there was a long stretch where as many as twenty-four oxen had to be hitched to a single wagon. After traversing this trail of bottomless mud, the train spent a day repairing damaged wagons and harness.

Soon arriving at the Big Blue River, the main tributary of the Kansas River, the flooded stream proved especially difficult to cross, because oxen were leery of water, particularly when pulling loaded wagons. "We doubled our teams," explained Billy, "cracked our whips, and forced the reluctant oxen into the torrent with a man on horseback swimming on each side of them, and in this way they swam and struggled to the further shore."[16]

A few days later the bull train struggled into Fort Kearny, established in 1848 on the Oregon Trail. The bull train struck the North Platte River and headed across the Plains with a military escort. "This meant that we were in a dangerous locality," realized Billy Dixon, who was in boyish hope "of seeing a war party of painted Indians, or a herd of buffaloes sweeping over the Plains. Neither had come to pass, and I was keenly disappointed."[17]

At the northeast corner of Colorado the bull train angled southwest and left Nebraska, soon passing through tiny Julesburg, where a fresh military escort took over. The South Platte, with a swift current and rocky banks, proved to be the most difficult crossing of the trip. Horsemen again had to be used to ride beside each team of oxen, some of the wagons had to be partially unloaded, and the crossing took the entire day.

After two and one-half months the bull train reached Fort Collins, and "I now saw mountains for the first time." At Fort Collins Billy also saw his first Indians, peaceful Utes in a camp near the fort. He admitted that "I was disappointed in not having engaged in a fight with Indians, and in not seeing a single buffalo."[18]

The empty wagons returned to Fort Leavenworth over the same route. The wagons were hitched three or four together, with the oxen being rotated — some harnessed to wagons, some being driven in a herd by bullwhackers, who took turns. When the bullwhackers were paid off at Fort Leavenworth, "many of us felt rich, and had enough to carry us through the winter if we were not extravagant."[19]

Dan Keller decided to spend the winter with his parents in Indiana, and Billy never saw him again. By that time Billy had become friends with another young bullwhacker, Johnny Baldwin. On the streets of Leavenworth they were offered jobs, but experienced bullwhackers warned them not to drive a train during a plains winter. So they accepted an offer of forty-five dollars a month from a man who was outfitting a government mule train during the winter. He was holding about one hundred and fifty mules on the farm of a man named McCall, located on Soldiers' Creek, near Holton, Kansas. Billy's chores in winter camp were helping the cook and, with other crew members, rounding up the mules in the evening.

Billy embraced another duty he was asked to assume. He had been given his first guns as part of his equipment by the government bull trains. Rifles and ammunition were provided in case of Indian attacks. Soon he was able to purchase a cap and ball revolver, along with all of the powder and shot he wanted. Billy was able to keep one of the government rifles he was issued, or perhaps he bought a shoulder gun of his own. In any event, now that he was armed Billy Dixon turned out to have a natural affinity for guns. He practiced at every opportunity during his bull train trips, and there were veteran frontiersmen who could provide tips in the handling of guns. He hunted small game whenever possible, and at the McCall farm he was asked to provide game for the mess.

"There were plenty of quails, rabbits, squirrels and prairie chickens, and I was in my glory," recalled Blly with relish. "I ranged the country, a youthful Daniel Boone [another boyhood hero], enjoying every moment of the time. I seemed to have a natural aptitude in the handling of firearms. It was my greatest ambition to become a good shot. In later years I was counted an expert marksman in any company, regardless of how proficient my rivals might be. I always attributed my skill with the rifle to my natural love for the sport, to steady nerves, and to constant, unremitting practice. Where other men found pleasure in cards, horse-racing and other similar amusements, I was happiest when ranging the open country with my gun on my shoulder and a dog at my heels, far out among the wild birds and the wild animal."[20]

Billy would exhibit a zest for "ranging the open country" for the rest of his life. He was a born outdoorsman and a marksman of exceptional gifts. Although only in his mid-teens, Billy Dixon developed rapidly into a man of the plains. "I had made up my mind to go west — and to keep going west until I could say I had seen it all, and had hunted buffaloes and fought Indians to my complete satisfaction." From the vantage point of his sixties, Billy reflected wryly on his youthful ambitions: "Little did I dream of how much of this sort of thing was in store for me in later years."[21]

The area was filled with farm families, and throughout the winter numerous parties and dances were held. The mule wranglers were invited, and fifteen-year-old Billy tagged along. "I went with the men, but I was too bashful to take part. I sat beside the fiddlers and looked at the pretty girls . . . and would have given a fortune — had I possessed one — for courage enough to walk boldly up to the handsomest, ask her to dance with me, and be able to dance without making blunders as the figures were called. Alas, such courage and assurance was quite beyond my strongest resolves."[22]

Bashful Billy was far more comfortable hunting in the fields than ducking girls at a party. Farmer McCall often went hunting with Billy, and bragged on the young sharpshooter for bagging the most game. Mr. and Mrs. McCall had two daughters and a son, Charley, who was a reckless and adventurous youngster. Mr. McCall offered Billy a job on his farm as an alternative to hiring on with another bull train.

Early in March orders came to drive the mules into Fort Leavenworth. The mule herd reached Fort Leavenworth the second day. Billy and the other herders ate at a mess hall and the quartermaster paid the men their accumulated wages. Now without jobs, Billy and a young friend went into Leavenworth, which was busy with bullwhackers and settlers who were headed west. Billy did not sign on with a bull train, however, deciding to accept the "kind offers" of the McCalls. Perhaps missing a home environment, "I remained on the farm about a year. During all this time Mrs. McCall was a mother to me, and the family treated me as if I were a son and brother. I am sure that the good influences of this home were helpful to me in after life."[23]

On the first day of July, 1866, a tragic event occurred at the McCall home. Mrs McCall was the sister of Mary Lane, who was the wife of the prominent — and controversial — Jim Lane. Lane — an Indiana attorney and congressman and veteran of the War with Mexico, moved to Kansas in 1855. A champion of abolitionism in "Bleeding Kansas," he led the Free State Army (or "Jayhawkers").

When Kansas was admitted to the Union in 1861 as a free state, Lane was elected as one of the two original U.S. Senators. Simultaneously, Senator Lane served as a Union brigadier general during 1861 and 1862. The infamous Quantrill raid on Lawrence, Kansas, targeted Lane, who made his home there. Lane managed to escape, although the town was burned. In 1864 Lane was a volunteer aide-de-camp during the Battle of

Senator Jim Lane, who also served as a Union general early in the Civil War, was a controversial figure in Kansas. While visiting at the McCall farm, Lane shot himself in the head, and Billy Dixon hurried to Fort Leavenworth for medical care. *Courtesy National Archives.*

Westport, when thirteen-year-old Billy Dixon was near enough to hear the gunfire and see explosions.

After the war Senator Lane became depressed — some said deranged — over political charges from fellow Republicans and by accusations of financial irregularities. On Sunday, July 1, while visiting his McCall in-laws, Senator Lane stepped out of his carriage, placed the muzzle of a pistol inside his mouth, and pulled the trigger. Although the bullet came out of the top of his head, Lane somehow remained alive. Billy Dixon raced to Fort Leavenworth and came back in an army ambulance, which transported Senator Lane into Leavenworth for medical aid. Lane lingered for ten days before dying on July 11, 1866. He was buried at Oak Hill Cemetery in Lawrence.[24]

That fall the McCalls persuaded Billy to attend school with Charley. "Prior to this, I had attended school only two terms," remarked Billy.[25] The McCall daughters were sent to a Catholic boarding school, but every weekday Billy and Charley walked to a rural school. Billy now was sixteen and was one of the largest pupils in the school — surely he was the only experienced bullwhacker in the student body. Surely, too, he needed a third term of schooling.

But when the spring of 1867 arrived Billy went to Fort Leavenworth to see what work was available. Mr. McCall urged him to continue his job at the farm, and Mrs. McCall implored him to stay with the family. "But my head was filled with dreams of adventure in the Far West," he confessed. "Always I could see the West holding its hands toward me, and beckoning and smiling."[25]

A government wagonmaster named Simpson was putting together a mule train that was to be shipped by the Kansas Pacific Railroad to Fort Harker, where "shave-tails" were to be trained in camp before hitting the trail. "Shave-tails" were wild, unbroken mules — only a few in the herd had ever been harnessed and driven. A great many of the drivers also were shave-tails, but Billy Dixon was not one of them. "By this time I could handle a team with as much ease as a man could."[26]

The wagons and harness were new. The mules, wagons, and harness were loaded onto railroad cars and, along with the crew, were shipped to Fort Harker. For ten days the shave-tails were broken in amid constant rodeo scenes. Mules ran away or, when harnessed, bucked and kicked. The drivers were issued breech-loading Sharps carbines and Remington Army revolvers, all recent models that now were Civil War surplus.

Of course, Billy's fine new guns and his presence at a frontier fort of the Indian Wars aggravated his disappointment at never having seen a buffalo herd — not even one shaggy beast — nor a party of horseback warriors. Little did he realize that at last he would be able to see both.

Chapter Three

Billy's First Buffalo and First War Party

*Here was the opportunity I had long looked for — to see
a big gathering of Indians close at hand, without
danger of getting scalped.*

Billy Dixon

"Alas, and again alas, up to this time I had never seen a buffalo! I could almost taste buffalo, so keen was I to behold one of these shaggy monsters, pawing the sandy plain, throwing dust high in air, and shaking his ponderous head at his enemies, defying them to battle."[1]

Billy Dixon's lament over the absence of buffalo finally was about to be ended. One morning during the shakedown period at Fort Harker, Billy crawled out of his blankets, began feeding his team of mules — and suddenly spotted a lone buffalo on the horizon to the northwest. "That was my buffalo," he thought excitedly. "I determined that I should get him, even if I had to twist my fingers in his shaggy mane and drag him back to camp."[2]

Billy grabbed his Sharps carbine, slipped a bridle onto his gentlest mule, and rode bareback toward the buffalo. The big beast launched into a lumbering gait away from his pursuer. The chase went on for eight miles, up and down hills and across gullies. Billy coaxed a final spurt from his panting mule and took a shot with his carbine. The gunshot startled the mule, but the buffalo fell dead.

"I had not only killed a buffalo," exulted Billy, "but had killed the first buffalo I ever saw." Three or four of Billy's fellow teamsters had followed the chase from camp, and they "were kind enough to exaggerate the distance of the shot." Billy and

Fort Harker, adjacent to the Kansas Pacific Railroad, was a busy shipping point for military supply trains. *Courtesy National Archives.*

his friends skinned the carcass and carved off choice hunks of meat.[3]

Within a few days orders came to load the wagons with supplies for Fort Hays, about ninety miles to the west. As a teamster Billy Dixon now was a "muleskinner" instead of a "bullwhacker." Rather than walking alongside his team, a muleskinner rode one of his mules, usually the one closest to the wagon. Mules pulled their wagons at two and a half miles per hour, while oxen generated two miles an hour. But mules had to be fed grain, which added expense to the trip, while oxen grazed their way across their journey. Furthermore, a pair of mules cost more than a pair of oxen, even though the trip could be made more rapidly with mules.[4]

En route to Fort Hays a band of warriors was sighted in the distance. Billy Dixon hoped to test his marksmanship with the Sharps again, but the war party soon disappeared over a ridge. During the trip buffaloes began to be seen in large numbers, and Billy killed several.

The trip to Fort Hays took only four days, and the mule train returned to Fort Harker to reload with supplies brought by the Kansas Pacific Railroad. Trips followed to Fort Wallace, Fort Lyon, Fort Zarah, and Fort Larned. With a great deal of Indian unrest across the plains, all of these outposts were being expanded and improved. Military escorts were provided for every trip, and west of Fort Dodge the teamsters saw horseback warriors wearing war paint.

During that busy summer of 1867, Billy Dixon witnessed his first buffalo breeding season. Billy observed that "at night and early morning could be heard the constant, low thunder of the bulls, their grunting rising into a roar that was one of the most striking of the natural phenomena of the Plains country."[5]

By October most of the government trains were camped at Fort Harker, awaiting orders. Directions came to make preparations to accompany peace commissioners who were going to conduct major negotiations with Southern Plains tribes. These negotiations were arranged to take place just above the southern Kansas border along the Medicine Lodge River. Seventeen-year-old Billy Dixon, who had only glimpsed horseback warriors a few times from great distances, was about to witness one of the most spectacular gatherings of warlike tribes in the history of the West.

In July 1867 Senator John B. Henderson from Missouri introduced a bill creating a peace commission to negotiate with Indians of the Southern Plains. Henderson's bill attempted to establish a "system for civilizing the tribes," and after passage by Congress it was signed by President Andrew Johnson before the month ended.

The chiefs insisted on a meeting site far from any fort or white settlement. The Medicine Lodge Valley, sacred to Kiowas, was agreed upon, while the first full moon in October was the time set for assembling the tribes and the peace commissioners.

The commissioners gathered at Leavenworth City early in October. Senator Henderson was present, along with Commissioner of Indian Affairs N.G. Taylor, Gen. William S. Harney, Gen. Alfred Terry, Kansas Governor Samuel Crawford, and other officials. Nine journalists were permitted to cover the trip, including Henry M. Stanley ("Dr. Livingstone, I presume") of the *Missouri Democrat*. There were numerous aides, secretaries, interpreters, ambulance drivers, and cooks. Transportation to Fort Harker was by rail.[6]

Nearby a great number of vehicles were clustered in the wagon park. Freight wagons were loaded with provisions and gifts, while army ambulances were configured to accommodate peace commissioners and other travelers. There would be three span of mules to each vehicle. But Billy Dixon's wagon was not loaded, and he feared he would not be included in this extraordinary expedition.

"I was eager to go, but as no orders had been given to my outfit, I was fearful that I might be left behind," remembered Billy. "Here was the opportunity I had long looked for — to see a big gathering of Indians close at hand, without danger of getting scalped. I had almost given up in despair, when an orderly galloped up from headquarters, saying that two more wagons must be sent forward at once."[7]

The wagonmaster quickly picked Billy and a muleskinner named Frickie. Billy ran to where his mules were eating, and in his haste to harness his lead mule he carelessly let himself be kicked. Billy sprawled onto the ground, and when he struggled to his feet he could not straighten himself. Frickie had to help him harness his mules, and the two muleskinners drove their wagons three miles in the gathering darkness to the assembly point.

The column pulled out the next morning, October 9, escorted by 200 troopers of the Seventh Cavalry. The journey to the Medicine Lodge Valley took four days. There were 211 vehicles and, according to Henry Stanley's count, 1,250 animals and about 600 men. The column stretched out for nearly two miles. Throughout the trip vast herds of buffalo were within sight.[8]

When the column reached Medicine Lodge River, an estimated 5,000 Indians already were arranged in tribal camps: Cheyennes, Arapahoes, Comanches, Kiowas, and Kio-

At the Medicine Lodge Treaty gathering, young Billy Dixon was particularly impressed by the "magnificent appearance" of Kiowa Chief Satanta. *Courtesy Fort Richardson Historical Museum.*

wa-Apaches. Everywhere there were tipis, horses, dogs, and Native American men, women and children. General Herney deployed the ambulances in a hollow square, reinforced by two Gatling guns, while the wagons were corralled nearby.

Billy Dixon was impressed "by a number of noted Indian chiefs, mounted upon their finest horses and arrayed in their most splendid costumes." He stated that these proud leaders "carried themselves with dignity and in every feature was revealed their racial pride and their haughty contempt for the white man." Billy especially recalled chiefs Kicking Bird, Black Kettle, and Satanta, who "rode a big black horse, and presented a magnificent appearance."[9]

There were several days of feasting and oratory. Leaders of the Comanches, Kiowas, and Kiowa-Apaches signed a treaty on October 21, 1867, agreeing to concentrate themselves on a large reservation in western Indian Territory. One week later the Cheyennes and Arapahoes agreed to occupy a reservation of their own. Seeds and implements would be provided to Native American farmers, while government teachers would instruct the young. White settlers were to avoid treaty lands. Wagon loads of presents — blankets, clothing, hats, sugar, coffee, and flour — were issued to the chiefs, who passed them out to their tribal families. A great deal of trading then commenced between the Native Americans and the soldiers and teamsters. Billy swapped his cap and ball revolver to an older Indian for three buffalo robes and small native items.

The teamsters soon harnessed their mules, and the column headed back to Fort Harker, arriving about the first of November. Most members of Billy's outfit had not left the camp, and the taciturn Dixon quickly grew "rather tired of telling the boys that had stayed behind all about the Medicine Lodge . . ."[10] But Billy always retained vivid memories of the historic, colorful, and large-scale Medicine Lodge assemblage.

The Peace Commissioners began planning similar negotiations with the Sioux and other warlike tribes of the Northern Plains. The Treaty of Fort Laramie was mediated in 1868. But by that time white men already were penetrating traditional Native American hunting lands, and war parties — armed with guns provided through the Medicine Lodge Treaty — began to strike back savagely. The Peace Commission assembled once more, in Chicago in October 1868, but following adjournment they never met again.

Meanwhile the frontier descended into all-out war, a warfare that would notably involve Billy Dixon at the height of hostilities. Across the West nomadic warrior-huntsmen refused to be transformed into sedentary agriculturists who assumed the values of white men. "Assigning Indians to reservations was one thing, but forcing them to live within narrow limits was quite another," observed frontier historian Ray Allen Billington. "Rather than trooping to their new homes, most younger warriors and many minor chiefs refused to abide by the treaties, denounced the leaders who signed them, and prepared to fight before surrendering their nomadic habits."[11]

In 1866 Gen. Winfield Scott Hancock, an excellent Civil War commander, launched preparations for an 1867 Indian campaign that became known as "Hancock's War." General

Hancock assembled as much artillery as possible, as he would have done for a Civil War campaign. But in the field against horseback warriors, cannons and gun carriages proved worse than useless. So the artillery was parked at Fort Harker. The big guns could have been transported by rail to Fort Leavenworth, but the cost would have been expensive, especially after a fleet of empty wagons arrived from Medicine Lodge Valley. Billy Dixon reflected that "inasmuch as the government owned the teams and wagons and was paying us by the month there was no good reason why we should not be hauling cannon to Fort Leavenworth."

The mule train followed the railroad tracks eastward, and on the first night barely escaped a prairie fire. The experienced hands set a backfire and beat out flames near their tents. Upon arriving at Fort Leavenworth the wagons were unloaded and the muleskinners were paid off. "I had a comfortable stake for a young fellow," recalled Billy, "and spent the winter in Leavenworth and Kansas City . . ." Billy visited his friends at the McCall farm on several occasions. And frequently he indulged in a favorite pastime, mingling happily with veteran frontiersmen "and listening delightedly to their incomparable tales of adventure."[13]

Railroad companies were promoting hunting trips into buffalo country. During the winter of 1867-68 Billy hired on with some of these excursions, assisting hunters who came from St. Louis, Chicago, Cincinnati, and other eastern environs. Billy already was a good shot but he was not yet more than a casual hunter of buffaloes. He said that he "went out from both Leavenworth and Kansas City with hunting parties." So Billy may have been employed more as a camp tender than as a hunting guide. "I thirsted for adventure, but as yet had seen only the mere fringe of it."[14]

In the spring of 1868 Billy hired out as a muleskinner to a Baxter Springs merchant named Powell. Baxter Springs was booming as a Kansas cattle town on the Shawnee Trail from Texas. Powell acquired a train of six freight wagons, each pulled by four mules, and he intended to supply his mercantile with regular trips to Leavenworth City, 170 miles due north. During the spring and summer of 1868 the population of Baxter Springs jumped to 1,500, including saloonkeepers, gamblers, and sporting ladies. Billy Dixon had been working for more than three years alongside rough bullwhackers, and muleskinners, but he swore that the raw cattle town "was infested by the most desperate class of men I ever saw . . . Baxter Springs supplied in abundance all that the most dissipated character could wish for in the way of whiskey, women, gambling, and fighting."[15]

After several months of working for Powell, Billy was at Fort Leavenworth when a big government mule train was being organized for a trip to Camp Supply in western Indian Territory at the junction of Beaver and Wolf creeks. "These were exciting times. The very air buzzed with news of Indian depredations,"

Camp Supply began as "Camp of Supply" in western Oklahoma. Billy Dixon was in and out of Camp Supply as a muleskinner and, later, as an army scout. *Courtesy National Archives.*

recounted Billy. "The Government was rushing troops and supplies to the front, as if the world was coming to an end."[16]

There were one hundred wagons and six hundred mules, and the wagonmaster — a man named Cox — hired Billy Dixon, by now a muleskinner with considerable experience. The Kansas Pacific Railroad had been extended all the way to Denver, so Cox transported his wagons, mules, and muleskinners by train to Fort Hays. The wagons and mules were unloaded from the railroad cars at Fort Hays on October 15, 1868, in cold and rainy weather. The mule train, once loaded with cargo, was ordered to depart for Camp Supply immediately. But Billy and his fellow drivers were dismayed to learn "that all the mules, big fellows from Missouri and Kentucky, were as wild as wolves, not one of them having been broke. Worst of all there was no time to break them."[17]

On the first morning the exasperated muleskinners harnessed and hitched their teams, amid crazed kicking and squealing and bucking. Once on the trail, however, the mules proved easy to drive because the loaded wagons were too heavy for them to run away. But on the third morning there was an epic stampede.

"The mules ran in every possible direction," described Billy in awe, "overturning wagons, and outfit colliding with outfit until it looked as if there would never be a pound of freight delivered to Supply. Many of the wagons were so badly demolished that they had to be abandoned and left behind." The cargo from these wrecked vehicles was distributed onto surviving wagons.[18]

The caravan passed Fort Dodge (there was not yet a Dodge City) and began to sight buffaloes. Between Bluff Creek and the Cimarron River a large herd of stampeding bison headed straight for the mule train. This wall of buffaloes might have overturned wagons and spooked the mules into a massive runaway. A troop of cavalry escort was deployed to try to turn the

A mule train in Denver. Each wagon is pulled by six mules, and each muleskinner is mounted on the left side mule closest to his wagon. Billy Dixon became an experienced muleskinner. *Courtesy National Archives.*

herd, and Billy Dixon and other muleskinners brought out their Sharps carbines. A great many buffaloes were shot down and the herd swerved aside, "which saved the mule train," pointed out Billy, "and filled our pots and skillets with fine meat."[19]

It took twelve days to reach Camp Supply, where the cargoes were unloaded onto the ground and covered with tarpaulins. The outpost had just been opened as a "Camp of Supply" to sustain the winter campaign of 1868. Eight hundred soldiers — five companies of infantry and eleven companies of George Armstrong Custer's Seventh Cavalry — hastily began throwing up a stockade and buildings.[20] This initial construction was supported by a 450-wagon supply train. When the mule train which employed Billy Dixon arrived, the train quickly was emptied and returned to Fort Hays for another load. Now back to full strength, the one hundred-wagon train delivered more cargo to Fort Hays.

On November 23 Lieutenant Colonel Custer led his column

out of Camp Supply in a snowstorm toward a hostile encampment thought to be on the Washita River. Within four days a large Cheyenne camp was found in a valley on the Washita. That night Custer divided his men into four squadrons, and at dawn on November 27 a general attack was signaled.

Chief Black Kettle was killed early in the charge, and more than one hundred other Native Americans were slain as warriors battled to cover the retreat of their fleeing families. In addition to fifty-three captives, soldiers collected 1,100 buffalo robes, 1,000 pounds of lead, and 500 pounds of gunpowder. In all, some 875 ponies were seized. Custer ordered troopers to pull down the lodges and pile up the food and clothing. The piles were set on fire, and men of four troops methodically shot the captured horses. Warriors crept back within range and challenged this winter destruction with sporadic but unsuccessful skirmishing.[21]

While Custer triumphed at the Battle of the Washita — a catastrophe for the Cheyennes — the mule train that included Billy Dixon experienced a spectacular catastrophe of its own. Returning again toward Fort Leavenworth with empty wagons, the muleskinners drove the wagons abreast.

"Nobody ever knew what scared one of the rear teams," related Billy, "but it certainly got scared, and that particular outfit was going in the direction of Missouri and Kentucky at the rate of about thirty miles an hour." The unexpected noise of the onrushing wagon, as well as the loud curses of the driver, caused panic and stampede among the mules that spread throughout the train.[22]

"So here we went, in every possible direction," said Billy. "It was impossible to hold the mules." For miles wagons were broken and scattered and overturned. Some mules were so badly injured that they had to be shot, while others tore loose from their harness and were never seen again. "The spectacle of those six hundred mules running away with their one hundred

When the Kansas Pacific Railroad reached Fort Hays, the outpost became a major shipping point for frontier military operations. *Courtesy National Archives.*

wagons was the most remarkable I ever witnessed." The mules afterward remained so skittish that they would bolt at "the flip of a prairie dog's tail."[23]

The train limped back to Fort Hays. When Billy first came to the "fort" it was all tents. But with the arrival of the Kansas Pacific Railroad, Fort Hays became the major shipping point for outposts to the south. So Billy remained at Fort Hays for a year, until the fall of 1869, working out of the quartermaster depot. "During the five years I had been making my way in the world," pointed out Billy, "I had worked for the Government most of the time."[24]

But Billy's years as a bullwhacker and muleskinner for government freight trains was at an end. He was about to become an independent buffalo hunter, a sharpshooting man of the plains who would experience all of the adventure as a hunter - and Indian fighter — he had long dreamed about.

Chapter Four

She Grew Up in the Old South

I'll be good Mother. I'll try so hard, and be good.

Olive King to her mother

Olive King was born on January 30, 1873, on Bent Mountain, Virginia. Bent Mountain, located eighteen miles southwest of Roanoke, was part of the Lewis Grant, which had been deeded by King George III of England to Olive's great-great-grandfather during the eighteenth century. Bent Creek Mountain Plateau stands more than 3,000 feet in elevation and offers a splendid view of the Roanoke Valley. (Little did anyone realize that Bent's Creek in the Texas Panhandle would flow just outside Olive's first home as a married woman.)

The King family was immensely proud of the Lewis Grant and of their illustrious ancestor, Gen. Andrew Lewis. Like Billy Dixon exactly a century later, Andrew Lewis would prove himself to be an outstanding Indian fighter. Andrew was born and raised in Ireland, but he and his brother came to Virginia with their father after he killed his landlord.

Andrew married and became the father of eight children. He was a farmer and a surveyor, and he served as a militia officer. During the French and Indian War Lewis was active on the frontier, fighting under Col. George Washington and winning promotion to major. Although the conflict with the French and Indians ended in 1763, the next year the Dunmore War (Lord Dunmore was Governor of Virginia) flared up on the mountainous frontier of Virginia. Lewis was elevated to colonel, and on October 10, 1774, led the colonials to a triumph over Shawnees at the Battle of Point Pleasant.[1]

A year later the American Revolution erupted, and in 1776

Andrew Lewis was commissioned a brigadier general. He also served in the Virginia House of Burgesses, but he died in 1780. Lewisburg, West Virginia, was named after General Lewis; there are statues of him; and a stretch of Interstate 81 is named "Andrew Lewis Memorial Highway."

Virginians always have been proud of being part of the first American colony and of the rich history of Virginia. Descendants of Gen. Andrew Lewis took deep pride in their illustrious ancestor and in the family's "Lewis Grant." General Lewis had been dead almost a century when Olive was born, but her grandmother, Catherine "Kitty" King, perpetuated his memory throughout the family circle. Lewis was Kitty's grandfather, and she inherited part of the Lewis Grant. Olive was told that when she was a baby, her grandmother solemnly pronounced: "Remember all your life, Olive, that you were born on the Lewis Grant."[2]

This military statue of Gen. Andrew Lewis stands in the Civic Center at Salem, Virginia. *Photo courtesy of Shay Joines.*

Closeup of General Lewis from his statue.
Photo courtesy of Shay Joines.

But Robert Woods King, Olive's father and Kitty's youngest son, could not support his family on the Lewis Grant. Olive was the eighth child born to Woods and Mary Jane Blankenship King. With the birth of Olive there were four girls and four boys. Tobacco cultivation is hard on the soil, and Woods King decided to move about twenty miles west, into Montgomery County, another mountainous, heavily wooded area. The family moved when Olive was two, but she would continue to be reminded that she was born on Bent Mountain in the Lewis Grant — in a log house built by her father.[3]

Woods King had followed the family military tradition and fought in the Civil War. Virginia was devastated by the war, and much of its soil was exhausted from tobacco cultivation. After the war Woods continued to farm tobacco, but yields did not produce prosperity. Olive's two oldest sisters married and moved away, but another little girl, Ida, was born, along with a tenth child, William. The oldest son, Joseph, moved out to try his luck farther west.

In 1880 Joseph returned home for a visit, but soon after his arrival he fell ill. Sadly he had brought smallpox into the house, and several family members contracted the deadly disease. Grandmother Kitty came over from Bent Mountain to help with nursing. Joseph recovered first, followed one by one by the sick children. Olive bore smallpox scars for years, finally outgrowing the pox marks.[4] But the disease killed Woods King, who was the only family member to succumb. Because of fears triggered by the epidemic, the coffin containing Woods King was prohibited from crossing county lines. Instead of being interred in the family cemetery at Bent Mountain, Woods was buried on his Montgomery County farm.[5]

Mary Jane King, whose father had died when she was a baby, sent for her widowed mother. Mrs. Blankenship would live with her recently widowed daughter. Joseph planned to send money home from his wages. Andrew, Albert, and Archie would take on the farm work. But these three boys were still youngsters, while Olive, four-year-old Ida, and nine-month-old William were just children. Maggie was the oldest of the seven who still lived at the farm, but it was arranged for her to move in with oldest sister Oceola and her husband, who made their home in Atlanta.[6]

The hardest deci-

General Lewis died in 1781 and was buried at East Hill Cemetery in Salem. The burial site once was part of his 625-acre estate. *Photo courtesy of Shay Joines.*

sion involved Olive. With the departure of teenaged Maggie to live with a married sister, the mother and two grandmothers decided to send Olive away also. The sons were needed on the farm, while little Ida — Olive's playmate — and baby William were too young to leave their mother. Of course, Olive was only seven and still in need of a mother, particularly since she had just lost her father. But Dora King Wade, a daughter of Grandmother's Kitty's oldest son, had a comfortable home in Decatur, Alabama. Dora and her successful husband, Miles Wade, had two sons, and in correspondence to relatives in Virginia she had expressed her disappointment at not having had a daughter. A letter was sent to Dora explaining the situation regarding Olive.

Dora replied with a letter of welcome and invitation. Grandmother Kitty pressed the point that living with her granddaughter Dora, Olive would be raised in a comfortable home with material advantages. And there would be one less mouth to feed on the farm. In pragmatic terms the decision was sound.

But seven-year-old Olive was horrified at this solution. To be separated from her mother and her siblings so soon after losing her father, to be sent away from her home to a cousin in a faraway state produced deep trauma and tears. Olive played with Ida, and she followed her mother around, and she wept. When she received final instructions from her mother, Olive replied pitiably through her tears: "I'll be good, Mother. I'll try so hard, and be good."[7]

Farm produce was sold to purchase Olive's train ticket. Her railroad journey was in the company of a cousin, Florence King Atkins and her two children. Florence was headed to Dallas to rejoin her husband, who had gone to Texas seeking opportunity. At the Decatur passenger depot several relatives had gathered to greet Cousin Florence and her children and little Cousin Olive. Soon Florence resumed her train journey and Cousin Dora brought Olive to her new home.

The north boundary of Decatur was the Tennessee River.

The town was incorporated in 1821 and was named after Commodore Stephen Decatur, a distinguished naval officer who had been killed in a duel the previous year. The strategic location of Decatur made it a battleground during the Civil War, and only four buildings remained standing after the war: a two-story brick bank and three private homes. The town had to be completely rebuilt during its postwar rebirth, which spelled success for building contractors such as Miles Wade.

The Wade home was a two-story frame structure with a broad central hallway and four large rooms opening off of the hall, both upstairs and downstairs. There was a kitchen wing presided over by a genial black woman named Winnie. A downstairs bedroom housed Miles Wade's mother, who habitually kept to herself. Olive's spacious room was upstairs above the dining room. Olive had never had a private bedroom, and the chamber was dominated by a tall four-poster bed. The boys, Henry and Alva, eleven and nine, slept in a bedroom across the hall. The front yard was well-groomed, and in the back was a barn and carriage shed. A black man named Henry tended the yard and the buggy horses and the milk cow.

Neighbors and friends came to the house to welcome the girl from Virginia, and Olive was gifted with more than a dozen dolls. Dora and Miles were the essence of hospitality and courtesy to Olive. The boys were on their best behavior, and she got on especially well with Henry, who easily took to the role of big brother. It was the spring of 1880, and Henry and Alva went off to public school every day. At age seven and raised in a rural area, Olive had not yet attended school. Dora enrolled her in a private, all-girls school operated by a spinster, Miss Greene, out of her home. The following fall Olive attended the local public school.[8]

Dora delighted in having a "daughter" in her home. She sewed dress after dress for Olive, and spent hours grooming her long hair. Although Miles did not play outdoors with his boys, he enjoyed shooting marbles in the yard with Olive. At Christmas, Olive and the boys were given roller skates, and the carpets in the upstairs hallway were removed to provide the children a skating rink. Olive attended Methodist services with the family at a church which stood catercorner across the street from their home.[9]

By the summer of 1882 Olive had been absent from Virginia for more than two years. Nine-year-old Olive was sent back for a visit by train to Christiansburg, the nearest rail stop to the King farm in Montgomery County. Her mother met her with open arms, and there was a delightful reunion with the siblings who were still at home. But most of the summer had to be spent in the fields, and at age nine Olive was expected to work full-time. Hay had to be raked and stacked, tobacco leaves were painstakingly checked for worms, weeds were hoed, and black-berries, huckleberries and dewberries were located and picked in the woods. At the end of the summer Archie borrowed a bug-gy from a neighbor and drove his sister to the depot in Chris-tiansburg. Olive's mother decided not to go to Christiansburg, perhaps finding the depot goodbye too painful. Olive would not return to Virginia for seven years.

Olive's arrival in Decatur was met with unrestrained affec-tion. Winnie proudly presented two dolls and almost two doz-en doll dresses she had stitched by hand. Dora upgraded the wardrobe of the growing girl, tirelessly fashioning dresses and undergarments of the finest materials. In school Olive became the center of a circle of friends who often met in the afternoons at the Wade home. While one girl sat at the parlor piano, the others would practice waltzes, polkas, and other popular danc-es of the day.

In 1881 Atlanta businessmen organized and staged the In-ternational Cotton Exposition, featuring more than 1,100 ex-hibits in large new buildings and an average daily attendance of 3,816 during the seventy-six days that the Exposition was open. Recognizing the potential of such events, a series of similar extravaganzas was held. The Piedmont Exposition of 1887 attracted a total attendance of 200,000, including President Grover Cleveland. Eight years later Atlanta's Exposition movement climaxed with the 1895 Cotton States and International Exposition, which included a notable speech by Booker T. Washington and music by the immensely popular band of John Philip Sousa.[11]

During Atlanta's Exposition era Dora and Miles planned a visit that would include Olive. Olive's oldest sister, Oceola, and her husband, William King, made their home in Atlanta. Sister Maggie still lived with Oceola and William, who now had two children of their own. One of Grandmother Kitty's older sons, Joe King, had moved to Atlanta before the Civil War, and there were other relatives in the growing city. When Dora and Miles arrived at the Cotton Exposition by train, they were greeted by a number of cousins, while Olive stayed with her sisters. A circus was in town, and the four youngsters enjoyed this special entertainment. From various cousins Olive received such gifts as a gold ring, a beaded purse, and a box of chocolates.[12]

By the summer of 1884, eleven-year-old Olive began to experience religious conviction. She had been a churchgoer since she was a little girl: "I remember well the old brick church close to my mother's home . . ."[13] Regular attendance at Methodist services with the Wade family exerted a maturing effect on her sense of spirituality. Olive talked with Dora about faith matters, and soon she joined the Methodist church during a Sunday service.[14]

The summer of 1888 brought tragic loss to the Wade family. An epidemic of typhoid fever broke out in Decatur during the summer heat and humidity. Henry, the oldest son, fell ill and died within a week. Dora tended the grave daily, often accompanied during that sad summer by Olive.[15]

A year later Olive finished high school. She enjoyed her

studies in literature and history, and applied herself with determination to mathematics. Her teachers urged her to go on to a normal school for teachers, and Dora offered to provide higher education for her beloved ward. But during the summer of 1889 Olive felt drawn to her native Virginia — the teachings of Grandmother Kitty ran deep. And Olive wanted to be with her mother and others of her immediate family.

Olive now understood the affection and advantages that had been lavished upon her for years by Dora and Miles, but her heritage called out to her. Olive expressed her deep appreciation to Dora, and after announcing her decision to leave both ladies wept and embraced. By the end of the summer sixteen-year-old Olive had left the Wade home and returned to Virginia.

Olive had not been to the Montgomery County farm since 1882, and the household had changed during the past seven years. Oldest brother Joe had become successful as a tobacco-curer and traveled constantly supervising various tobacco sheds. Brother Andrew also worked away from home a great deal of the time.

Albert and Archie, the older brothers closest in age to Olive, had left the tobacco farm to become Texas cowboys. Like tobacco farmers, cowboys engaged in hard, often monotonous work. But cowboys rode horseback, herded ornery longhorn cattle utilizing skills with a lariat, and wore big hats, high-heeled boots, chaps, bandanas, and other colorful attire. Cowboying was the great American adventure for young men in the post-Civil War West, and during the 1880s Albert and Archie headed for the ranch country of the Texas Panhandle. When Olive returned to the farm in 1889, the only one of her five brothers who was still at home was nine-year-old Will.

Maggie, like Olive, now was back at home, because Oceola's husband had died. Maggie suddenly was a burden in Atlanta to her widowed sister, and so she returned to Virginia. The youngest of the five sisters, Ida, was still at home. The second oldest sister, Catherine, had married Henry Correll and started a family. But Catherine King Correll died, and her daughter Grace had moved in with her grandmother, Mary Jane Blankenship King. Mary Jane's mother, Olive's Grandmother Blankenship, still lived at the farm. With the return of Olive, there were six females — of a broad age range — and one boy living at the worn-out tobacco farm.[16]

But Olive and Maggie, as young ladies newly returned to the neighborhood, attracted the notice of young men. Maggie began to keep company with Charles St. Clair, while Olive was courted by Kemper Lawrence. The courtship of Olive and Kemper did not accelerate into romance, but in 1890 Maggie became Mrs. St. Clair. Charles St. Clair found work in a West Virginia coal mine, and Olive moved with them to keep her sister company in a mining town. A year later the St. Clairs were parents of a baby boy. Olive helped her sister with the baby and the house work, but when Maggie returned to full strength Olive realized it was time to return to her mother's farm.[17]

In 1892 news came from Texas that Archie and his wife, Sena Walstad King, now had a baby boy in their Texas Panhandle sod house. Learning of Olive's return to the Virginia farm after keeping Maggie and her baby company in West Virginia, Archie sent an invitation for her to visit in their Panhandle home with Sena and their baby. Olive, who would turn twenty early in 1893, adventurously agreed to travel to cowboy country.[18]

But first Olive wanted to visit Decatur. She had not seen the Wade family in nearly four years. Dora had a grandbaby in the house, the son of Alva and his wife. In her loving fashion, Dora doted on her grandson. But she was elated when Olive arrived. Olive once again enjoyed the gracious hospitality of the Wade home. Olive and Dora caught up on family events while sewing and gardening together. Olive visited her school friends. The visit extended to two months, and Dora invited Olive to move back in permanently. The offer of providing college education was renewed.[19]

But Olive already had made this decision — in 1889. Now, as a twenty-year-old, she was determined to embark on an adventure in the West. The first leg of that adventure was a reunion with the loving family in Decatur. But now she had the opportunity to visit her cowboy brother — and a new sister-in-law and baby nephew — in the wide-open spaces of the Texas Panhandle. Once again she bade farewell to the Wades and, with a sense of anticipation, boarded a train for the Lone Star State.

Chapter Five
Buffalo Hunter

*I felt the cold driving into my very bones,
and realized my danger.*

Billy Dixon

Billy Dixon had struck out on his own at the age of thirteen in 1864. Although his first employment was as a bullwhacker, he had to have help from full-grown men in order to yoke his oxen. By the fall of 1869, however, five years of hard work — often under dangerous conditions — had produced a mature, impressive young man. "I was now eighteen years old, in perfect health, strong and muscular, with keen eye-sight, a natural aptitude for outdoor life, an excellent shot, and had a burning desire to experience every phase of adventure to be found on the Plains."[1]

In November 1869 Billy and a couple of muleskinner pals, Tom Campbell and George Smith, decided to fit up an outfit to hunt and trap throughout the winter. Smith was a veteran trapper, and Billy Dixon evidently did not want to waste the winter months — as he had the previous year — hanging out idly in Leavenworth and Kansas City.

The trio purchased a wagon and team, provisions and traps, and guns and ammunition. Working their way north along the Saline River, they fashioned a dugout where there was a good supply of firewood. They trapped beaver and otter, as well as a great many wolves. In addition to selling their pelts, at intervals they sold game in Hays City, where a load of elk brought twenty dollars apiece.

"My happiness now seemed complete, and I enjoyed to the fullest every moment of my life." Billy revelled in the outdoor existence, and he earned good money. He enjoyed their "warm, comfortable dugout," and besides, "I had no wish to return to a city."[2]

The winter months of 1869-70 as a hunter and trapper in Kansas propelled Billy Dixon into the promising life of a buffalo hide hunter. By early 1870 eastern hide-buyers were sending agents to Fort Hays and other Kansas frontier communities. "The first offers were $1 each for cowhides and $2 each for bull hides, which enabled us to make money rapidly." Recounting in later years the offers of hide-buyers, Billy still seemed astounded at his good fortune. "As the slaughter increased, and the buffalo grew scarcer prices were advanced, until $4 was being paid for bull hides by the fall of 1872."[3]

The buffalo is the largest mammal in North America. Bulls weigh up to 2,000 pounds and often are six feet tall. Cows are four to five feet tall and weight up to 1,000 pounds. Buffalo calves are born from late March through May and weigh from thirty to seventy pounds at birth. Despite their massive size, buffaloes are surprisingly agile and fast, capable of speeds up to thirty-five miles per hour. When Billy Dixon ventured to the frontier, there were tens of millions of buffaloes ranging across the West. Native American tribes which had mastered horses based their culture upon the buffalo: food, clothing, tipi coverings, saddle coverings, bridles, saddlebags, weapons, tools and utensils of every sort.

Buffalo hides were in demand as trade items. The thickest hides came from old bulls, which might live to an age of twenty. Bull hides went into warrior shields and belts and moccasin soles and, later, the boots of white men. The thinnest and most flexible leather came from unborn calves and was utilized for small bags and underclothing. The intermediate thickness of cowskins provided tipi covers, dresses, leggings, and a great variety of other items. Rawhide (untreated skins) was tough, but after tanning it was used for lariats, hackamores, picket ropes, pole hitches, tie strings, saddlebags, even snowshoes.[4]

By 1840 there were more than one hundred trading posts through-out the West, and Na-tive Americans began to swap well over 100,000 buffalo hides annual-ly — as well as ponies —for their needs. Buf-falo robes, with the hair on, were popular in the East for lap robes. At first Anglo hunters did not have to go very far into the West to kill buf-faloes for hides and for tongues, which could

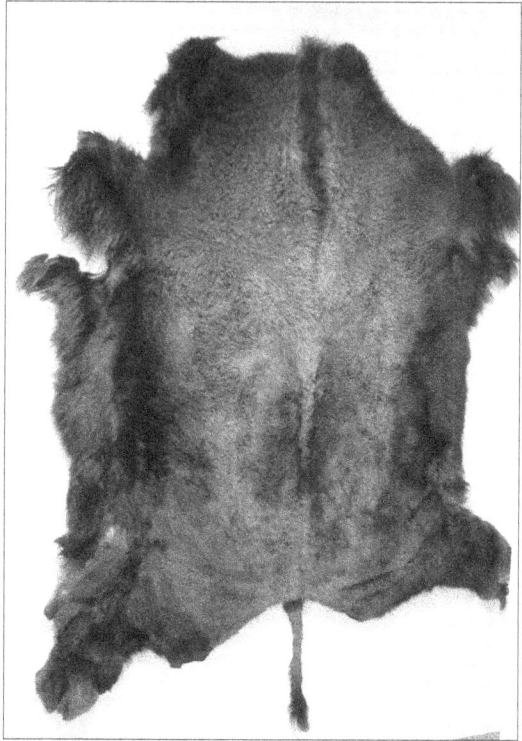

The thickest buffalo hides came from old bulls. *Courtesy Hutchinson County Museum, Borger.*

be smoked and shipped to the East as culinary delicacies. As railroads penetrated the West, travelers banged away at near-by buffaloes from train windows. Five-day railroad excursions were advertised, promising buffalo shooting along the tracks. Easterners organized trips to the West, small sporting expedi-tions of the type that young Billy Dixon hired on to support in the winter of 1867-68. After the first transcontinental rail-road was completed in 1869, hides could be shipped profitably to tanneries, and the vast numbers of buffaloes were divided into a northern and a southern herd. The southern herd, which ranged deep into Texas, was the largest.

By the 1870s Europeans were developing tanning process-es which accelerated demand for buffalo hides, and Americans quickly adapted these processes. America's Industrial Rev-

Buffalo skinner at work. *Courtesy of the University of Texas Institute of Texan Cultures, San Antonio.*

olution soon discovered that thick buffalo leather was excellent for machine belting, as well as for shoes and luggage and other commercial uses. It was at this point, early in 1870, that the agents of eastern hide-buyers began to offer one dollar for cowhides and two dollars for bull hides and, within a couple of years, four dollars for bull hides.

Dixon and his two companions apparently encountered the hide-buying agents in Hays City, "and quickly abandoned trapping for buffalo hunting." During the winter months of early 1870 Dixon and the others hunted mainly along the Republican River and its tributaries in western Kansas. Dixon and his friends fashioned a dugout as a headquarters site for the outfit. "The only kind of dugout worth having was one with a big, open fireplace, near the edge of a stream of good water, with plenty of wood along its banks." explained Dixon. "We often occupied the same dugout for a month or more. Then, as the buffaloes grew less plentiful, we shifted our camp and built a new dugout, which was easily and quickly done."[5]

Dixon, Smith, and Campbell skinned the buffaloes where

they had fallen and hauled the hides to camp, where they were staked out on the ground with the meat side down. When the green hides had dried they were stacked in four piles: bull hides, cow hides, robe hides, and calf hides. Loaded into wagons, the hides were transported to town, or buyers came to camp with freight wagons. By the end of the summer Smith and Campbell decided to quit, and Dixon bought them out. Although Dixon still was only nineteen, he decided to lead his own outfit as the principal hunter.

Dixon realized that "there were very few men who could excel me in marksmanship, which possibly was a natural gift supplemented by more or less constant practice." Perhaps Smith and Campbell quit because Dixon monopolized the shooting, relegating his partners to the nasty odiferous activity of skinning. "I always did my own killing," insisted Dixon, "and generally had two experienced men to do the skinning. A capable man could skin fifty buffaloes a day, and usually was paid $50

Engraving of a buffalo hunters' camp from *Harper's New Monthly Magazine*, 1879, p. 716. *Courtesy of the University of Texas Institute of Texan Cultures, San Antonio.*

a month. I have paid as much as twenty-five cents a hide to a good skinner." After buying the outfit, Dixon "straightaway hired two men to work for me, and started out killing buffaloes more energetically than ever."[6]

In the fall of 1870 Dixon moved his camp south, about ten miles below Hays City. A large dugout was built along with a picket house. The camp was on a well-traveled road, and Dixon established a road ranch. Stocking his roadside store with whiskey, tobacco, and groceries, Dixon hired a former muleskinner named Billy Reynolds to run the place, "while I devoted my time to killing buffaloes."

Reynolds and Dixon had known each other at Camp Supply in 1868. "Many a jolly company gathered at the road ranch," said Dixon, as the whiskey flowed freely under the jovial management of Reynolds. But after several months, following two weeks on the hunt, Dixon returned to his road ranch to find the building empty of merchandise and Billy Reynolds vanished. Dixon commented dryly, "during my absence Reynolds sold the whole outfit and skipped the country, without even telling me goodbye."[8]

But Dixon was making good money as a hide hunter, and he formed another partnership with a former teamster pal named Finn. Finn invested in Dixon's outfit and brought a good team to the partnership. Dixon and Finn hunted together for a year, usually aided by a hot-tempered skinner known as "Fighting" McCabe, who also was an incurable gambler. McCabe worked for Dixon for three years, and was with Billy at Adobe Walls. Finn proved to be good company at the end of the day. "He was a good story-teller, and when the day's work was done and we were comfortably seated around the fire, nothing pleased me more than to get Finn started telling stories."[9]

Since boyhood Billy Dixon enjoyed hearing the campfire tales of frontiersmen. Perhaps because he was such an avid listener, he stayed on congenial terms with a rugged set of companions. On the frontier he was in the company of riverside woodcutters, bullwhackers, muleskinners, buffalo hunters, hide skinners and, later, cowboys. Many of the men Billy Dixon grew up with were hard-drinking, coarse-mannered, foul-mouthed, quick fisted. But somehow the soft-spoken youngster formed a camaraderie with his fellow frontiersmen, in great part because he clearly admired these rough men of the West. As a young man it was Dixon who earned the admiration of his fellow Westerners for his courage and exceptional skills with firearms. Certainly these were the people he was comfortable with throughout his life.

In November 1871 Dixon drove his wagon into Hays City, intending to bring a load of supplies to his dugout. But at his hotel he encountered an express agent who hired him — and his empty wagon and team of mules — to haul a load of freight to Fort Dodge, one hundred miles to the south and west. The need for supplies at his camp was not pressing; besides, "I also wanted to look that country over for buffaloes."

After loading 1,500 pounds of express, Dixon headed south, staying that night at a road ranch. The next morning the weather was frigid, "and by 10 o'clock it was spitting snow and getting colder every minute." Dixon dismounted from his mule and walked, trying to stay warm. "I felt the cold driving into my very bones, and realized my danger." When he reached the crest of a long divide, Dixon remounted and sent his mules down the slope at a gallop.[10]

Fortunately another road ranch soon came into view. "I was scarcely able to speak when I drove up and found half a dozen men coming to meet me, all eager to hear the news from town, whatever it might be." But Dixon's jaws were locked and he could not speak. He was hustled into the road ranch dugout and extra wood was thrown on the fire, and finally Dixon recovered. "This was my first experience with killing cold." It was not to be the last.[11]

Resuming his journey the next day, Dixon began to sight buffaloes along the way. He reached Fort Dodge on the third night, and learned that the recent blizzard had driven buffaloes by the thousands to the outpost. Officers ordered the discharge of artillery to keep the massive beasts from breaking down the corrals and walls of buildings. Billy determined to find the location of this great herd.

Billy had brought his saddle horse along, as he usually did ("in case of trouble I had a better show of getting away on horseback"). The next morning he rode west for more than thirty miles up the Arkansas River, sighting locations in every direction where the buffaloes had bedded down, but not spotting a single bison. Frustrated, he rode north toward the open plains, and at a high point he caught his breath in astonishment. "As far as I could see there was a solid mass of buffalo . . . At no other time in my life did I ever see such a vast number of buffaloes. For miles in every direction the country was alive with them."[12]

The following day Dixon headed back to Hays City, where many buffalo hunters had sought shelter from the winter storms. "I told them of the black ocean of buffaloes I had seen northwest of Fort Dodge," recalled Dixon, "and set every man to overhauling his outfit." Of course Dixon "was impatient to reach my camp, so I loaded up with supplies and pulled out."[13]

Months of steady hunting followed. In May 1872 Dixon and his men moved their camp north of the Kansas Pacific Railroad, and soon Billy had a rare experience: "I got completely lost, so badly that I had no idea of direction." Billy was with a skinner named Perkins, who was of no help. The two men had to make a dry camp, but they shot four buffalo bulls and made a warm bed of two hides, turning the fur inside.

"In after years I thought many times of that night on the Plains," reflected Billy. "Of how tired we were, of how the wind whistled past us, of how the cold seemed to come down out of the sky, heavy and chill, and of how icily the moon shone as she sailed westwind. Save for the occasional howling of wolves and coyotes, the night was supernaturally silent . . . It was the stuff that makes a man in a warm bed under a roof feel like getting up to saddle his horse and ride away to the Land of Nowhere. Once in the blood, it can never be lost. Home-sickness for the Plains and their free, open life stings like a hornet."[14]

It was late in life that Billy Dixon expressed these feelings to his wife/biographer. One wonders how many times in his latter years Dixon, while shouldering the responsibilities of a large family, awakened in a warm bed under his roof with a drowsy longing to saddle his horse and ride into plains country which still was covered with buffalo herds. This "Home-sickness for the Plains and their free, open life." once was expressed by the great Kiowa leader, Chief Satanta. At the Medicine Lodge peace negotiations in 1867 (seventeen-year-old Billy Dixon was present but probably did not hear the chief speak), a translation from Satanta was printed by a *New York Times* reporter. "I love the land and the buffalo," said Satanta emphatically. "I love to roam over the wide prairie . . . and when I do I feel free and happy."[15] As Billy Dixon said, "Once in the blood it can never be lost."

Dixon and Perkins slept late in their makeshift bed of freshly skinned buffalo robes. Billy heard something "scratching and clawing on the hide," and he feared it was a skunk ("I would have preferred being bitten by a rattlesnake"). He kicked the hide violently, but instead of a skunk, "I was astonished to see a big eagle that had been trying to get his breakfast by picking the meat off the fresh hide." The eagle also was astonished and flopped desperately before managing to take flight. Perkins was startled out of a deep sleep. "He told me that he was sure Indians had nailed us, and that his scalp-lock twitched all day."[16]

Throughout the summer of 1872 Dixon and his outfit hunted along the Saline and Solomon rivers. That fall they headed south to the small cluster of new buildings that comprised

Dodge City. Recalling the names of the first businesses, Dixon listed four saloons, a drug store, Wright & Company General Store, and Zimmerman's gun and ammunition store. Zimmerman's did a roaring business arming the hundreds of buffalo hunters who were outfitting in Dodge City.

Zimmerman's featured a powerful new rifle known as the Sharps Big Fifty. The Sharps Rifle Manufacturing Company was located in Hartford, Connecticut, and the company introduced a succession of military and sporting rifles, carbines, and shotguns, as well as a variety of cartridges. More than 100,000 firearms were manufactured by Sharps for the Union Army during the Civil War. The Model 1874 Sharps Sporting Rifle actually was introduced in 1871 and was produced until 1881. This single-shot breech-loader was available with octagon, round, or round/octagon barrels from 26-inches to 30-inches long, although extra-long barrels could be ordered. Double-set triggers and globe-and-peep sights were popular features. There were several cartridge possibilities, but the most powerful loads were the .45-120, the .44-90, and the .50-90. The .50-90 in a 2 ½-inch case came out in mid-1872 and gained an immediate following among the buffalo hunters for the "Big Fifty."[17]

Buffalo hunter J. Wright Mooar killed an estimated 20,000 bison, including the only albino ever slain in Texas. He kept two of his Big Fifties throughout his long life (1851-1940), and carefully described these prized rifles and their performance. "The weapon was a gun weighing from twelve to sixteen pounds, and the caliber was .50-110. One hundred and ten grains of powder, in a long brass shell, hurled from the beautifully rifled muzzle of the great gun a heavy leaden missile that in its impact and its tearing, shattering qualities would instantly bring down the biggest bison, if properly aimed, and that reached out to incredible distances for rifles of that period."[18]

Because a buffalo hunter might fire more than a hundred rounds in a day, factory loaded ammunition was a luxury that gave way to the reloading of cartridge cases by hunters (some outfits employed a reload man). Some hunters might reload fewer grains of powder so that a heavier bullet could be used, and a .50-90 case could be stuffed with 110 grains of powder with a lighter bullet. For the resulting .50-110 cartridge or a similar high power load, hunters often preferred an octagonal barrel for strength. The heavy weight of octagonal barrels also helped absorb the recoil of heavy charges, and so did a large buttplate.[19]

The Sharps Big Fifty was the preferred rifle of Billy Dixon, along with a great many other buffalo hunters. With a Big Fifty and his uncanny accuracy, Dixon could shoot from five hundred yards and drop a buffalo with every round. At close range buffaloes might stampede from the noise and the smell, although most hunting was done downwind of the herd. Buffaloes were near-sighted and, perhaps because of their great size, hard to scare. Experienced hunters would spot and shoot the leader of a herd, then shoot buffaloes on the outside of the herd, while the other animals seemed not to notice falling buffaloes. But wounded buffaloes would run around wildly and start a stampede. A good marksman aimed for vital organs. "The buffalo was a hard animal to kill instantly," said Billy, "as a vital point had to be struck."[20]

Legendary hunter J. Wright Mooar killed an estimated 20,000 bison, including the only albino ever slain in Texas. *Courtesy Scurry County Museum, Snyder.*

With a broadside shot a

During a vicious blizzard a buffalo stampede imperiled fencing and even buildings at Fort Dodge. *Courtesy National Archives.*

soft lead slug would be driven into the lungs, or with an angle from the rear a high-powered bullet could be fired behind a shoulder blade into the heart. But veteran hunter J. Wright Mooar had seen buffaloes shot through the heart "run one to two hundred yards, and by that time the whole herd was stampeded beyond stopping." Mooar therefore preferred a lung shot. "A buffalo shot through the lungs immediately sank to his haunches, rocked sidewise, as his air passages filled with blood, and finally he rolled over and expired."[21] Head shots often were unsuccessful, because soft lead slugs rarely penetrated the thick skulls. Many hunters learned these lessons in Kansas during 1872 and 1873.

"During the fall and winter of 1872 and 1873 there were more hunters in the country than ever before or afterwards," testified Dixon, who was among their number. "This was the beginning of the high tide of buffalo hunting, and buffalo fell by the thousands." Dixon estimated that 75,000 buffaloes were killed within sixty to seventy-five miles of Dodge City that season. A line of camps radiated out of Dodge. "The noise of the guns of the hunters could be heard on all sides," remembered Dixon, "rumbling and booming hour after hour, as if a heavy battle were being fought."[22]

The buffalo population, of course, was reduced in the vicinity of Dodge City. Dixon and two men working with his outfit ventured into Dodge, "taking in the sights" for a few days before heading out again in search of new hunting grounds. Going west along the Arkansas River, Dixon led his outfit south

Buffalo hunter at work with a Sharps Big Fifty with an octagonal barrel. *Courtesy NRA Museum in Springfield, Missouri.*

across the river into range that had been reserved at Medicine Lodge for Native American hunters. The army was supposed to patrol the Arkansas River, but Dixon had no trouble in crossing into the southern range. Although testy encounters with angry Native Americans inclined Dixon to retreat back to the north, the sudden appearance of thousands of buffaloes tempted the men to hunt for two or three days. Their hunt extended for more than a week, and three trips were required to haul the hides into Dodge City, where they were paid $2,000.

It was early 1873 and bitter winter weather soon would strike. "Each man bought himself a supply of warm winter clothing," said Dixon, "and with lots of supplies and ammunition, we again went in search of the shaggy buffalo." But a sweeping hunt turned up few buffaloes, and a vicious blizzard sent the outfit to the shelter of a road ranch, where other hunters congregated as well. "We were a jolly crowd," reminisced Billy happily. "What sport we had, telling stories of our hunts, drinking whiskey, playing cards and shooting at targets. I was especially fond of the latter."[23]

"Whiskey-drinking was a pastime or diversion in which few men did not indulge," observed Billy, apparently including himself. "I cannot boast of having been an altogether perfect man in my conduct in those wild, free days, but there were two popular forms of amusement in which I did not indulge — dancing and gambling. I never bet a nickel on cards nor gambled in any form in my life though I saw all these things going on every night when I was in a border town, especially at Dodge." But from his earliest years in the West, he realized that "a man who did not take at least one drink was considered unfriendly . . . Inviting a man to drink was about the only way civility could be shown, and to refuse an invitation bordered upon an insult." Billy offered this explanation of frontier drinking etiquette to his biographer — who also was his wife and a devout Methodist — at a time when prohibition was a popular cause.[24]

When winter weather moderated a bit early in 1873, Dixon and a partner named Jack Callahan and a couple of skinners left Dodge City and headed west, hoping to find buffaloes in large numbers. At one point the outfit camped one night at Sand Creek, Colorado, site of the infamous Chivington Massacre of Cheyennes in 1862. "We could see bones still scattered over the battleground," noted Dixon. But after a long, circular sweep, their hunt produced scant returns. Several days were spent col-

Hide wagons.
Courtesy Scurry County Museum, Snyder.

lecting a pile of hides left in one place and other piles left else-
where. The hides were hauled to Dodge City in the spring of
1873.[25]

Callahan decided to quit buffalo hunting, opening a saloon
in Granada, Colorado. Dixon found that many others who had
hunted around Dodge in 1872 and 1873 also had abandoned
the hide business. "I did not have enough of the buffalo game,
however," related Dixon. Ranging into western Kansas with
two skinners, "We prospered, as buffaloes were plentiful." The
hides were hauled into Granada, just inside the Colorado line.[26]

In the fall of 1873 Dixon loaded up on supplies for an expedition to the south. Billy led his outfit, including two wagons,
along the Cimarron River to a site near Wagonbend Springs,
where he planned to spend the winter. A dugout was erected
and buffalo proved numerous. But warriors also were numerous. Cheyenne braves rode by in small bands of as few as three
or four, "but if fifteen or twenty came in sight, heading for our
camp, we signaled for them to pass around without stopping."
Dixon did not want a superior force to get at close quarters.
"Occasionally, upon approaching, the Cheyennes would lay
down their guns, and advance unarmed, to show that they did
not intend to offer us injury. We always fed them well." After
one visit Dixon noticed that his field glasses has been stolen. He
angrily gave chase, but when the warriors scattered into broken
country, Dixon prudently turned back to camp.[27]

Deciding to hunt farther to the west, Dixon led his outfit
as far as the present-day town of Guymon, Oklahoma. Several
small bunches of buffaloes were killed and skinned. Riding to
the southwest, the outfit came to Al Frio, or Coldwater, a series
of springs which form pools of water and a cluster of timber,
including cottonwoods, elm, and willows. This oasis attracted
buffaloes and became known as Buffalo Springs.

When the enormous XIT Ranch was organized in the
1880s, the northernmost division was headquartered at Buffa-

Buffalo hunters' camp.
Courtesy Scurry County Museum, Snyder.

lo Springs. Buffalo Springs was located just below the border of the Texas and Oklahoma panhandles, and years later Billy Dixon would establish a homestead claim just above the Oklahoma line and within sight of Buffalo Springs.

At Buffalo Springs during his scouting trip of 1873, Billy Dixon ventured into Texas for the first time. "This was a new country to all of us," said Billy, "and as strange to us as if we were its first visitors." The outfit found a pool that was alive with fish, and deer and wild turkeys could be found "in all directions." Everyone in the outfit wanted to camp at this inviting spot. "As a fisherman I never had any luck," allowed Dixon, who "left the sport to his outfit."[28]

Dixon soon gathered up his outfit, and resumed exploratory travels. They crossed the South Canadian River, struck Palo Duro Creek below the waterfalls, then established a camp at the headwaters of Mullberry Creek. Later the party angled eastward, striking the Canadian River about twenty miles west of where the town of Canadian later would be established. During their travels the outfit had not sighted a single human being, "only a vast wilderness," remembered Dixon, "inhabited by game — truly the hunter's paradise." Of course, one of the reasons for the winter exploration was the likelihood of not encountering horseback warriors, who stayed close to camp during winter months, and whose grass-fed ponies were in poor shape during the winter.[29]

Finally running low on supplies, Dixon and his outfit headed back to Dodge City, arriving in February 1874. "We had seen enough to satisfy us that the thing to do would be to go down on the Canadian as soon as the weather settled." In the interim Dixon led his outfit northwest of Dodge to his old hunting grounds. "It was the last hunting I ever did north of the Arkansas," stated Dixon, who now was thinking about the Texas Panhandle he had just reconnoitered. "My face was set toward the forbidden country, where the Indians were looking for the scalps of white men."[30]

Chapter Six

Adobe Walls

A man's gun and his horse were his two most valuable possessions, next to life, in that country in those days.

Billy Dixon

Following his sweeping exploration of the Texas Panhandle, Billy Dixon led his outfit back to Dodge City in February 1874. Dixon quickly resupplied his outfit, but after hunting northwest of Dodge for a week, he returned to town in March. "There was lots of talk about the increasing scarcity of buffaloes on the old range," discovered Dixon, "and all of us agreed that we would have to drift further south to make buffalo-hunting a paying business."[1]

Charles Myers, a former buffalo hunter who now operated a mercantile in Dodge City, had come to the same conclusion regarding his business. Although a growing number of hunters were willing to venture into Texas, the distance back to the hide markets in Dodge City — approximately 150 miles — posed a problem. Myers decided to establish a trading post in the midst of the new hunting region. He had a couple of wagons and teams, and he bought more. But for the quantity of merchandise Myers needed in order to stock his frontier store, far more wagons would be required.

Since each outfit would bring at least one wagon, Myers offered a "liberal freight rate" to anyone who carried a load of his merchandise. And once his mercantile encampment was established, Myers announced that all sales to hunters would be at Dodge City prices. "The organizing of this expedition caused much enthusiasm among the hunters at Dodge," remembered Dixon, "and many wanted to go."[2]

Billy Dixon guided Myers and his caravan of about thirty wagons into the Panhandle, crossing into Texas at the mouth of Palo Duro Creek in Hansford County. Dixon had a grand time during the trek, with "singing, dancing, music, and telling of tales" around the campfires each night. "There were always fiddlers in a crowd like ours, perhaps an accordion, and a dozen fellows who could play the French harp."

Dixon became friends with the youngest member of the expedition, twenty-year-old Bat Masterson. At twenty-three, Billy was close in age to Bat. "There was never a happier lot of men in the world," rhapsodized Billy, who was in his element. "If there was a care of any kind, it was too light to be felt. We ate like wolves and could have digested a dry buffalo hide with the hair on. Spring was on the way, and the air was light and buoyant, making the days and nights an endless delight."[3]

The general destination was "somewhere on the Canadian . . . where grass, timber, water and buffaloes most abounded." After entering Texas, the expedition began to encounter buffalo hunting outfits already camping in likely locations. (Texas was not off-limits to buffalo hunters — who did not know or care — because the federal government did not own public lands in the Lone Star State, thanks to unique characteristics of the treaty which admitted the Republic of Texas as the twenty-eighth state in the Union.)

The Myers caravan pushed onto the South Canadian River, camping a couple of miles below the future town of Plemons. The grass seemed inadequate, however, so there was another move along West Adobe Walls Creek, a clear stream which soon became known as Bent Creek.

A mile above the mouth of the creek stood the walls of a short-lived trading post known as Adobe Walls. William Bent, who was instrumental in erecting Bent's Fort in 1833 on the Santa Fe Trail in Colorado, put up the adobe walls of a Texas Panhandle trading post in 1842. Within a few years the Adobe

Walls outpost was abandoned and began to fall into ruins. In 1864 Col. Kit Carson led a punitive expedition from New Mexico into the Texas Panhandle. Pursuing Comanche and Kiowa war parties, on November 25, Carson and his four-hundred-man Federal column battled a far superior force of warriors in the vicinity of the Adobe Walls ruins. Indeed, Carson's two mountain howitzers were positioned at the site of the old trading post, and these artillery pieces turned the tide of this First Battle of the Adobe Walls.

A decade later, when buffalo hunter Billy Dixon and his companions camped at this historic location, he observed that "there were parts of walls still standing, some being four or five feet high."[4] Little did Dixon realize that later he would make his home at this site, a home to which he would bring his bride.

The day after camping at Adobe Walls, several riders found an excellent location for the trading post a little more than a mile to the north, on East Adobe Walls Creek. Charles Myers and his partner, Fred Leonard, decided to build their store at this site.

Good wages were offered to anyone who was willing to aid in construction work for a few weeks, and about forty men agreed to help. By late April work began on the Myers and Leonard Store, a sod structure seventeen feet wide and seventy feet in length, north to south. A flanking bastion was built at the northeast corner. Myers and Leonard also erected a large picket corral, extending more than 130 feet east to west, and 210 feet north to south. Loopholes four feet high were placed at intervals along the picket walls. A picket mess hall, measuring twelve by twenty-nine feet, was built at the southwest corner of the corral. Just to the north of the mess hall stood a stable which could accommodate about forty horses. The picket corral provided exterior walls for these structures, while the seventy-foot east side of the stable was open. A large area of the corral enclosure would serve for hide stacks.[5]

Basic construction materials at "Adobe Walls" were sod and picket, rather than adobe. Adobe was used in the 1840s at the original Adobe Walls trading post a mile to the south, while sod and picket buildings were not common in the upper Panhandle. The texture of Panhandle soil and grasses were generally unfavorable to sod construction, while the lack of timber discouraged picket walls. But the proximity of the Canadian River and several nearby tributaries made available grassy, slightly damp soil suitable for peeling off sod bricks from the surface. And cottonwood logs for picket construction "were hauled across the Canadian, from Reynolds Creek, a distance of about six miles, and was a laborious undertaking," pointed out Billy Dixon.[6] Therefore none of the structures at "Adobe Walls" were built of adobe; the name was adapted from the nearby trading post. Besides, sod and picket buildings could be erected rapidly, and Adobe Walls was not being built for the ages.

Other frontier entrepreneurs soon arrived at Adobe Walls from Dodge City. Charles Rath and Robert M. Wright were partners in a general merchandise business in Dodge City, along with an operation to buy and sell hides. Rath and Wright each invested $4,000 in the Texas Panhandle enterprise, and they engaged twenty-eight-year-old James Langston to manage their trading post. Charles Rath accompanied his caravan to the Texas trading site, leaving Dodge

Charles Rath, one of the Dodge City entrepreneurs who was instrumental in establishing the Adobe Walls trading community. *Courtesy Scurry County Museum, Snyder.*

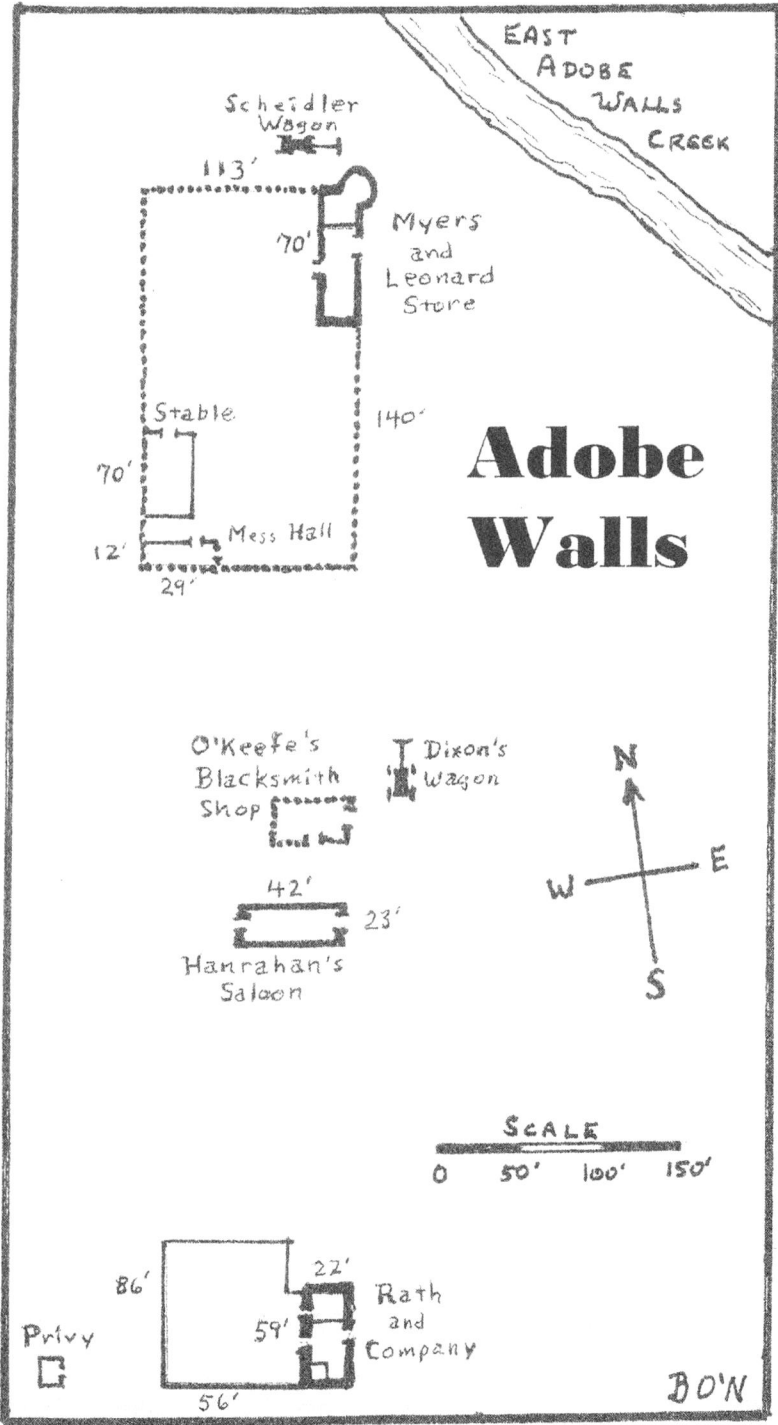

EAST ADOBE WALLS CREEK

Scheidler Wagon

113'

70'

Myers and Leonard Store

Stable

70'

140'

12'

Mess Hall

29'

Adobe Walls

O'Keefe's Blacksmith Shop

Dixon's Wagon

N

W — E

S

42'

23'

Hanrahan's Saloon

SCALE

0   50'   100'   150'

Privy

86'

22'

59'

Rath and Company

56'

BO'N

City late in April and arriving at East Adobe Walls Creek early in May. Rath intended to supervise construction of the store before returning to Dodge City.[7]

Work began immediately on the "Rath & Company Store," located 380 feet south of the Myers and Leonard Corral. The sod building faced east and was fifty-nine feet long, north to south, and twenty-two feet wide. A room at the north end would serve as a restaurant, operated by Mrs. William Olds, wife of one of the firm's employees. Mr. and Mrs. Olds lived in a room at the south end of the building. A sod corral, eighty-six feet by fifty-six feet, was begun but not completed. A large privy was built sixty-six feet west of the southwest corner of the corral.

Rath made an agreement with an experienced frontiersman named James Hanrahan to open a saloon at Adobe Walls. Rath returned to Dodge City to dispatch a load of building materials for the saloon. Hanrahan's Saloon was erected by Rath's builder, Andy Johnson, and was located more than 200 feet north of the Rath & Company Store. The sod structure opened on the east; the front and rear walls were twenty-three feet wide, while the side walls were forty-two feet long. Blacksmith Thomas O'Keefe arrived and built a shop thirty-five feet north of the saloon. The small picket building had a six-foot wide door opening to the east.

The precise measurements and locations of the Adobe Walls buildings were determined by five seasons of archaeological excavations that commenced in 1975. Billy R. Harrison, Curator of Archaeology for the Panhandle-Plains Historical Museum, supervised the excavation work, which produced a large collection of artifacts from 1874. Many of these items are on exhibit at the Panhandle-Plains Historical Museum, as well as displays at the Hutchinson County Museum in Borger. There are tools, bowls, bottles, buttons, combs, smoking pipes, coins, bullets, cartridge cases, arrowheads, horseshoes, lanterns, along with building materials brought from Dodge City, which include

Lamps were found by archaeologists at the Adobe Walls buildings. *Courtesy Panhandle-Plains Museum, Canyon, Texas.*

door knobs, hinges, and window sashes with glass pane remnants. Substantial tangible remains recall the world of Billy Dixon and the other Adobe Walls adventurers of 1874.

Within a few weeks the structures of Adobe Walls were completed. On a north to south line extending for 650 feet stood four structures: the Myers & Leonard Store, O'Keefe's Blacksmith Shop, Hanrahan's Saloon, and the Rath & Company Store, along with a picket corral and a few outbuildings. "Thus," observed Billy Dixon, "a little town was sprouting in the wilderness — a place where we could buy something to eat and wear, something to drink, ammunition for our guns, and a place where our wagons, so necessary in expeditions like ours, could be repaired."[8]

But Billy took no part in the construction of the little frontier hamlet. "While all this hammering and pounding and digging was going on, I started with three companions and rode the country as far down as where the present town of Clarendon, Texas, now stands." Billy "was impatient to be about my own business, which was to find a good buffalo range and begin hunting." But buffalo were scarce, and Billy and his men returned to Adobe Walls after fifteen days.[9]

At Adobe Walls more hunters had arrived, and freight wagons were making regular trips to and from Dodge City. But spring weather was late in arriving in the Panhandle, and the hunters felt that the buffalo herds had not yet migrated north from their winter range on the *Llano Estacado*.

At the end of May, Billy Dixon impatiently ventured out from Adobe Walls, intending to establish a hunting camp. Southwest of Adobe Walls Dixon saw buffalo sign near what would be named Dixon Creek, and he began to build a camp. There were two Englishmen with him as skinners: Charley Armitage and a man incongruously called "Frenchy," who also served as camp cook. After a couple of days Billy awoke to the bellowing of countless bulls. Arousing Frenchy and Armitage, Billy galloped out of camp, and after several miles he sighted an immense herd.

"As far as the eye could reach," remembered Billy with relish, "south, east, and west of me there was a solid mass of buf-

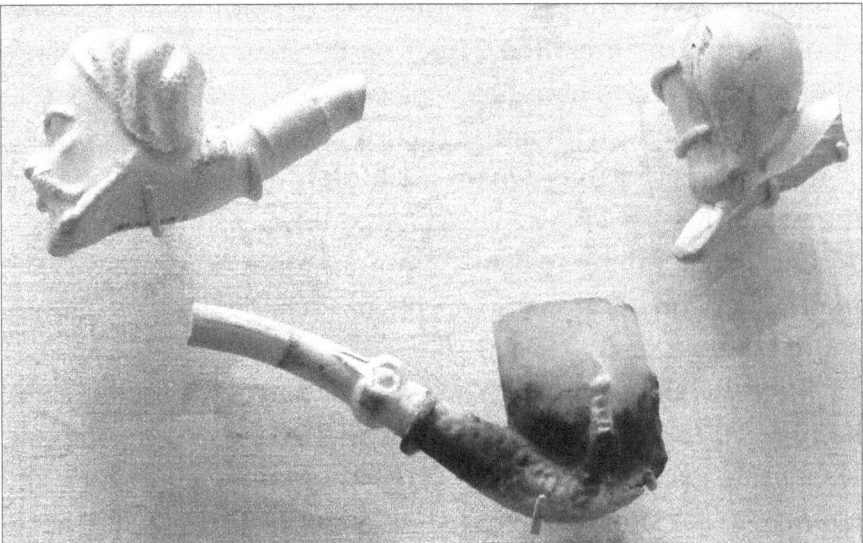

Pipes were retrieved from the excavations at Adobe Walls. *Courtesy Panhandle-Plains Museum, Canyon, Texas.*

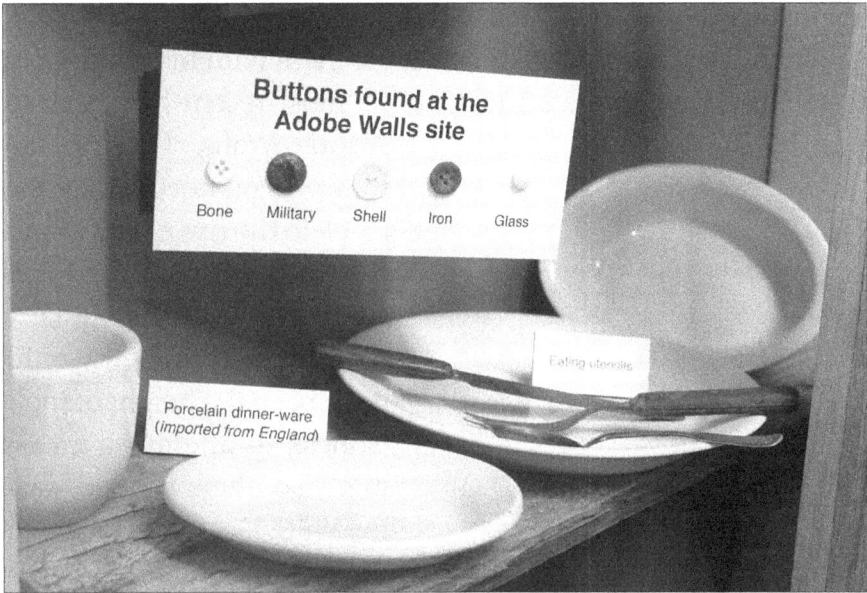

Buttons found at the Adobe Walls site. *Courtesy Hutchinson County Museum, Borger.*

faloes — thousands upon thousands of them — slowly moving toward the north."[10]

Hastening back toward camp, Billy shot thirty-five or forty bulls, putting Frenchy and Armitage to work with skinning knives. "Business has now begun in earnest," said Billy, "and we would soon be enjoying a steady income, to offset our winter's expenses."[11]

By nightfall buffaloes were passing within range of the camp, and the next morning Billy shot enough to keep Frenchy and Armitage busy for several days. Billy next drove his wagon to Adobe Walls, hoping to hire more skinners. But almost everyone had left town for the range. Only one man remained who was unemployed, and he was committed to an employer within a couple of weeks. Billy offered him twenty-five cents per hide — the most he ever paid a skinner — while promising to deliver him back to Adobe Walls.

Once back in camp, Billy killed as many buffaloes as his three skinners could handle. "This was a deadly business," remarked the buffalo hunter, "without sentiment; it was dollars against tender-heartedness, and dollars won."[12]

But after several days of doing business with his Sharps Big Fifty, Billy was obligated to take his most recent hire back to Adobe Walls. Driving the hide wagon north along the creek to the river, they found the treacherous Canadian swollen and turbulent. Dixon remarked that "it would have been the height of foolishness to attempt a crossing," so they headed east to White Deer Creek, which flowed into the Canadian a few miles south of Adobe Walls. Billy decided to unhitch the two mules from his wagon, leave the vehicle on the south bank until the Canadian subsided, and each man would cross the river by swimming with the mules about fifty or sixty yards to the north side.

At that point, however, two men from Adobe Walls appeared on the north side of the Canadian and shouted the news that two buffalo hunters had been killed by Indians about twenty-five miles to the east, near Chicken Creek. Billy Dixon promptly changed his

Intact bottle of the popular Dr. J. Hostetter's Stomach Bitters. *Courtesy Hutchinson County Museum, Borger.*

tactic. "If the Indians were on the warpath," he reasoned, "we knew it would be foolish to leave our wagon, as they would destroy it beyond doubt, so we decided to risk trying to take it across the river regardless of the wide stretch of rolling water."

The mules were hitched back to the wagon and, "hoping for the best," the team was driven into the Canadian. Within moments the wagon and team were carried away by the current, and the mules frantically began swimming. "In water a mule has less sense than a horse," explained Billy, "and the ginger is soon knocked out of him if his ears get full of water. Having smaller feet, the mule cannot equal a horse in traversing quicksand."

The wagon began to be whirled around uncontrollably. Billy and his hired man cut the harness so that the mules would not be dragged beneath the waters and drowned. The wagon was swept away and lodged against the riverbank about sixty yards downstream. With desperate efforts the two men and mules emerged on the north bank, but one mule lay down and died. "When we lined up on the north side of the river we were a sorry looking lot — two bedraggled, unarmed men and a water-logged mule three miles from Adobe Walls . . ." Dixon had lost his hat in the river, and his clothing was covered with mud and sand. Leading the mule, Old Tobe, they trudged forlornly to Adobe Walls.[13]

On first sight, the men at Adobe Walls thought that Dixon and his skinner were survivors of an Indian attack. "We found Adobe Walls buzzing with talk about Indians," said Dixon. Grisly details were exchanged about the recent killing and mutilation of hunters Dave Dudley and Tommy Wallace about fifteen miles southeast of Adobe Walls. Their skulls were broken open, the brains cleaned out, and the cavities stuffed with grass. Ears, fingers, toes, noses were cut off. Stakes were driven through their torsos, pinning Dudley and Wallace to the ground, and their hearts were cut out.[14]

Furthermore, James Hanrahan and his teamsters were struck on their second day out of Dodge City, hauling liquor to the Adobe Walls saloon. There were no casualties, but all of their horses were stolen. A passing caravan led by Charles Myers helped bring the liquor to Hanrahan's Saloon. Meanwhile, word reached Adobe Walls that two other hide men, an Englishman called "Antelope Jack" and a German known as "Blue Billy" Muhler, had been slain and mutilated in their camp near the Canadian. They were staked to the ground and their disfigurements were ghastly.[15]

J. Wright Mooar and his outfit skirmished with warriors on multiple occasions. During one clash Mooar held the war party at bay with his Big Fifty while his men rounded up the outfit's livestock. There was a general retreat across Red Deer Creek, and a sudden thunderstorm flooded the crossing with twenty feet of water and thwarted the pursuit of the war party. Reaching Adobe Walls on June 11, the Mooar brothers heard of the recent killings in the field. Coming on top of their encounters on the range, the Mooar brothers decided it was prudent to move with their outfit to Dodge City. En route to Dodge the Mooar party came in contact with other men who had grisly news. A teamster named Warren was killed and scalped not far from Dodge City. Horses were stolen from several camps. Hunter Emanuel Dubbs returned to his camp to find all three of his men slain and mutilated. Shaken, Dubbs immediately headed to Adobe Walls.[16]

When the Mooar party met teamster Isaac "Ike" Scheidler en route with a loaded wagon for Adobe Walls, Ike was warned that his scalp was in danger. The Mooars reached Dodge City on June 29 — two days after Ike Scheidler and his brother, Shorty, had been killed and scalped at the Second Battle of Adobe Walls. During their trek to Dodge the Mooars hosted Charles Rath and Charles Myers in their camp for one night. Rath and Myers had left their Adobe Walls stores in charge of James Langston and

Fred Leonard, respectively, while they rode on horseback to Dodge City.[17]

Billy Dixon did not join the exodus to the safety of Dodge City, and neither did most of the other hunters. "Every man of us was dead set against abandoning the buffalo range," asserted Dixon. "The herds were now at hand, and we were in a fair way to make a pile of money. Furthermore, the buffaloes were becoming scarcer and scarcer each year . . ."

The day after Dixon's near-catastrophic crossing of the Canadian River he returned with help and dug out his wagon. But everything in the wagon was swept away, including his Sharps Big Fifty and other rifles. "We could dig out the wagon, but not the guns, and somewhere in the depth of the Canadian they are rusting to this very day."[18]

The best replacement rifle Dixon could find in Adobe Walls was a round barrel Sharps. He persuaded a noted hunter, Brick Bonds, to accompany him to his camp, and it took several days to haul all of the hides to Adobe Walls. There was general agreement among the hunters to take extra precautions on the range and even to combine two or three outfits in one camp. But the hunters were not afraid to continue their profitable assault on the buffalo herds.

"After all," pointed out Dixon, "it was not unusual to hear of two or three buffalo-hunters being killed and scalped every year, and perhaps there would be no further outbreaks by the Indians."[19] An occasional attack by raiders was an occupational hazard for far-ranging buffalo hunters, and Dixon and most of the others were optimistic that the recent murder raids were isolated incidents.

Billy Dixon decided to shift his operations to the north side of the Canadian River. He hired three skinners and bought supplies for two months. Billy was approached by James Hanrahan who wanted to partner in the hunt with a big outfit that would include seven skinners, which would make a total of ten hide

In the murder raids by war parties a teamster named Warren was killed and scalped near Dodge City. *Courtesy National Archives.*

men. Billy assured Hanrahan that he was capable of keeping twenty hunters busy. Hanrahan offered Billy half of the profits, and the partners readied their wagons and crews for departure on Saturday morning, June 27, 1874.

Billy was not satisfied with the replacement rifle he purchased after losing his Sharps Big Fifty in the Canadian River. In the Rath & Company Store he found a new .44-90 Sharps, "which was next best to a '50.'" But James Langston, managing the Rath & Company Store, told Billy that a hunter in the field had spoken for the gun, agreeing to pay $80 for the rifle.

Later in the evening, however, Langston sought out Billy, telling him he had just heard that a freight train from Dodge was camped only a couple of days away, and the cargo included a large order of hunting rifles. Langston agreed to sell Billy the Sharps .44-90. Billy followed Langston right back to the store and paid for the new gun and a case of ammunition. "For some reason which I cannot explain, even to myself, I left the case of ammunition with Langston, little dreaming how greatly I would regret my carelessness."[20]

Billy hurried to Hanrahan's Saloon to show his partner the new gun. Several hunters came into Adobe Walls that Friday, "and we planned to stay up late that night, celebrating our return to the range, telling stories of past experiences and joking about how much money we would have when the hunt was over." There was a lively time in the saloon, and Billy pointed out that "Hanrahan did a thriving trade."[21]

Thomas O'Keefe had repaired Billy's wagon, and the vehicle, now loaded with provisions, was parked near the blacksmith shop. During the evening Billy brought his saddle horse to the wagon, tying him with a long picket rope to a nearby stake. It was a sultry July night, and most of the men bedded down outside. Billy spread his blankets near the wagon. "I placed my gun by my side between my blankets, as usual, to protect it from dew and rain."

"Every door was left wide open" for air circulation as the lamps began to go out at Adobe Walls. "There was not the slightest feeling of impending danger."[22]

Chapter Seven

The Second Battle of Adobe Walls

War-whooping had a very appreciable effect
upon the roots of a man's hair.

Billy Dixon

The First Battle of Adobe Walls was the U.S. Army's largest engagement against Indians during the Civil War. On November 25, 1864, Col. Kit Carson and four hundred men desperately battled 1,300 or more Comanche, Kiowa, and Kiowa-Apache warriors. Although outnumbered more than three to one, Carson had fought in at least twenty-seven engagements against Indians during thirty-five years on the frontier, and he was familiar with the old Adobe Walls trading post, having been employed by William Bent two decades earlier. Colonel Carson suffered six men killed and twenty-five wounded, while holding off a superior force during a perilous fight for survival.[1]

The Second Battle of Adobe Walls was an even more desperate fight for survival. On June 27, 1874, about twenty-eight buffalo men were almost overwhelmed by perhaps five or six hundred Comanche, Cheyenne, Kiowa, and Arapaho warriors.[2] Although the numbers on both sides were far fewer than those of the 1864 battle, the defenders of 1874 were outnumbered by at least twelve or fifteen to one. Buffalo hunter J. Wright Mooar, who missed the battle, was inspired to call it "The Alamo of the Panhandle."[3] Of course, the defenders of the Alamo, also outnumbered by great odds, were slain to a man. But the Adobe Walls defenders of 1874 missed the fate of the Alamo heroes of 1836 by the narrowest margin of timing.

As at the Alamo, the Adobe Walls attackers moved into po-

The Panhandle of Billy and Olive Dixon

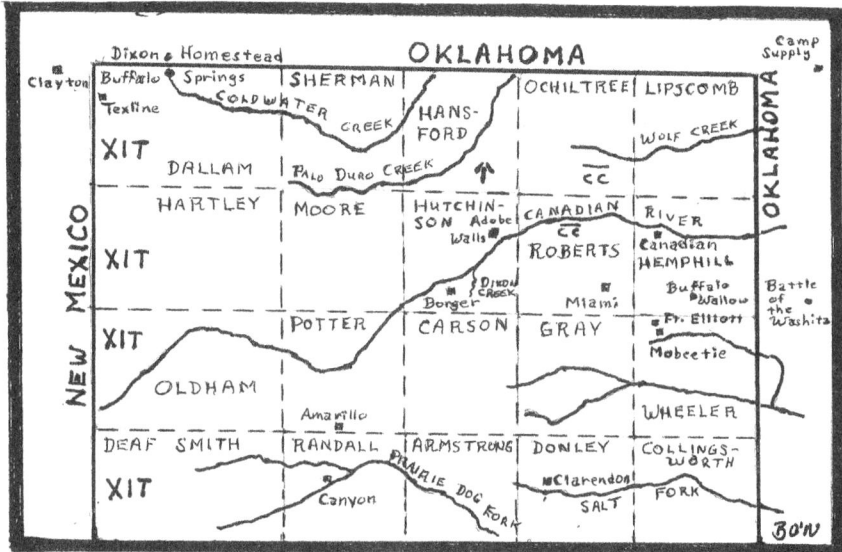

Dixon Homestead

OKLAHOMA

Camp Supply

Clayton Buffalo Springs SHERMAN OCHILTREE LIPSCOMB

Textline COLDWATER CREEK HANS-FORD WOLF CREEK

XIT DALLAM PALO DURO CREEK

HARTLEY MOORE HUTCHIN-SON Adobe Walls CANADIAN cc RIVER

XIT ROBERTS Canadian HEMPHILL

Dixon Creek Borger Miami Buffalo Wallow Battle of the Washita

XIT POTTER CARSON GRAY Fr. Elliott Mobeetie

OLDHAM Amarillo WHEELER

DEAF SMITH RANDALL ARMSTRONG DONLEY COLLINGS-WORTH

XIT Canyon PRAIRIE DOG FORK Clarendon SALT FORK 80'N

NEW MEXICO

OKLAHOMA

sition during the predawn hours, and began their charge while darkness still shadowed their target. The attack on the buffalo hunter community was the culmination of months of effort by two young, ambitious Comanche leaders, who burned to reverse the decline of their people. *Isa-tai* was a medicine man who skillfully used magical tricks to convince observers of his miraculous powers. Quanah was a physically impressive warrior who tirelessly recruited braves to join him in a major foray against whites. *Isa-tai* and Quanah often traveled together from one Comanche band to another, and to other tribes — Kiowa, Cheyenne, Arapaho.

Fierce, proud, horseback warriors who long ruled a vast region known as *Comancheria*, Comanche bands began to suffer reversals during the 1850s at the hands of pistol-wielding Texas Rangers, the U.S. Army, and white settlers who were determined to advance the Texas frontier. The Comanche population was reduced through losses in battle and the ravages of white man's diseases.

But during the American Civil War the large number of

Quanah was a young Comanche war leader who relentlessly recruited fellow warriors for an all-out assault on buffalo hunters. *Author's collection.*

Texas military forts were abandoned by blue-coated soldiers and not reoccupied until 1867, two years after the white men stopped fighting each other. During these unprotected years the "Wild Tribes," Comanches and Kiowas, came back with a vengeance, forcing the abandonment of a great many frontier ranches. But the soldiers finally returned, rebuilding their forts and creating new ones. The U.S. Army invaded *Comancheria*, marching under Col. Ranald Mackenzie and other capable, implacable leaders. And then the buffalo hunters came to Texas, slaughtering the enormous herds on which their nomadic, warlike lifestyle was based. By this time there were only a few thousand Comanches, and two-thirds lived at least part of the time on a reservation in western Oklahoma. Food that was issued often was inadequate and fouled, and reservation dwellers were plagued by whiskey peddlers and horse thieves.

Quanah, who was raised as a traditional Comanche horseman and hunter and warrior, was horrified as he watched his way of life vanishing before his eyes. He was the son of war chief Peta Nocona and Cynthia Ann Parker, who was abducted by Comanches during an infamous 1836 attack on Parker's Fort in central Texas. Cynthia grew up as a Comanche, married a leader, had three children. But while Quanah was still a youngster his father was killed and his mother and little sister were recaptured during a Texas Ranger raid in 1860. He lost his

As dawn was breaking on June 27, 1874, hundreds of mounted warriors galloped past the southerly butte at right, angling northwest (right to left) toward the buildings of Adobe Walls. *Photo by the author.*

family, and then he began to watch his native lifestyle disappear. By the time he became a young man he yearned to lead a vengeance raid, such as the famous 1840 rampage that swept through Victoria all the way to the Gulf of Mexico.

Quanah and *Isa-tai*, who promised medicine that would protect warriors from the bullets of hunters, relentlessly recruited warriors for a large-scale raid. A massive sun dance was staged in 1874, and enthusiasm for a major attack became widespread. A council of Comanche elders, however, ruled that instead of a raid against the Texas frontier, the assault should be directed against buffalo hunters in their new community not far west of the reservation. Quanah and *Isa-tai* readily agreed to the directive of the council. They, too, hated the hunters, and one success should lead to another. Scouts were sent out and plans began to be developed for a major assault. [4]

As braves were aroused to a fighting pitch, small parties attacked buffalo hunter outfits in the countryside, as we have seen. When *Isa-tai* and Quanah and various war leaders organized the war party, on the reservation about twenty miles north of Fort Sill, scouting parties ranged ahead and were in

Adobe Walls bullet types

50-70 Gov. Cartridge

50 Cal. Bullet

40-70 W.R.A. or Sharps

45-70 Gov. Carbine

45-70 Gov. Rifle

44-77 Bottleneck

Spencer 56-56

Colt -45

44-Henry Rim Fire

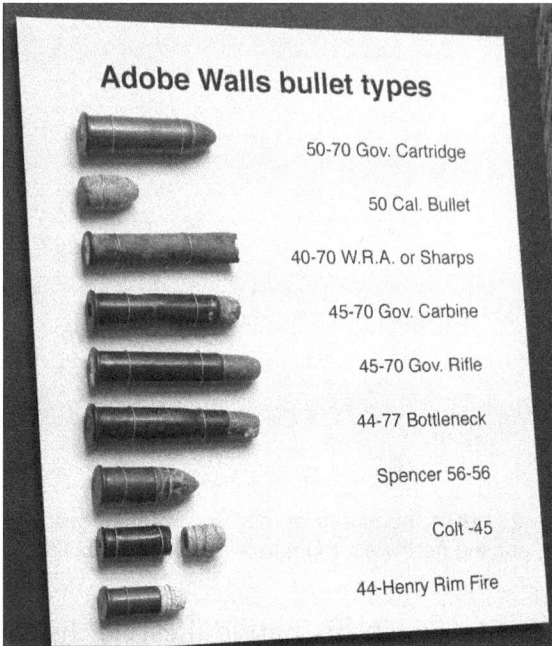

Bullet types used by the Adobe Walls defenders. *Courtesy Hutchinson County Museum, Borger.*

the vicinity of Adobe Walls by Friday, June 26. The advance guard killed some buffaloes east of Adobe Walls, providing fresh meat to the main body of warriors as they arrived.

"We shot some buffalo . . . the day before," recounted a young Comanche named Yellow Fish, "and stopped and cooked them. Then we rested that night, on the south side of the river. We came on across the next morning, walking and leading our horses. Then, [when] we were just a few hundred yards away we mounted and rode forward in long lines."[5]

The mounted advance began just as the sky in the east began to lighten. *Isa-tai* had promised that the warriors would be able to club the white men to death where they lay. But many of the whites already were awake. About two hours after midnight in Hanrahan's Saloon there was a sharp report, like the cracking of a ridge pole — or the discharge of a pistol. Each of the buildings had a ridge pole supporting a heavy earthen roof, and every plains settler was aware of the danger of a collapse of a weighty sod roof.

Sleeping in the saloon were bartender Oscar Shepherd and Mike Welsh, one of Hanrahan's skinners. Shepherd and Welsh enlisted several men, including Billy Dixon, to help prop up the ridge pole, while others climbed up to shovel dirt off the roof

Bat Masterson was only twenty when he stood side by side with Billy Dixon firing out of the same window at Hanrahan's Saloon. *Courtesy Scurry County Museum, Snyder.*

and lighten the weight. Half the men in camp were busy in the saloon, and after a couple of hours Hanrahan offered everyone a free drink.[6] (An unlikely rumor later developed that Hanrahan had been tipped off about the pre-dawn Indian attack and he fired a revolver shot to arouse everyone with a story about a cracked ridge pole. It is hard to believe that anyone who knew about the pending attack would not spread a general alarm.)[7]

Some of the men went back to their bedrolls, but Hanrahan and Dixon decided to get an early start to their hide-hunting expedition. Hanrahan sent a skinner, Billy Ogg, to bring up the horses, which were grazing off to the southeast along East Adobe Walls Creek.

Billy Dixon rolled up his bedding and tossed it into his wagon. As he picked up his rifle he glanced toward the horses along the creek. In the dim distance he spotted movement of some sort. "Then I was thunderstruck," he remembered. "The black body of moving object suddenly spread out like a fan, and from it went up one single, solid yell — a war whoop that seemed to shake the very air of the early morning. Then came the thudding roar of running horses, and the hideous cries of the individual warriors, each embarked in the onslaught. I could see that hundreds of Indians were coming."[8]

The warriors were in a headlong charge at full gallop, trying to reach the white men while they still were outside, before they could arm themselves and fort up inside the buildings. In the darkness horses tripped on prairie dog holes, tumbling to the ground and sending their riders sprawling.

Billy Dixon's saddle horse was lunging violently against his picket rope, and Billy secured the mount to his wagon. Assuming that the warriors were riding to steal the horses grazing beside the creek, Dixon moved forward "to get a few good shots before the Indians could turn to run away." He triggered one round before realizing that the warriors "were coming straight as a bullet toward the buildings, whipping their horses at every jump."[9]

Dixon broke into a dead run for Hanrahan's nearby saloon. "War-whooping had a very appreciable effect upon the roots of a man's hair," Billy remembered. From a quarter of a mile away Billy Ogg also sprinted for the saloon. With bullets kicking up dust near his feet, Dixon reached the saloon only to find the door shut and barred. Finally responding to his shouts, the men inside opened the door. Dixon scrambled inside, just as Billy Ogg raced through the open doorway and sprawled panting onto the floor.[10]

There were nine or ten men inside Hanrahan's, each armed with buffalo rifles or Winchester repeaters. These riflemen included such crack shots as Dixon, Hanrahan, and Bat Masterson. Almost 300 feet to the north, at the Myers and Leonard Store, were ten more armed men. Almost 200 feet south of the saloon stood Rath and Company, with only six men, none of them hunters. (James Langston, store manager; the bookkeeper; two other store employees; blacksmith Tom O'Keefe; clerk William Olds). A non-combatant also was present, Hannah Olds, who was frantic at the assault by savages. The three sod buildings were spread along a 650-foot north to south line, and the riflemen in the saloon would be able to provide flanking fire to each of the buildings at north and south. No one took refuge in Tom O'Keefe's blacksmith shop, a small picket building with an open front.

As if by preplanning, the big war party broke into three divisions to attack each of the three sod buildings. A fourth band of riders raced to round up the horses along the creek. The defenders frantically worked to barricade doors and window openings. In the two stores bags of flour and grain were piled against the doors.

"We were scarcely inside before the Indians had surrounded all the buildings and shot out every window pane," said Dixon. "Some of the men were undressed, but nobody wasted any time hunting their clothes, and many of them fought for their lives all that summer day barefoot and in their nightclothes."[11]

The first half-hour of the battle was a furious firefight at close quarters. The hard-riding warriors enveloped the sod structures only moments after they were barricaded. Yellow Fish saw Quanah arrive just in time to thrust his lance into a partial door opening.[12] Other braves fired revolvers, carbines,

Newspaper drawing of the Adobe Walls attack in the *Kansas City Star*, Sunday, July 7, 1929.

and arrows at the windows and doors. Panes were shattered in all of the narrow windows, while cans and bottles on the shelves of the stores were punctured. "I could never see how we escaped," reflected Billy Dixon, "for at times the bullets poured in like hail and made us hug the sod walls like gophers when a hawk was swooping past."

Positions On The Morning Of June 27, 1874

Scheidler Wagon

Ike Scheidler, teamster	Shorty Scheidler, teamster

Myers And Leonard Store

Fred Leonard, store owner	Billy Tyler, skinner
Charley Armitage, skinner	Mike McCabe, skinner
Fred Myers, hunter	Frenchy, skinner and cook
Old Man Keeler, store cook	James Campbell, skinner
Henry Lease, hunter	Edward Trevor, skinner

Hanrahan's Saloon

Jim Hanrahan, owner, hunter	Mike Welsh, skinner
Billy Dixon, hunter	Billy Ogg, skinner
Bat Masterson, Myers employee	Jim Carlyle, hide yard
Oscar Shepherd, bartender	Hiram Watson, skinner
Dutch Henry Born, hunter	James McKinley, skinner

Rath And Company

James Langston, store manager	Andy Johnson, laborer
George Eddy, bookkeeper	Sam Smith, store employee
William Olds, clerk	Thomas O'Keefe, blacksmith
Hannah Olds, restaurant	

There is uncertainty about the presence of a few of these men, while there are a few other men who claim to have been present. There also is uncertainty about the occupations of a few of those men.

Courageous warriors rode up to the buildings and pounded the doors with their rifle butts. Dixon described the first moments, when "a good many of the Indians jumped off their

Nearby warrior corpses were decapitated, and several heads were placed on the picket corral fence. Illustration from Miles, *Personal Recollections*, 163.

horses and prepared for a fight on foot." Some warriors backed their ponies against the doors, hoping their weight would force an entrance.[13]

During this opening stage of battle many of the defenders went to their revolvers for a better rate of fire at close range. The powerful hunting rifles were single shot breech loaders that had to be reloaded after every shot. Later in the fight these weapons would be decisive in keeping the superior force at a distance. But in the first moments of battle rapid-firing revolvers, along with lever-action Winchesters, halted the braves from overrunning the buildings by sheer force of numbers. The low, barricaded buildings quickly filled with clouds of gunsmoke. Adding to the frustration of the warriors, these hulking low buildings with earthen roofs could not be set on fire. The walls were three feet thick at their base tapering to two feet toward the low roofs. Despite the volume of fire poured at the buildings, not a single defender was killed inside the walls.

But when the opening charge struck Adobe Walls, two men were caught outside the walls. Teamster brothers Ike and Shorty Scheidler were sleeping in one of their wagons when the war party charged. The canvas-covered wagon was parked north of the Myers and Leonard picket fence, and the slumbering brothers realized the danger too late. Ike and Shorty tried to conceal themselves, guns at the ready.

A young Comanche warrior, *Tim-bo*, testified decades later that none of the braves near the wagon knew there was anyone inside. "Then *Mihesuah*, a warrior of own tribe, lifted the wagon cover with his bow. Immediately, a shot was fired from the wagon, badly wounding the warrior." The wagon cover promptly was riddled with spears, arrows, and bullets. The Scheidler brothers were scalped, and these bloody trophies were proudly waved about. When the black Newfoundland dog of the Scheidlers tried to defend his masters, he too was slain. As an honor to the fighting dog, a warrior "'scalped' him by cutting a piece of hide off his side."[14]

A large number of warriors dismounted and took up firing positions outside the Myers and Leonard picket stockade. They aimed their guns between the cottonwood posts, and rained lead on the rear or west side of the store. Billy Tyler for some reason was in the hide yard, and when he paused to re-enter the rear door, he turned to fire a parting shot. But at that instant a bullet ripped into his lungs. Although he was pulled indoors, Tyler died within thirty minutes.

Following half an hour of combat, the fury of the initial assault was broken. The relentless gunfire from the revolvers, carbines, and rifles of the defenders took a steady toll on the war ponies and braves. Wounded and dead warriors were removed from the field of battle by braves riding at a dead gallop under fire. One warrior raced in on a white horse and pulled an injured comrade up behind him. But as the two braves rode away, a rifle bullet broke one of the horse's hind legs. "Both Indians began whipping the poor brute," described Dixon, "and lurching and staggering on three legs, he carried them away." A group of warriors "would pour a hot fire into the buildings, [while] other Indians on horseback would run forward under the protection of this fusillade" to retrieve the wounded and dead.[15]

Quanah reputedly galloped in, lifted a fallen warrior from the ground, and rode off to safety. Quanah and a few other warriors clambered up on the earthen roofs and tried to gouge holes to shoot through. His bold leadership was appropriate for a young war leader who was in great part responsible for organizing the big war party. But early in the fight his horse was shot out from under him. He scrambled to a place of cover, but while he was hunkered down a bullet — apparently a ricochet shot — struck between his shoulder blades. Quanah remained pinned down for a considerable time, and the loss of this courageous leader at a key point in the battle unquestionably exerted a demoralizing effect throughout the war party. Indeed, by the afternoon of the first day Isa-tai was utterly discredited, and the disgraced medicine man was insulted and threatened by angry warriors.[16]

By mid-morning the headlong charges had ended as the warriors fell back to safer distances. But while those distances seemed safe enough for the Winchesters many braves carried, they were easily within range of buffalo rifles. "The power and range of the buffalo hunters' guns surprised and bewildered our people," remembered the Comanche warrior Yellow Fish.[17]

Billy Dixon yearned for a Big Fifty to fire at these distant warriors. When the heat of battle lessened, Billy noticed that bartender Oscar Shepherd was brandishing Jim Hanrahan's Big Fifty. But Shepherd was not much of a gun handler, so Billy offered his new .44-90 to Hanrahan. "Here, Jim, I see you are without a gun; take this one." Now Billy was without a rifle, but "it was rather to the interest of all of us that I should have a powerful gun," and he easily persuaded Shepherd to hand him the Big Fifty.[18]

Billy and Bat Masterson found themselves firing from the same window in Hanrahan's Saloon. There were few windows in Hanrahan's, or in either of the other sod buildings, but this particular aperture must have been an especially lethal firing position. Masterson and Dixon would become legendary figures of the West, and expressed admiration of each other. "'Bat' Masterson should be remembered for the valour that marked his conduct," said Billy. "He was a good shot, and not afraid." Bat enthusiastically returned the sentiment: "Billy Dixon, who occupied half the window with me during much of the thickest of the fight, was a remarkable man, always cool, a dead shot no matter what the distance, never saying a word, always alert . . ."[19]

Warriors now stationed themselves in positions to the east and to the west, related Dixon, "maintaining a more or less steady fire all day on the buildings." Of course, these sniping positions drew return fire from the buffalo hunters. From his vantage point at Hanrahan's window, Dixon noticed a war pony standing at the corner of a tall stack of buffalo hides behind Rath's store. "We could see that an Indian behind the hides was holding the pony by the bridle, so we shot the pony and it fell dead." ("We" apparently was Dixon and Masterson.) The fall of this pony left the warrior somewhat exposed, and he drew fire from riflemen in both Hanrahan's and Rath's. "We had him jumping like a flea back and forth behind the pile of hides." Dixon carefully aimed his Big Fifty at a corner of the pile of hides and the powerful round blasted through the hides and wounded the crouching warrior. The injured brave jumped straight up and, "howling with pain," zigzagged for thirty or forty yards before dropping into the tall grass.[20]

By noon the men in Hanrahan's were running low on ammunition. Dixon and Hanrahan decided to run to Rath's store, which had thousands of rounds of ammunition in stock — including the case which Billy had purchased the previous evening. The two men crawled out of a window and sprinted to Rath's, a distance of about seventy yards. Bullets began to kick up dust, but a door opened and "we got inside without a scratch, although badly winded." Dixon and Hanrahan now realized there were only six men in Rath's store, and not a one was a hunter. The inventory of provisions and ammunition certainly needed to be defended, and so did Hannah Olds. "The boys begged me to stay with them," said Dixon. Dixon agreed to remain in the store, while Hanrahan hustled back to his saloon with a towsack full of ammunition. Meanwhile, Bat Masterson had scampered from the saloon to the Myers and Leonard Store.[21]

Dixon found a firing position at the west door of the restaurant in Rath's store. The door was strongly barricaded with sacks of flour and grain, but just above the door was a transom. There was no glass in the transom, and Dixon wanted to take advantage of this firing point that was elevated more than six feet above ground level.

Climbing to the top of the barricade, Dixon peered through the transom and saw a warrior crawling in the tall grass. With the weight of his body resting on one knee, he quickly leveled his rifle and squeezed off a shot. But Billy's perch on the sacks was precarious, and the powerful recoil of the Big Fifty sent him flying. "As I went down I struck and dislodged a washtub and a bushel or two of cooking utensils which made a terrific crash as they struck the floor around me. I fell heavily myself, and the tumbling down of my big '50' did not lessen the uproar. The commotion startled everybody. The boys rushed forward believing that I had been shot, even killed." Billy immediately crawled back to the transom, but his second shot hit just beyond the target. On his third try, however, he scored a center hit.[22]

Early in the afternoon the warriors fell back to the foothills and began to ride back and forth across the valley, which exposed them to rifle fire. "So we began picking them off," said Dixon. "They were soon riding in a much bigger circle . . ."[23]

During the early morning attacks a bugler was signaling the warriors — charges, assembly, retreat. Many of the defenders assumed that the bugler was a Negro deserter from the army. "The bugler was killed late in the afternoon . . . ," related Bat Masterson, "as he was running away from a wagon owned by the Shadler [sic] brothers . . ." Charley Armitage, stationed in the Myers and Leonard Store, drilled the bugler as he retreated from looting the wagon. He had his bugle with him. "Also he was carrying a tin can filled with sugar and another filled with coffee, one under each arm."[24]

About four o'clock in the afternoon James "Bermuda" Carlyle (who, as a deputy sheriff, would be slain in 1880 during the Lincoln County War) ventured outside of Hanrahan's Saloon to pick up an Indian trinket which he had spotted from a window. Carlyle was not shot at, so he soon came outside again. Other defenders emerged outdoors and began to collect souvenirs. Several scalps were found, adorning shields and bridles. Billy Dixon pried open the jaws of a dead war pony to retrieve a silver-mounted bridle, along with a rawhide lariat. He also collected a lance, an old army Springfield rifle, a shot pouch with fifteen cartridges, a powder horn, and a bow and quiver. But when Dixon returned to the store, Hannah Olds asked for the lance, and he graciously handed it over to her. Dixon later gave away the other items to people in Dodge City. "I always regretted that I did not keep the relics I picked up at Adobe Walls."[25]

The bodies of the Scheidler brothers were found in their wagon. A large grave was dug north of the corral. The corpses of Ike and Shorty Scheidler and of Billy Tyler were wrapped in blankets and buried in the common grave. Thirteen dead warriors lay so close to the buildings that it would have been suicide for other braves to try to carry off the bodies. The corpses were beheaded, and the severed heads were displayed on the stockade gatepost.

Part of the strategy of the war party was "to put every man of us afoot, thereby leaving us without means of escape and powerless to send for aid . . ." At the first charge as many of the white men's horses as possible were seized. After that all remaining horses around the compound were shot with bullets or arrows. Five horses that were left in the stockade were killed, and so were four tied to a wagon at Rath's. A tamed mustang colt that had been given to Hannah Olds was shot with an arrow. "My own saddle horse," said Billy Dixon, "which I had owned for years and highly prized, was among the first to be shot, and still lay tied to the wagon when I found him."[26]

During the fighting wounded horses stood near the buildings. "A horse gives up quickly when in pain," explained Dixon, "and these made no effort to get away. Even those that were at a considerable distance from the buildings when [they] received their wounds came to us, as if seeking our help and sympathy. It was a pitiable sight, and touched our hearts, for the boys loved their horses."[27]

Of course, many dead and wounded horses were war ponies, shot in battle. "We counted fifty-six dead horses scattered in the immediate vicinity of the buildings . . . ," recalled Dixon. There also were twenty-eight head of dead oxen that were owned by the Scheidler brothers.[28]

By the time the Scheidlers and Billy Tyler were buried, darkness gathered, and the defenders "returned to the protection of the buildings, completely exhausted by the strain and excitement of the day's fighting." Inside the stores juices from the bullet-punctured cans attracted hordes of flies, and broken glass was everywhere. But it was not considered safe to sleep outside, and during an unusually quiet night many combatants surely experienced nightmares. "I doubt if any of us slept soundly that June night," said Dixon. Billy's sleep was interrupted by troubled dreams; "the bloody scenes of the day passing in endless procession through my mind — I could see the Indians charging across the valley, hear the roar of the guns and the blood-curdling war-whoops, until everything was a bewildering swirl of fantastic colours and movements."[29]

The opening charge made an indelible impression. "Hundreds of warriors, . . . mounted upon their finest horses, armed with guns and lances, and carrying heavy shields of thick buffalo hide, were coming like the wind. Over all was splashed the rich colours of red, vermillion and ochre, on the bodies of the men, on the bodies of the running horses. Scalps dangled from bridles, gorgeous war-bonnets fluttered their plumes, bright feathers dangled from the tails and manes of the horses, and the bronzed, half-naked bodies of the riders glittered with ornaments of silver and brass. Behind this head-long charging host stretched the Plains, on whose horizon the rising sun was lifting its morning fires. The warriors seemed to emerge from this glowing background." Dixon had only a moment before running for cover and getting his gun into action, but he never forgot the spectacular scene. "There never was a more splendidly barbaric sight. In after years I was glad that I had seen it."[30]

By the second day the decomposing animal carcasses and the dead warriors were sending up "an awful stench" in the summer heat. "As we had no teams with which to drag them away, we rigged up several buffalo hides and tied ropes to them, then rolled the bodies onto the hides and pulled them far enough away . . . In this way three or four men could move a horse." The bodies of livestock "and the Indians were dragged off on the prairie and left to the coyotes and buzzards." Between the saloon and Rath's store lay a dozen horses. A large pit was dug and the animals were rolled in and buried.[31]

Warriors were rarely seen throughout the second day. One group appeared in the valley east of the buildings. Some of the hunters opened fire with buffalo rifles, and the warriors tried to shoot back. But the range was too great for any guns the Indians had, and the warriors soon rode out of sight. Defenders worried, however, that the war party was awaiting reinforcements for another assault. Loopholes were punched out at likely points along the walls, and small lookout posts were added to the roof of each of the two stores. Piles of hides were unstacked so that they could not again be used as cover by attackers.[32]

The defenders knew that a large number of war ponies had been killed, and that at least thirteen braves were dead. James Langston counted the same number of nearby corpses as Billy Dixon. "The Indians were very brave; for hours they kept in range, and carried their dead and wounded off the field, all but thirteen."[33]

In addition to the dead and injured warriors who were carried off by brave comrades, other warriors or their mounts had been wounded and left the field of battle under their own power. But the effects of the soft lead slugs used by the buffalo hunters often were devastating. At the very least injured warriors and war ponies were put out of action for the remainder of the battle. Although it can never be determined with any precision how many warriors died at Adobe Walls, the most likely of the estimates is seventy killed and perhaps a similar number of wounded. Defenders of a protected position always have an advantage over attackers, especially when the defenders are well armed. However heavy the casualties, the war party had expected a quick and total victory with their initial assault, and being repulsed with numerous dead and wounded was completely disheartening. There would be no attacks on the second day.

On the first day the thunder of battle was heard in several hide camps. Some outfits packed up and headed for Dodge City, while others went to the sound of gunfire. Brick Bonds, bringing in a wagon load of hides, unhitched his team and hid out until evening, before driving on to Adobe Walls after dark. A day later George Bellfield led his outfit into the battered settlement, telling the defenders that he had not seen a sign of the war party. But when the Cator brothers, Jim and Bob, brought their large outfit in later in the day, there was a long range rifle duel with a band of warriors along the way.[34]

While work went on to improve the fortifications at Adobe Walls, buffalo hunter Henry Lease agreed to try to slip past the Indians and seek help at Dodge City. He was paid a fee — reported at $125 or more — and provided a horse by George Bellfield. Lease took his Big Fifty and a brace of pistols, along with a couple of ammunition belts. Lease shook hands all around before riding into the night. "I doubt if there was a man who believed that Lease would get through alive," admitted Billy Dixon.[35]

Chapter Eight

Billy Dixon's Shot

On the third day Billy Dixon made what became the most famous single shot in the history of the West.

S.G. Gwynn

Empire of the Summer Moon

Monday, June 29, 1874, was the third day of the siege at Adobe Walls. It also was the day that Billy Dixon triggered a long-range round from a Sharps Big Fifty that became the most celebrated shot in the history of the Old West. It was a feat of marksmanship that Dixon shrugged off as a "scratch" shot — a lucky shot.

Indeed, several remarkable shots already had been made from Adobe Walls on the first day of battle. Although fewer than half of the defenders were professional hunters, these men were armed with high-powered hunting rifles and they were accustomed to hitting targets at great distances. Throughout the first day countless shots were fired at hundreds of warrior targets, and quite naturally a few of the big slugs found a distant mark.

Tim-bo and Yellow Fish, who in 1874 were teenaged braves participating in their first battle, revisited the Adobe Walls site in 1939. Tim-bo pointed out to a reporter a low hill a few hundred yards northwest of the former trading post — basically to the rear of the now-vanished sod buildings. "That's where we went," said *Tim-bo* through an interpreter. Behind the hill the warriors regrouped, then charged past the sod buildings, before galloping back to the hill. But the last rider was shot as he slowed down at the crest. "He reached the top going at a slow trot. The whites weren't able to shoot much from that side.

We'd noticed them digging at the chinks in one of the houses, and I guess a white man poked his rifle through there and took good aim, for he dropped him dead, shot squarely through the back. We got his body and dragged it behind the hill." Timbo and Yellow Fish both agreed on the accuracy of their opponents: "They were good shots."[1]

One group of braves was talking, while riding, about how to rescue some of their fallen comrades when, "suddenly and without warning, one of the warriors fell from his horse dead." Dismounting to examine their friend, the warriors found that a bullet had torn through his skull. But the rifleman was so distant that they had not even been able to hear the report. "Buffalo hunters had awful long range," remarked a Comanche warrior named *Co-hay-yah*. "Sometimes we wouldn['t]t be thinking of it and they would kill our horses . . . No wonder they could kill the buffalo!"

As previously mentioned, during the first afternoon braves began riding back and forth across the valley to the east. "So we began picking them off," said Dixon, shooting the braves or at least their horses, and the riders retreated out of range. During a council of leaders "on a distant mound" some of the sharpshooters opened fire, and the horse of *Isa-tai* was killed. *Isa-tai* had promised that war paint on a horse would protect the animal from bullets, and the dismayed medicine man tried to point out that the slug had hit his pony where there was no paint. But this incident only intensified the disgrace of the medicine man.[3]

There were other accounts of long-range hits, real or imagined. Enough warriors or war ponies were struck by sharpshooters to keep them backed off to considerable distances. And on the second day, when a group of mounted braves appeared on a distant bluff to the east, hunters opened fire at long range. The warriors scattered, and prudently the raiders made no more appearances during the day.

So there were enough shots at great range to generate wary respect among the war party. But it was Billy Dixon's shot on Monday, June 29, that achieved legendary status.

"On the third day a party of about fifteen Indians appeared on the side of the bluff, east of Adobe Walls Creek, and some of the boys suggested that I try my big '50' on them. The distance was not far from three-fourths of a mile. A number of exaggerated accounts have been written about this incident," cautioned Billy as he dictated this important story to his wife. He certainly had described this event to Olive before, but he made it clear that he did not want exaggeration of this key story in his book. Indeed, the written account took up only a single paragraph in the Dixon book. "I took careful aim and pulled the trigger. We saw an Indian fall from his horse. The others dashed out of sight behind a clump of timber. A few moments later two Indians ran quickly on foot to where the dead Indian lay, seized his body and scurried to cover . . . I was admittedly a good marksman, yet this was what might be called a "scratch" shot.[4]

A "scratch" shot. When the caravan set out for the Texas Panhandle from Dodge City the previous April, a tenderfoot named Fairchild came along, inevitably becoming the butt of practical jokes by veteran frontiersmen. Fairchild yearned to fight Indians and to hunt wild game. "By 'scratch' shots," reported Dixon, "Fairchild managed to kill several antelope and he swelled up with pride until he was almost unrecognizable."[5] Fairchild banged away at wild animals and managed to bring down several with "scratch" shots — lucky shots. And Billy Dixon compared his most famous feat of marksmanship to a tenderfoot's "scratch" shot.

It should be taken into consideration that Dixon used a borrowed Big Fifty for his epic shot. He estimated the distance at three-fourths of a mile, and certainly he was experienced at estimating shooting distances. He would not have attempted such a lengthy shot from an offhand stance. Probably he used

Sharps Big Fifty with a Creedmore tang sight. *Courtesy NRA Museum in Springfield, Missouri.*

a window ledge as a rest, perhaps from a seated position. The borrowed Sharps probably had a Creedmore tang sight behind the breech of the gun, allowing the eye to line up naturally with the front sight. The Creedmore could be elevated for distance shooting, and adjusted side to side for windage. Billy pulled the set trigger and was ready to touch off the big cartridge. "I took careful aim and pulled the trigger."

The sight elevation raised the barrel and the slug exploded from the muzzle at an upward angle. Billy was trying to drop the bullet into the middle of the fifteen or so mounted warriors on the distant bluff. Of all people Billy Dixon understood that calculated luck was involved in a shot of such great length. But when an Indian in the faraway group tumbled off his horse, it was not just luck — it certainly was more than a "scratch" shot.[6]

While the men who had urged him on watched expectantly, Billy accounted for extreme range and windage and, with considerable barrel elevation, he arched a heavy slug into the midst of a group of horseback warriors — on his first try. He thus made a shot that galvanized the admiration of those who saw it and of those who heard about it. It was the kind of shooting feat to be expected when a small band of frontiersmen fought off hundreds of warriors. Billy Dixon's shot was the best of a great many fine shots that were made by fewer than thirty men while they fought for their lives against overwhelming numbers. And Billy's extraordinary shot was not forgotten — not during his lifetime and not in the more than a century that has followed his death.

Many firearms enthusiasts enjoy shooting antique weapons. Black powder shooters have a passion for firing nineteenth-century pistols and rifles. SASS (Single-Action Shooters Society) stage fast-draw competitions in imagined emulation of quick-drawing Old West gunfighters. A favorite competition is long-range target shooting with reproductions of Sharps buffalo rifles. Owners of these rifles regard buffalo guns not as antiques but as excellent competitive weapons. Manufacturers, both in the United States and abroad, have a long waiting list for these frontier reproductions, and one of the favorite models is the "Billy Dixon" in .45-70, .45-90, or .50-70 calibers. Manufactured by Pedersoli, the "Billy Dixon" has a 32-inch octagonal barrel and weighs 10 ½ pounds. (Of course, Billy preferred a Big

Looking from the site of Adobe Walls toward the north butte with two "warriors" standing atop the mesa. *Photo by the author.*

A modern shooter prepares to fire a Sharps Big Fifty at the north butte. *Photo by the author.*

Fifty, which weighed 16 pounds and fired a .50-90 cartridge.) A favorite distance of these competitions is 1,000 yards.[7]

There is uncertainty about the length of Dixon's legendary shot. Billy, true to his taciturn nature, rarely talked about his most famous feat as a sharpshooter. He told Olive for her record that the "distance was not far from three-fourths of a mile" — which would be about 1,320 yards. In the Dixon book a photograph of the northernmost plateau east of Adobe Walls is captioned: "High bluff east of Adobe Walls on which Dixon killed Indian at 1200 yards." The author has seen two men atop this plateau, and they looked like tiny black specks. But there is speculation that the southern plateau is where the fifteen or so Indians stood, and this site is significantly farther. A post-battle survey conducted by U.S. Army surveyors under the orders of Gen. Nelson A. Miles indicated the distance was 1,538 yards, about nine-tenths of a mile. As part of the fiftieth anniversary celebration of the battle, the shooting site was pointed out to a civilian surveyor in 1924 — more than a decade after the death of Billy Dixon — and the distance was recorded at 1,028 yards.[8]

If indeed the distance was the estimated maximum, 1,538 yards, the bullet would have been 5.3 seconds in flight. Warriors gathered on the south plateau might have noticed the puff of smoke when Dixon pulled the trigger, and 4.1 seconds later the report would have reached their ears. Another 1.2 seconds and the slug would have toppled a brave from his horse.[9] Whatever the distance — 1,538 yards, 1,320 yards, 1,028 yards — this impressive shot earned Billy Dixon a lasting place in Western lore.

The men who saw the shot almost immediately were able to tell others about Billy Dixon's deed. First, there were men at Adobe Walls who did not witness the shot, and they were quickly, excitedly informed. And soon there was a stream of new arrivals. On the same night that Henry Lease slipped away to try to reach Dodge City, two other men set out to alert the outfits in the countryside. Soon buffalo hunters and skinners were "coming in like blackbirds from all directions —" remembered Dixon. "By the fifth day enough hunters had arrived to make us feel comparatively safe." and by the sixth day more than one hundred men had reached Adobe Walls.[10]

But on the fifth day — Wednesday, July 1 — tragedy struck at Adobe Walls. William Olds was manning the new lookout station on the roof of Rath's store, where he clerked. Billy Dixon recalled that a lookout at the Myers and Leonard store, nearly six hundred feet to the north, "shouted that Indians were coming, and all of us ran for our guns and for shelter inside the buildings." Dixon headed for Rath's store, entering just in time to see Olds scrambling down the ladder from the roof, grasping his rifle awkwardly. Somehow the rifle discharged, "tearing off the top of Olds' head," said Dixon. "At the same instant Mrs. Olds rushed in from an adjoining room — in time to see the body of her husband roll from the ladder and crumple at her feet, a torrent of blood gushing from the terrible wound."[11]

Olds was dead when he hit the floor, and his wife Hannah

The grave of William Olds, who mishandled his rifle and inflicted a fatal wound within view of his wife Hannah. *Photo by the author.*

was overwhelmed with anguish. "Her grief was intense and pitiable," said Dixon. "A rough lot of men, such as we were, did not know how to comfort a woman in such distress." Meanwhile, the twenty-five or thirty warriors who caused the alarm apparently were only riding away from Adobe Walls, and soon they were out of sight to the east. William Olds was buried just southeast of Rath's store. He was the fourth man from Adobe Walls to die.[12]

The bad-luck rifle that belonged to William Olds promptly was borrowed by Bat Masterson, who had loaned his own gun to another defender. But a day later the widowed Hannah Olds sent word for Bat to return the rifle. Bat replied that he would return the gun to Mrs. Olds the next morning. Concerned that she might somehow lose possession of her husband's fine rifle, Hannah asked a man named Frank Brown to bring her the gun.

Brown brought up the matter-spiced with profanity - in Hanrahan's Saloon, where the owner gave his personal guarantee that the rifle would be returned in the morning. Billy Dixon was one of the onlookers. "Brown crowded matters until Hanrahan grabbed him by the neck, shook him as a bulldog would a rabbit, and then threw Brown out of the saloon . . .'Get out of my building, you _____ _____!'" Angrily Hanrahan drew his revolver, but Dixon and several others intervened before gunplay could erupt.[13]

The next morning Bat Masterson brought the rifle to Hannah Olds, but it was too late to avoid an ugly flareup among the men at Adobe Walls. Tensions had been strained for a week.

Following a fight for their lives against heavy odds, the defenders realized that they were trapped at Adobe Walls and that reinforced warriors might return at any time, and feelings became stretched to a breaking point. When Fred Brown demanded the return of the Olds rifle he threw blasphemy at James Hanrahan, who threw it right back. Hanrahan impulsively roughed up Brown and whipped out his sixgun for good measure.

"The row spread ill feeling among a number of the men," reported Dixon, "and though blood that had been split in fighting for each other was scarcely dry on the ground, yet some were now ready to begin fighting each other. This was the way of the west in those times . . ."[14]

Shortly after this incident the war party disappeared from the vicinity. Although life and death anxiety thus was eased, everyone at Adobe Walls had to face a new economic reality. Thousands of buffalo hides had been unstacked and scattered on the ground. The two stores no longer were buying hides, which put the hunters and skinners out of business. The stores would have to close, and so would the saloon and the blacksmith shop. James Hanrahan, without a future at Adobe Walls as either a saloonkeeper or a hide hunter, began to organize a caravan to retreat to Dodge City. The war party had not destroyed wagons, but draft animals had to be procured from the hide men who continued to come to Adobe Walls from their camps. Men had to be employed by the storekeepers to stay at the stores; other men decided to stay without recompense.

On Monday, July 13 — more than two weeks after the original attack — a large caravan pulled out of Adobe Walls — heading up Short Creek until they reached the plains. There they left the well-traveled road to Dodge City and, as a precaution against a possible ambush, went westward until they reached the headwaters of Palo Duro Creek, where they made camp. On Tuesday, by making a long trek, the caravan encamped at San Francisco Creek.

There they found a recently - abandoned hide-hunters' camp and the mutilated corpse of Charley Sharp, who had been dead about a week. The men of Adobe Walls would learn that after the battle the war party broke up into small bands and raided isolated camps. Charley Sharp was a partner of Henry Lease, who had left camp to buy supplies at Adobe Walls, before riding to find help at Dodge City. Sharp's remains were buried by men of the caravan.

On Wednesday the caravan angled to the northeast, again reaching the Adobe Walls road, along the Cimarron River. Thursday's travel led to Crooked Creek, and on Friday the caravan pulled into Dodge City. Up and down the Arkansas River near Dodge were the camps of buffalo hunters who had fled to town after hearing of the assault at Adobe Walls.

"Ours was the first crowd to reach Dodge City after the fight at Adobe Walls," said Billy Dixon, "and the whole town turned out to see us. Everybody was anxious to learn the particulars, and we were asked thousands of questions." They learned that a party of about forty buffalo hunters and men of Dodge, led by Tom Nixon, already had ridden to the relief of Adobe Walls.[16]

Some of the refugees from Adobe Walls left the caravan and bought train tickets "for their homes in the east. They had enough of the Indians to last them several years, and they were not ashamed to stand up and say so." But Billy Dixon and many of his pals were "locoed" with the land where "the customs [were] wild." Once again he expressed how he was drawn to the rugged plains frontier. "Drouth, scarcity of water-holes, 'northers,' rattlesnakes, Indians, even the United States Army, could not have driven us east of the ninety-ninth meridian of longitude."[17]

When Billy Dixon and his fellow frontiersmen reached Dodge, they found that the town was hitting its raucous stride as the "Bibulous Babylon of the Plains." Billy and other veterans of Adobe Walls "were soon entering into the fun at Dodge with the greatest enthusiasm, forgetful of the perils and hardships that so lately beset us."[18]

While Billy Dixon was enjoying the pleasures of Dodge City, Tom Nixon and his men reached Adobe Walls. Hannah Olds and most of the men departed with Nixon and his group. But more than a dozen men decided to stay at Adobe Walls. Their horses were kept in the stockade, and hay was cut in the nearby creek bottom. These men had plenty of provisions from the remaining stocks in the old store buildings. Staying close to the buildings, these men remained at Adobe Walls for two more months.

Two months later, while scouting for an army column, Billy Dixon and Bat Masterson arrived at Adobe Walls and were treated to a good supper by the inmates. The troopers, led by Lt. Frank Baldwin, soon arrived and pitched tents. Dixon gave Lieutenant Baldwin and most of his men a guided tour of the battlefield. And during their stay, Dixon and the soldiers were astonished at the sudden appearance in the distance of a war party which darted from cover to kill a civilian named George Huffman. From a mile away, Dixon watched a warrior lance Huffman and steal his horse. Huffman and a companion, Tobe Robinson, had ridden to the Canadian River to hunt wild plums when they were jumped. Robinson managed to outrace his pursuers. Huffman's body was retrieved and buried at Adobe Walls.[19]

The group of men who had stayed at Adobe Walls left when Lieutenant Baldwin led the troopers away. "Ours was the last party of white men ever to leave Adobe Walls," remarked Dixon. Actually on September 7 an Eighth Cavalry detachment, led by Lt. Henry Farnsworth, rode by the abandoned buildings at the start of the campaign known as the Red River War. Farnsworth found a large supply of corn in one of the stores and he hauled off 5,500 pounds for the use of the column.[20]

The next visitors were warriors who vengefully destroyed

the Adobe Walls complex. The picket blacksmith shop was
burned. The sod structures were supported by a wooden frame-
work, including a big ridge pole in each building. Doors, window frames, wooden barrels, furniture, and other flammable
materials, including a wagon box without wheels, were piled
up in each store and set ablaze. A number of the scattered buffalo hides were draped over the picket corral fence, and as the
cottonwood poles began to burn the fat in the skins added to
the flames.[21]

Scout Dixon returned in October with a large column commanded by Col. Nelson A. Miles, but only the old saloon walls
still stood. "The ruins were still smoking," commented Dixon.
Both Lieutenant Baldwin and Colonel Miles, who each were
ambitious, highly competent professional soldiers, took the
opportunity to quiz Dixon in detail about the battle at Adobe
Walls. Baldwin requested a walking tour of the battlefield and,
accompanied by many of the troopers, the men hiked "about
a mile." Of course there were questions about the already famous shot, and Colonel Miles ordered a measurement of the
distance.[22]

Nearly a century and a half has passed since Billy Dixon,
at the urging of his comrades , triggered an extraordinary shot
before eyewitnesses. The post-battle questions about distance
and location and other details are still being asked today. The
trajectory of the shot is studied by computers, and the performance of Sharps rifles at long range is continually tested by
sharpshooting competitors. The shot at Adobe Walls earned
Billy Dixon a permanent place in the saga of the Old West and
called attention to his other frontier exploits — including the
award of a Congressional Medal of Honor for another exceptional combat adventure at a lonely site that became known as
Buffalo Wallow.

Chapter Nine

Buffalo Wallow

Forward! If any man is killed I will make him a corporal.

Captain Adna R. Chaffee
to his troopers

Billy Dixon reached Dodge City from Adobe Walls on July 17, 1874, and he lost no time in carousing with pals through the growing number of saloons and dives. "Things at Dodge were run for the fullest enjoyment of the present —" he reminisced with pleasure.[1] Everyone asked about the fighting at Adobe Walls, and Dixon was talked out of all of his Indian plunder by eager souvenir-seekers.

Soon Billy encountered an old friend, Jack Callahan. A major military expedition was being organized to converge on the Texas Panhandle. As a newly-appointed wagon master for a column that was forming in Dodge City, Callahan offered Dixon a job as his assistant. Dixon was inclined to accept this position, but just down the street, he ran into another old acquaintance from his teamster days, John Curley, who was corral master at Fort Hays in 1868. Curley told Dixon that he believed he could help Billy become part of a special scouting unit that was being established for the expedition by Col. Nelson A. Miles. Dixon immediately expressed interest, and Curley led the way to headquarters. Curley introduced and recommended Dixon. "After asking me a few questions, General Miles turned to his adjutant and told him to put my name down." Billy Dixon became a civilian scout, guide, and dispatch rider on August 6, 1874.[2] Five weeks and two days later, at the Buffalo Wallow Fight, Dixon found himself in even greater peril than at the recent Battle of Adobe Walls.

Because of the mounting depredations on the Staked Plains, William T. Sherman, Commanding General of the United States Army, telegraphed orders on July 20, 1874, that launched the Red River War. The strategy was to send five columns from as many directions into the Texas Panhandle. The army had orders to drive all roaming bands of Comanches, Kiowas, Southern Cheyennes, and Arapahos onto their reservations in Indian Territory. One column would be led by Col. Nelson A. Miles who had distinguished himself during the Civil War as a Major General of Volunteers. The reduction of the military after the Civil War demanded that Miles accept a colonelcy to remain in the regular army.

On July 27, 1874, Colonel Miles was directed to organize his column in Dodge City, where railroad connections sped up the military assembly. Miles commanded the Fifth Infantry, based at Fort Leavenworth. Colonel Miles brought four companies with him, and he established his headquarters at Fort Dodge. The Sixth Cavalry would add eight mounted troops in two battalions. Miles assigned Lt. Frank Baldwin of the Fifth as chief of scouts. An outstanding soldier, Baldwin was a combat veteran of the Civil War, earning a Medal of Honor during the Battle of Atlanta and ending the war as a twenty-three-year-old lieutenant colonel. An artillery unit added Gatling guns and mountain howitzers to the column. In all, Miles would command 744 men.[3]

Colonel Miles (he commonly was addressed as "General" Miles, from his brilliant Civil War service) paid special attention to the "trailers, guides, and scouts" he placed under Frank Baldwin. "This force was composed of [twenty] friendly Delaware Indians and a body of twenty-five frontiersman made of expert riflemen, pioneers, and plainsmen; men of known courage and intelligence, and possessing the best attainable knowledge of that remote and unsettled country."[4] Billy Dixon was qualified on all counts.

Miles wrote to his wife, Mary — the daughter of Senator John Sherman and the niece of General William T. Sherman — about his civilian scouts. "I find no trouble in getting all of that class of men I want, and though they are a rough set of individuals they will be valuable for what I want them for."[5]

In the end, Miles did not find quite as many of these men as he originally intended. Instead of twenty-five plainsmen, he enlisted seventeen, along with twenty Delaware men from their reservation in

Lt. Frank Baldwin was tasked with organizing a special scout force for the campaign of 1874. Baldwin earned a Medal of Honor during the Civil War, and he was awarded a second Medal for leading the rescue of the German sisters in 1874. *Courtesy National Archives.*

southern Kansas. The Delawares were led by a trusted chief, Falling Leaf, who was more than seventy years old.

Miles encamped his command away from the fort, creating a tent camp on the Arkansas River, which ran just south of Dodge City. On August 9 Miles personally conducted a target practice for the plainsmen. At the riverside, Miles indicated snags and stones and other targets, and he called out the name of each shooter. Miles was impressed at the quality of long-range shooting, and Dixon was pleased that "I never missed a single time."[6]

Bat Masterson joined the scouting unit a few days after Billy Dixon, who may have helped to recruit his friend. The scouts were paid seventy-five dollars per month, plus an additional fifty dollars for carrying dispatches across dangerous territory. They were furnished firearms, ammunition, and provisions. One man listed as a "scout" was J.T. Marshall, a newspaperman brought along by Miles to provide news to the public. The scouts were tasked with locating bands of Indians who were off their reservations, almost always with their women, children and elderly. By checking the reservation rolls, it was estimated that the enemy on the Staked Plains consisted of 2,000 Comanches, 1,800 Southern Cheyennes, and 1,000 Kiowas, numbers which included about 1,200 warriors.

Miles intended to conduct his march into Texas across a broad front, with the Delaware scouts deployed to provide a loose connection between the columns. A cavalry battalion marched out of the Dodge encampment on August 11, leading the way toward the Texas Panhandle. Lieutenant Baldwin, civilian scouts Dixon and Masterson, six Delawares, and a platoon of cavalrymen were assigned to conduct a sweeping probe, riding along the North Canadian to Palo Duro Creek, then following the hidemen's trail to Adobe Walls, before proceeding along the Canadian River until contacting Colonel Miles. Miles was the last to depart, leading the infantry and artillery south almost one hundred miles to Camp Supply. After reprovisioning, he would march into Texas and conduct his command along the planned strategic advance from the northeast.[8]

Lieutenant Baldwin led his eight scouts and eighteen troopers, who were commanded by Lt. Austin Henely, on a five-day ride to Adobe Walls through withering August heat. They were accompanied by a wagon drawn by a six-mule team and carrying bedding, provisions, and a cook outfit. On the afternoon of the fifth day, Baldwin sent Dixon and Masterson ahead to alert the men at Adobe Walls "that the troops were coming." This precaution was taken so that the mounted force would not be mistaken for a war party and fired upon. Dixon rode within shouting distance and waved his hat, and "they gave me a hearty reception." A hot supper was provided, "and I was telling them stories of the outside world when the soldiers arrived around 9 o'clock."[9]

There was almost no water in East Adobe Walls Creek, so with the guidance of Dixon, camp was made a mile south, near the original Adobe Walls ruins and Bent Creek, which did not have water. The next morning was when Lieutenant Baldwin asked Billy Dixon for a walking tour of the Adobe Walls battlefield. And later in the day two men from Adobe Walls, George Huffman and Tobe Robinson — feeling safe because of the nearby troopers — rode down to the Canadian River to collect wild plums. As previously mentioned, they were attacked by a concealed war party, and Huffman was killed with a lance thrust. By the time the scouts and soldiers rounded up and saddled their horses the war party had vanished. Huffman's corpse was brought back to Adobe Walls for burial. The next day, when Lieutenant Baldwin broke camp and resumed the march with his patrol, the final residents of Adobe Walls rode out with them.

The little column headed south, crossing the Canadian River. When they reached Chicken Creek, they found two warriors who had built a fire and stopped for noon, tying their horses to sagebrush. A quick attack resulted in the death of one brave, but the other warrior leaped onto his pony and galloped away, somehow eluding a rain of gunfire that followed him.

"The noise of our guns stampeded a big bunch of buffaloes further up the creek," related Dixon. "They kicked up such a cloud of dust that we thought a war party of Indians . . . was coming for us, and that we had stirred up the worst kind of trouble. Happily, we were soon able to see the buffaloes, and the world soon looked brighter." But the cook, trailing behind with the wagons, knew nothing of the buffaloes. Assuming that there were warriors ahead, he whipped his mules furiously to catch up with the column. "When almost upon us," said Dixon, "his mules took fright and ran away, and could not be stopped until men rode to his assistance."[10]

The rendezvous point was Cantonment Creek. Once Colonel Miles was able to reorganize his command, he pushed his men hard across the dry plains in continuing heat. Many dogs expired of thirst, and on one occasion Miles' setter, Jack, led the men to a small water hole after they noticed his damp fur. On August 28 abandoned Native American baggage was discovered on the trail. Miles detailed two troops to guard the slow-moving supply train, then pushed ahead with the balance of his command. He covered sixty-five miles in two days, and on August 30 he took up the march at four o'clock in the morning.

Baldwin and his scouts were two miles in advance as the troops approached the Cap Rock Escarpment near the entrance to Palo Duro Canyon. As the scouts entered the hills, two hundred or more concealed Cheyenne warriors suddenly attacked from the bluffs. Miles stated that "Baldwin handled his men with consummate skill . . ." The scouts, including Billy Dixon and Bat Masterson, "quickly took position, dropped on the ground, and used their effective rifles to the best advantage." The Delawares went into action, with Chief Fall Leaf riding up and down his line, exposing himself to enemy fire. Baldwin's "little force held its ground until reinforced by the rapid advance of the cavalry . . ."[11]

Both cavalry battalions deployed at the gallop and the Gatling guns opened up on the warriors' position. The braves fell back to a defensive position reinforced by perhaps four hundred more Comanches and Kiowas. The six hundred warriors gave ground grudgingly as Miles pressed the attack. "Forward!" ordered Capt. Adna R. Chaffee of the Sixth Cavalry. "If any man is killed I will make him a corporal."[12]

Aggressively Miles advanced all day across the rugged, waterless region. By nightfall, many of his men were so parched that they slit veins in their arms and wet their swollen tongues by sucking their own blood. The command suffered only two soldiers wounded during the fighting, but the men were exhausted, and the following dawn revealed that the entire band of Indians had disappeared. Pursuit was not possible without resupply, and Miles decided to hold his current position while sending his wagon train eastward.

Capt. Wyllys Lyman commanded thirty-six empty wagons, a company of infantry, and a cavalry detachment. Colonel Miles, through couriers, arranged for a supply train to come down from Camp Supply and transfer provisions to Lyman's wagons. Lyman pushed hard, traveling 120 miles in five days. By the time the connection and transfer were made with the Camp Supply caravan, it was September 9 before Captain Lyman started back, and almost immediately he was tracked by hostiles. There were long-range potshots and other harassment, and by the next day, a full-scale assault was launched on the caravan, which now was just north of the Washita River in modern Hemphill County.

Lyman circled his large wagon train against a hillside, dug rifle pits twenty yards outside his perimeter, and secured his animals within the enclosure. The soldiers took casualties but conducted a skillful defense. Lyman sent a courier to Camp Supply requesting "quick aid" because "I am corralled by Comanches, two miles north of the Washita . . ." The scout entrusted with this message made a narrow escape past the attackers on September 11, a day of constant attacks by mounted warriors, whose numbers were estimated in the hundreds by Lyman.[13]

On the next day Billy Dixon, carrying dispatches with a courier detail, chanced into contact with a large contingent of the attacking force. Miles, facing a precarious supply situation, moved his command to McClellan Creek, and on September 10 he assigned scouts Dixon and Amos Chapman to carry dispatches to Camp Supply. Four enlisted men were directed to ride as escorts: Sgt. Z.T. Woodhall, and Privates Peter Rath, John

Harrington, and George W. Smith. Miles offered as large an escort as the two scouts wanted, but they preferred the smallest number possible.

"Leaving camp," related Dixon, "we traveled mostly at night, resting in secluded places during the day. War parties were moving in every direction, and there was danger of attack at every turn."[14]

Amos Chapman, thirty-seven, was a veteran frontiersman. Of mixed white and Native American parentage, he married Mary Longneck, a daughter of Cheyenne chief Stone Calf, and lived on occasion with the tribe. Chapman was at Camp Supply when Miles arrived from Dodge City, and he volunteered to join Baldwin's scouting force.

Chapman and Dixon led the way eastward, moving rapidly even though traveling primarily during two nights. But at dawn on Saturday, September 12, the six-man detail topped a rise between the Washita River and Gageby Creek and came "almost face to face with a large band of Kiowa and Comanche warriors." Dixon and his companions had no way of knowing that they were only five miles south and slightly west of the besieged supply train, although the Washita River lay in between. The war party, numbering perhaps 125 braves, immediately galloped to encircle their white foes. "We were in a trap."

Dixon and his comrades realized they could not make a run for it, because they could be cut down one by one by swarming warriors. "We also realized we could do better work on foot, so we dismounted and placed our horses in the care of George Smith."[15]

When cavalrymen fought on foot, one of every four troopers became a horse holder. But the customary number of fours did not work in this case, so Private Smith held all six horses while the other five men unlimbered their guns. But within moments Smith was shot through the left lung beneath his shoulder blade. The impact of the bullet toppled him face down. Smith dropped his service revolver and, of course, lost his grip on the six sets of reins. The horses stampeded, carrying off coats and canteens and rations.

The warriors apparently had ridden away from the near-by wagon train fight and were providing a large screen for their families, who were moving camp. The war party poured a heavy fire into their outnumbered opponents, and Private Smith collapsed, which enabled the warriors to chase down six horses. But Dixon had his Big Fifty, and the others had carbines, as well as revolvers. The warriors circled around the trapped white men, "or dashed past," said Dixon, "yelling and cutting all kinds of capers." At times "Indians would ride toward us at headlong speed with lances uplifted and poised, undoubtedly bent upon spearing us." Colonel Miles reported that sometimes the attackers closed to such "short range that [the defenders] sometimes used their pistols, retaining the last charge to prevent capture and torture . . ."[16]

Amos Chapman was struck by a bullet which shattered his left knee. "Billy, I am hit at last," he gasped. Dixon also took a slug in the calf of his leg, but his movements were not impaired. "I was wearing a thin cashmere shirt, slightly bloused," said Dixon. "The shirt was literally riddled with bullets." Sergeant Woodall and Private Harrington both were shot, while Private Rath suffered a minor wound. Dixon realized "that I was in closer quarters than I had ever been in my life . . ."[17] Even closer than Adobe Walls.

Everyone exposed atop the little hill been hit, but Billy finally spotted a buffalo wallow which might offer a modicum of cover. Buffaloes roll in the dirt to deter biting flies and to shed fur, and bulls wallow during mating season to display their strength and to leave their scent. Dixon ran to the wallow at top speed, while the warriors shot at him without effect. "The wallow was about ten feet in diameter," he reported. "I found that its depth, though slight, afforded some protection." He shouted at his comrades to join him, and as each man arrived at the wallow, he drew his knife and began throwing dirt around the perimeter. The land was sandy, and the cover piled up quickly, although the men were "constantly interrupted by the necessity of firing at the Indians as they dashed within range." During an advance one of the wounded men raised up and yelled, "No use, boys, no use; we might as well give up." The others shouted at him to get down. And at that instant, a bullet slammed into the

Scout Amos Chapman, whose leg had to be amputated after the Buffalo Wallow Fight. *Courtesy Roberts County Museum, Miami.*

soft bank near him and filled his mouth with sand. Billy could not suppress a laugh.[18]

Amos Chapman did not join the other four men in the buffalo wallow. One man called out to him to come over, but Chapman announced that his knee was shattered and he could not walk. Dixon started toward Chapman's position, but a warrior volley drove him back into the buffalo wallow. He was driven back two or three more times before finally running to Chapman's side. Dixon hoisted Chapman onto his back, drew both legs in front of him, then carried his wounded friend to the wallow. "We began digging like gophers with our hands and knives to make our little wall of earth higher, and shortly had heaped up quite a little wall of dirt around us." With only a limited amount of ammunition, the battered defenders fired deliberately, and were "not unmindful of the fact that every once in a while there was another dead or wounded Indian."[19]

At mid-afternoon, a thunderstorm struck, and the accompanying norther dropped the temperature precipitously. Everyone's coat was tied behind his saddle, and the horses had stampeded. "I was heart-sick over the loss of my coat," said Dixon, "for in the inside pocket was my dearest treasure, my mother's picture . . ." The warriors sat forlornly on their ponies out of rifle range, "with their blankets drawn tightly around them." All fighting stopped in the face of thunder and lightning and sheets of rain.[20]

Buffaloes compact the soil as they wallow, and the shallow depressions they create therefore hold more water than surrounding undisturbed soils. Soon there were a couple of inches of water in the bottom of the wallow, although it was muddy and stained with the blood of the wounded. The drenched men,

This fine depiction of the Buffalo Wallow Fight is on display in the Roberts County Museum. Billy Dixon is in the foreground, wearing a white shirt. *Courtesy Roberts County Museum, Miami.*

shivering from the cold, drank the foul water.

Late in the afternoon, with ammunition running low, someone suggested retrieving Private Smith's revolver and cartridge belt. Private Rath volunteered to go but soon returned with the astounding news that George Smith was still alive. Rath and Dixon hurried to Smith's side and helped him to the buffalo wallow. A massive wound was discovered beneath Smith's shoulder blade. Dixon recorded that "when he breathed the wind sobbed out of his back beneath the shoulder blade." Nearby Dixon found "a stout willow switch" that a warrior had been using as a makeshift quirt. "With this switch, a silk handkerchief was stuffed into the gaping bullet hole in Smith's back." Before darkness fell, Dixon put the willow switch to double duty, using it to clean all of the guns.[21]

Everyone was cold and hungry, and the four seriously wounded men could not be expected to rest in two inches of water. Dixon and Rath collected tumbleweeds, crushed the stiff twigs, and created a rudimentary bed across the bottom of the wallow, laying the wounded men atop the twigs and above the water. A quick conference of war demanded that a messenger try to go for help, and Billy stated his confidence that the trail to Camp Supply was nearby and that he could find it. But the wounded men insisted that Dixon should stay with them. Rath agreed to go, but two hours later he returned without having found the trail.

By this time George Smith was asking to be put out of his misery, while Billy Dixon considered cutting his long black hair to make a less tempting scalp. About ten o'clock Smith fell asleep, and he died within an hour. "We lifted the body of our dead comrade and gently laid it outside the buffalo wallow on the mesquite grass," said Dixon, "covering the white face with a silk handkerchief."[22]

Following a miserable night, "all the men were willing that I should go for help, and I at once started." Of course, now Dixon had to make his way in daylight rather than under cover of darkness. He brought his Big Fifty and proceeded carefully. He still had no knowledge of the nearby presence of Captain Lyman and the supply caravan, and he assumed that Colonel Miles was still seventy-five miles to the west. But within half an hour Dixon found the trail to Camp Supply, and a short distance farther he saw a large body of mounted men approaching from the northwest. Warriors or soldiers? Within moments he could tell that they were troops.

"I never felt happier in my life," exulted Billy. He fired his Big Fifty twice. The entire command came to a halt, and two troopers rode forward. The column was an Eighth Cavalry force from Fort Bascom, New Mexico, under the command of Major W.R. Price. The approach of Major Price broke up the siege of Captain Lyman's wagon train, which probably is why the courier detail encountered 125 warriors on September 12. "The Indians had just given up the attack when we ran into them," reasoned Dixon.[23]

Major Price rode to Dixon, and after learning the condition of the courier detail, he sent his surgeon and two men toward the buffalo wallow. While reporting to Major Price, Dixon noticed that the surgeon's detail was veering too far south. He fired his Big Fifty again and made a signal which sent the detail in the right direction. But the three shots from Billy's Big Fifty alarmed the men in the wallow, and when the surgeon's detail rode into view, one of the wounded men nervously fired a shot which felled the horse of one of the surgeon's men.

The angry surgeon gave no more than a cursory examination of the wounded men. He did not even bandage the wounds nor leave any medicines, an outrageous and inhumane violation of medical duty. Price, who had lost a cavalry horse, also was irritated and refused to provide a protective detail or even to leave guns and ammunition. (The Buffalo Wallow defenders had nearly exhausted their ammunition, and the Eighth Cavalry were issued different firearms.) "For this [Price] was afterwards severely censured, and justly," related Dixon with satisfaction. As Price led his column away, some of his troopers sympathetically handed rations to the starving, wounded men.[24]

The men at the buffalo wallow suffered throughout the rest of September 13 until midnight, when they heard the faraway note of a bugle. "We fired our guns, to let them know where we were," said Billy, "and soon the soldiers came riding out of the darkness."

The relief column, dispatched as soon as Miles learned of their plight from a Price courier, built a fire and cooked a hot meal for Dixon and his comrades. The next day the four badly wounded men were sent to Camp Supply, where Amos Chapman's left leg was amputated above the knee. "Amos was as tough as second growth hickory and was soon out of the hospital and in the saddle," remarked Billy. "Chapman could handle a gun and ride as well as ever, the only difference being that he had to mount his horse from the right side, Indian fashion."[25]

Once Colonel Miles received a thorough report on the Buffalo Wallow Fight, he promptly began action to secure military recognition for the courageous men of the courier detail. On September 24, 1874, from his camp on the Washita River in the Texas Panhandle, he composed a lengthy letter to the United States Adjutant General, with copies to the Assistant Adjutant General and the Headquarters Departments of the U.S. Army and of the Missouri Division.

In his opening sentence Colonel Miles declared: "I deem it but a duty to brave men and faithful soldiers to bring to the notice of the highest authority, an instance of indomitable courage, skill and true heroism on the part of a detachment from this command, with the request that the actors may be rewarded, and their faithfulness and bravery recognized, by pensions, medals of honour, or in such way as may be deemed most fitting."[26]

THE VICTORY OF THE PRIVATES.

The Victory of the Privates" is an illustration of the Buffalo Wallow Fight in Miles, *Personal Recollections*, 175.

Miles went on to describe the action in several subsequent paragraphs. The final paragraph featured eloquent admiration from Miles: "The simple recital of their deeds, and the mention of the odds against which they fought, how the wounded defended the dying, and the dying aided the wounded by exposure to fresh wounds after the power of action was gone, these alone present a scene of cool courage, heroism, and self-sacrifice which duty, as well as inclination, prompts us to recognize, but which we cannot fully honour."

Honour. Heroism. Cool courage. Self-sacrifice. These words aptly summed up the valor shown at the Buffalo Wallow Fight. And beneath the signature of Miles was a notation: "Official copy respectfully furnished William Dixon. By command of Bvt. Maj. Gen'l Miles." Miles had every intention that the Buffalo Wallow defenders were to be properly honored — especially Scout William Dixon.

The Congressional Medal of Honor was not created until the outbreak of the Civil War. In 1847 a Certificate of Merit was authorized to acknowledge courageous actions during the War with Mexico. No medal was awarded, just a certificate — it was believed that Americans should avoid such extravagant European trappings as medals. But with the explosion of hostilities between North and South, there was a sudden groundswell to offer tangible rewards to those who protected American so-

Billy Dixon's Medal of Honor was presented to him by Col. Nelson Miles in a camp only a few miles west of Adobe Walls. *Courtesy Panhandle-Plains Museum, Canyon, Texas.*

ciety. In 1861 a Navy Medal was authorized, and early the next year an Army Medal of Honor for enlisted men was proposed. President Lincoln signed it into law on July 12, 1862, and the following year it was amended to include officers and to become retroactive to the opening of the Civil War.

But until 1868 only three medals had been awarded to participants in the Indian Wars. For the next two decades and longer, more than 400 soldiers distinguished themselves with sufficient valor to be honored with the medal. The branch which predominated in such awards, not surprisingly, was the cavalry. Many infantry regiments never recorded a single Medal of Honor, and those which did posted just one or two. But the Fifth Infantry of Col. Nelson A. Miles posted forty-five medals, the majority during the Red River War.[27]

It should be mentioned that company commanders sometimes recommended large numbers of men for the Medal of Honor. In 1876, however, General Alfred E. Terry disapproved many of these recommendations, emphasizing that "Medals of Honor are not intended for ordinarily good conduct, but for conspicuous acts of gallantry." That was the first step in establishing a strict body of regulations and legislation which would insure and enhance the dignity of the Medal of Honor. An immediate result of Terry's action was the appointment of a board of officers to review the recommendations. Of course, by any standard, the actions of Billy Dixon at the Buffalo Wallow Fight qualified him for the nation's highest award for valor.

On November 6, 1874, notification was dispatched by the Adjutant General's Office authorizing the medals requested by Miles for the action at the Buffalo Wallow, including a posthumous Medal of Honor for Pvt. George Smith. Delivery of Medals of Honor to Indian fighters usually was by registered mail. Although a few medals had been presented during the Civil War amid troop formations, after the war recipients were simply mailed their medals. The Adjutant General's Office mailed a Medal of Honor to Scout William Dixon on November 19, 1874.[28]

A proud moment came, apparently on Christmas Eve, 1874, when Miles insisted upon a personal presentation after the medals arrived from Washington: "With his own hands he pinned mine on my coat when we were in camp on Carson Creek, five or six miles west of the original ruins of Adobe Walls." Miles also presented a personal letter to Dixon, which Billy kept for the rest of his life:[29]

Headquarters Ind. Ter. Expedition
Camp on Canadian, Texas
December 24, 1874

Mr. William Dixon,
Sir:

I take pleasure in presenting to you a Medal of Honour, as a recognition by the Government of your skill, courage and determined fortitude, displayed in an engagement with (5) others, on the 12th of September, 1874, against hostile Indians, in overwhelming numbers.

This mark of honour, I trust, will be long worn by you, and though it in a small degree compensates for the hardships endured, yet it is a lasting emblem of distinguished services, well earned in a noble cause. It will ever recall the fact to you and yours, of having materially aided in clearing this fair country of ruthless savages, and freeing it from all time to civil settlements. This must be an ever increasing gratification to you. This badge of honour is most worthily bestowed.

Respectfully, &c,
Nelson A. Miles,
Bvt. Maj. Gen'l. U.S. Army,
Commanding.

Through General Orders No. 28, dated January 24, 1875, Miles announced to his entire command "his pleasing" to bestow the "medal-of-honor" to the five survivors of the Buffalo Wallow Fight. [30] When the scouts had signed up in Dodge City, they were promised a bonus of fifty dollars for courier duty in dangerous territory. Certainly, the mission that climaxed at Buffalo Wallow qualified as dangerous, and Lt. Frank Baldwin did not forget the promise of "a reward promised you for the extraordinary service performed by you as Guide and Scout while under my command . . ." In the summer of 1875, from his

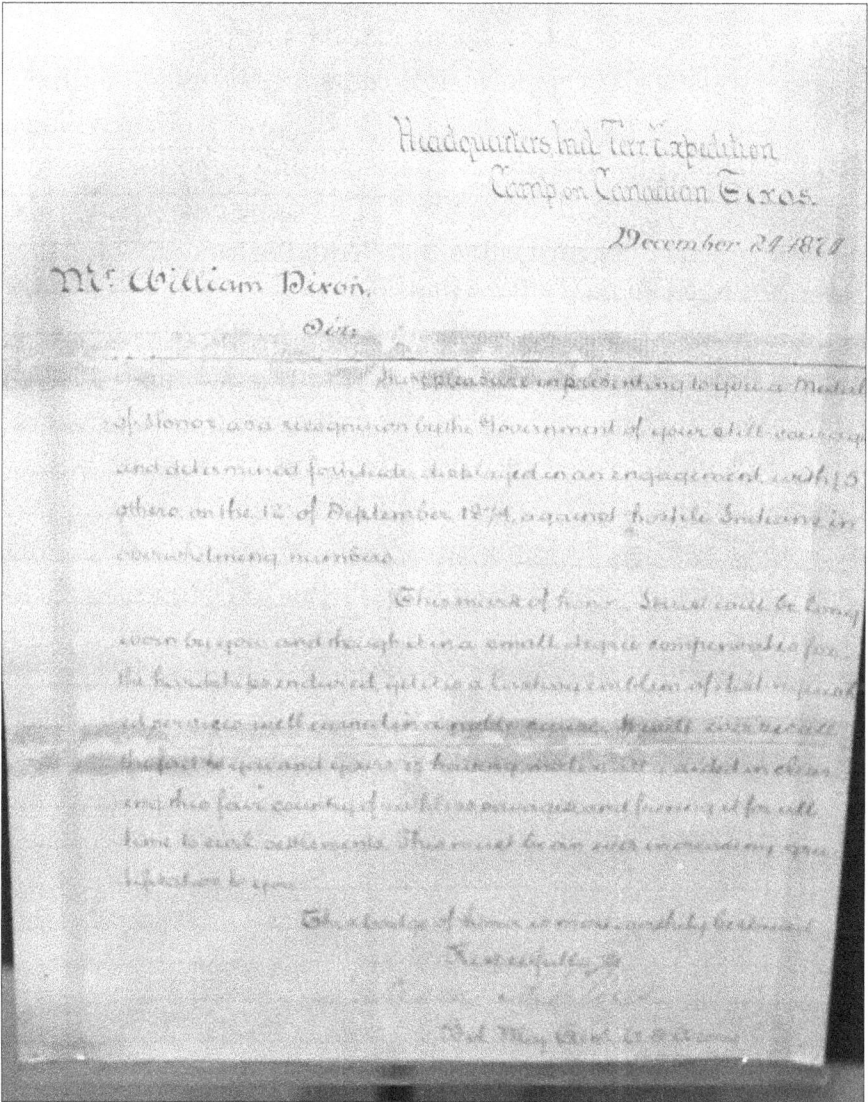

Letter of congratulations from Miles to Dixon, written on Christmas Eve, 1874. *Courtesy Panhandle-Plains Museum, Canyon, Texas.*

new duty station at Fort Leavenworth, he corresponded with Dixon, asking him to sign enclosed vouchers, and two months later Billy was sent a check for fifty dollars.[31]

Less welcome correspondence came in 1917 when authorities decided to rescind Medals of Honor awarded to civilians. As civilian scouts, Amos Chapman and Billy Dixon both were on this list. Billy was deceased by 1917, but he had strongly expressed to Olive his conviction that he had earned the Medal of Honor. "I have always felt that I did some good work that day," he said in an understatement.[32] Olive simply did not return the medal, and eventually, she donated it to the Panhandle-Plains Historical Museum. (In 1989 the Army Board for the Correction of Records reversed the 1917 decision, which applied to five Indian War civilian scouts.)[33] Today Billy Dixon's Medal of Honor may be viewed at the Panhandle-Plains Museum in an exhibit case which also displays the original letter to Dixon from General Miles.

Chapter Ten

Army Scout

The charge was spectacular, grand, and most effective in results.

Lt. Frank Baldwin,

Chief of Scouts

Billy Dixon signed on as a civilian army scout on August 6, 1874. Immediately he became acquainted with Col. Nelson A. Miles, who was destined to become Commanding General of the Army. Miles was impressed by the courage and skills displayed by Dixon, and became the scout's admirer and advocate.

Dixon's first weeks as an army scout were packed with action and danger. The Miles column was organized rapidly, and Billy Dixon accompanied a hard-riding patrol that brought him to Adobe Walls and to two small-scale actions. Soon the scout detachment was in the van when the Miles command was attacked by hundreds of warriors, and Dixon fought in a day-long battle across harsh terrain.

Just days later Dixon and another scout, along with a four-man escort, were sent with dispatches, only to be intercepted by a war party that outnumbered the surviving combatants twenty-five to one. Yet Dixon and his comrades fought off the warriors, and each man was recommended for the Medal of Honor. All of this martial activity took place in just over five weeks of service.

Shortly after the Buffalo Wallow Fight, Billy Dixon resumed his post with Lt. Frank Baldwin's scouting company. The Red River War now was at full scale, with five columns of troops crisscrossing the Panhandle in pursuit of war parties and their dependents. The warriors often eluded their pursuers, sometimes fighting rearguard actions to cover the retreat of their fam-

Billy Dixon during his period as an army scout.
Courtesy Roberts County Museum, Miami.

ilies. But during these actions tipis, camp equipment, food, and sometimes horses had to be abandoned, and early in the fall small bands began to return to their reservations.

Late in September Col. Ranald Mackenzie, commander of the crack Fourth Cavalry, located Palo Duro Canyon, the great Indian sanctuary of the Staked Plains. On the floor of the half-mile deep canyon, Mackenzie and his men destroyed villages, food stores, and camp equipment, while capturing more than 1,400 horses. Two weeks later Col. George Buell, on successive days in October, located and burned deserted camps of 75 and 475 lodges.

Meanwhile, Colonel Miles finally resupplied his column. Lieutenant Baldwin's scouts reported that several bands were camping in the northwestern reaches of the Staked Plains. Miles recorded that "by establishing small supply camps on the Canadian, the Washita, and the tributaries of the Red River, I was enabled to keep my command in very fair order and use it against the Indians whenever they could be found in that remote country."[1]

In October Dixon rode with troops that were commanded by Colonel Miles. Moving along the Canadian River, this force camped within sight of the Adobe Wall battlefield. As previously mentioned, a war party recently had burned the buildings, which were still smoldering. Colonel Miles asked Dixon "hundreds of questions about the fight appearing curious about every detail."[2]

The troopers avidly searched everywhere for mementos of the battle. "The soldiers picked up everything they could find in their hunt for souvenirs, even bones, which I am sure were mostly horse bones," said Billy. "The Indians had gathered up all the bones of their dead and wrapped them in new blankets, depositing them at the foot of the hills on the east side of the valley of Adobe Walls Creek. The soldiers threw away the bones and carried off the blankets."[3]

When Adobe Walls was attacked in June, all of the dogs at the trading post raced to safety. The dogs which disappeared included Billy Dixon's setter bitch named Fannie. To Billy's astonishment, in October Fannie wandered into the military camp. Soon she left, but promptly came back with "a fat, bright-eyed little puppy in her mouth. Dropping the little fellow gently on a pile of bedding, she frisked about with delight as each of us tried to get hold of the pup and fondle it." Fannie made three more trips, and soon all four puppies "were playing with each other on our bedding." Dixon declared that the father of the pups was the big Newfoundland that died defending the Scheidler brothers. When the column pulled out, "Fannie and her babies were given a snug place in the mess wagon."[4]

The column — including Fannie and her pups — resumed the campaign trail. "Our operations lasted during the autumn, and even into the winter," reported Colonel Miles. "They resulted in nine different engagements and affairs with the Indians by different detachments and under different officers . . ." One of these engagements included Billy Dixon and attracted considerable attention.

"Lieutenant Baldwin with his detachment, and Troop D of

the Sixth Cavalry, and Company D of Fifth Infantry, attacked a camp of the [Cheyenne] chief, Gray Beard . . . on the north branch of McClellan Creek on November 8, and in a spirited engagement drove the Indians out of their camp to the Staked Plains again."[5]

The Battle of Adobe Walls had triggered retaliatory raids by smaller war parties, and these attacks were not limited to the Texas Panhandle. Two weeks after the charge on Adobe Walls and about one hundred miles to the north, a Cheyenne named Medicine Water led a murder raid on the family of John and Lydia German. John was moving west toward Colorado when he began to receive warnings about Indian unrest. Traveling up the Smoky Hill River stagecoach trail, the Germans camped on September 10, just one day's journey from Fort Wallace in western Kansas. There were two ox-drawn covered wagons, a few head of cattle, and a chicken coop. But on the next morning, shortly after beginning the day's journey, John and Lydia and their seven children were attacked by war-whooping braves emerging from the river bed.

John was shot down immediately, and Lydia was tomahawked to death. Also killed and scalped were older daughters Joanne and Rebecca Jane, and Stephen, the only son. Left alive were Catherine (age seventeen), Sophia (twelve), Julia (seven), and Addie (five). "For awhile there was a wild exhibit of dancing, screeching Cheyennes, as they searched the wagons to see what they could find," reported Olive Dixon, who interviewed two of the sisters in later years. "After taking everything they considered of value the Indians set fire to the wagons." The livestock were killed, and after a meal of beef the entire party headed south. Several days of hard riding led the band to a large Cheyenne village in Indian Territory.[6]

The four captive girls were taken before the chiefs, Stone Calf and Gray Beard. "The two older sisters were real prizes from the Indian way of thinking, " related Olive Dixon. Indeed, seventeen-year-old Catherine related that she was gang-raped by young braves. When Stone Calf eventually marched in a southerly route toward the Staked Plains, he took Catherine and Sophia with his band. Gray Beard moved north and west in a nomadic ramble, bringing little Julia and Addie with him. The children later said that they had not been mistreated by the Cheyenne men. "The squaws, however," said Billy Dixon, "had forced them to work beyond their strength."[7]

Grey Beard encamped on the north bank of McClellan Creek, about ten miles south of the modern town of Pampa. The village was found by scouts of Lt. Frank Baldwin, who commanded a column consisting of his scouting detachment, a troop of cavalry, a troop of infantry, and twenty-three empty supply wagons he was escorting. The size of the village — at least one hundred lodges — indicated that the soldiers would be seriously outnumbered, and Baldwin's command was hardly a textbook attack force. But Baldwin put infantrymen in the wagons and placed the supply train in the center of a line, flanked by cavalry and the mounted scouts. He also had a mountain howitzer in the center. Baldwin rode ahead a short distance to the top of a divide, and spotted the village less than a mile away.

"The troops having reached the crest of the divide," described Baldwin, "the trumpeters sounded the charge, and as the clear, shrill note of that thrilling call echoed through the valley . . . , every trooper, wagon train and all, rushed down the slope, into and through the Indian camp like a hurricane. The charge was spectacular, grand, and most effective in results." The Cheyennes immediately abandoned the village and their possessions, retreating westward and soon reaching the *Llano Estacado*. Baldwin pressed the attack, but three hundred warriors formed a defensive position, enabling the women and children to flee. Baldwin re-formed his line and attacked again, but the warriors fell back until they could establish a new defensive position. This hit-and-run battle went on for twelve miles and four hours, before the Cheyennes scattered and disappeared. "The pursuit was then discontinued," said Baldwin, "owing principally to the utter exhaustion of both men and animals."[8]

Baldwin's wild, reckless charge drove Gray Beard and his large band onto the Staked Plains with the complete loss of lodges, camp equipment, provisions, and a great many ponies. Baldwin was awarded his second Medal of Honor for his bold leadership on November 8, and he became the only man to win the Medal during the Civil War and again during the Indian Wars. (After World War I regulations specified that no soldier could be presented more than one Medal of Honor. Three soldiers won two Medals during Indian War service, while Lt. Tom Custer was the only man to earn two Medals during the Civil War. A lifelong bachelor, Tom casually allowed various sweethearts to wear his Medals.)[9]

The most notable event of the battle was the recovery of Julia and Addie German. As Billy and his scouting comrades rode through the hastily abandoned village, "somebody noticed that a pile of buffalo hides seemed to be moving up and down. Pulling the hides aside, we were astonished at finding two little white girls, who proved to be Julie and Adelaide." The Cheyennes fled so rapidly that the white children were left behind. "They were pitiable objects," continued Billy. "Hunger and privation had reduced them to mere skeletons, and their little hands and fingers . . . resembled bird's claws. The children were trembling with fright, but upon seeing that we were white men their terror changed to a frenzy of joy, and their sobs and tears made hardened frontiersmen turn away to hide their own emotion."[10]

An infantryman with a paternal instinct took charge of the children "and gave them a thorough washing." Colonel Miles sent the girls back to Fort Leavenworth in the care of an army surgeon. At Fort Leavenworth a photograph was taken of Julia and Addie. Determined to rescue the older girls, in January 1875

Colonel Miles sent friendly Indians to find the camp of Chief Stone Calf with a message to bring his band to the reservation, but if the German sisters were killed no surrender would be accepted. The chief had a special tipi for the sisters placed next to his large lodge, so that they would not be harmed. A copy of the photos of Julia and Addie with a note on the back was sneaked to Catherine: "To Misses Germaine: Your little sisters are well, and in the control of friends. Do not be discouraged. Every effort is being made for your welfare." From his village near the New Mexico border, Chief Stone Calf led his people through a bitter Panhandle winter during January and February. After struggling for two hundred miles, Chief Stone Calf surrendered to the army on March 1, 1875, at a point about seventy-five miles west of the Darlington Agency. Catherine German later wrote: "Just before the sun set, we came to the soldiers' camp. They stood at the side of the trail cheering. We stopped, but I could hardly say anything, and when I think of it now a lump rises in my throat."[11]

Colonel Miles arranged to be appointed guardian of the four German sisters. "I secured a provision in an appropriation of Congress diverting ten thousand dollars from the offending Indians to be given to them." The annual interest was applied to their support. A family in Kansas took them into their home, and each girl received $2,500 when they reached their majority. They all married, settling in Kansas, Colorado, and California.[12] And decades later two of the sisters returned to the Texas Panhandle, where they received a warm welcome and met Olive Dixon.

Late in 1874 and early in 1875 more and more bands yielded to ice and snow and subzero temperatures and straggled back to the agencies at Fort Sill and at the Darlington Agency. Of course, the army columns were struggling through the same conditions. "Horses died by the score at the picket lines," related Indian Wars historian Robert Utley. "Frostbite produced

long casualty lists. Col-
umns moved slowly and
painfully, when they could
move at all. Men lived in
constant discomfort."[13]

Lt. Col. John W. David-
son called off his winter
operations in November,
arriving back at Fort Sill on
November 29. Col. George
P. Buell led his column into
Fort Griffin a few days later. Col. Ranald MacKenzie
went back to Fort Con-
cho late in December. Col.
Nelson Miles persisted in
the field the longest, but
in January 1875 he sent

Col. Ranald Mackenzie was a key military leader of the Red River War. *Courtesy National Archives.*

the Eighth Cavalry companies to their base in New Mexico.
Miles and the balance of his command headed east — singing
"Marching Through Georgia" with perverse humor — to a cantonment that had been established on Sweetwater Creek. There
Miles stationed four companies of his Fifth Infantry and four
companies of the Sixth Cavalry, an initial garrison of 422 men
commanded by Maj. James Biddle. Lt. General Phil Sheridan
had ordered the placement of this cantonment in the eastern
Panhandle so that troops could be positioned to cut off or pursue any breakouts from the two reservations to the east. Regular patrols could be sent on surveillance duty along the nearby
border of Indian Territory.

Billy Dixon remained at the cantonment as a scout. Lt.
Frank Baldwin, who returned to regimental headquarters at
Fort Leavenworth, wrote to Billy in September 1875 with the
address: "Mr. William Dixon, Cantonment, Texas."[14] Soon the

cantonment became a permanent post, Fort Elliott, and Scout Dixon would be based at this outpost for eight years.

Cheyenne, Kiowa, Arapaho, and Comanche bands relegated themselves in large numbers to reservation life. On June 2, 1875, Chief Quanah led more than four hundred Comanches into Fort Sill. With satisfaction Nelson Miles evaluated the results of the recent convergence campaign as "the complete subjugation of four powerful tribes of hostile Indians. The tribes that had gone out in the summer splendidly equipped with all the grand paraphernalia for an Indian campaign, with beautiful lodges and thousands of ponies, came back in the winter, many of them on foot in abject poverty, leaving most of their horses dead upon the plains as well as many of their people."[15]

Of course, no one knew when a raiding party of young braves might break out of their reservation and head for the Staked Plains. As directed, Major Biddle selected a permanent site for the outpost on a plain that overlooked Sweetwater Creek to the west. The Sweetwater was a spring-fed stream

Scout Billy Dixon was provided with this trapdoor Springfield U.S. Model 1873 "Officer's Rifle." Also visible in this exhibit is Dixon's Medal of Honor, and, at right, his congratulatory letter from Col. Nelson A. Miles. *Courtesy Panhandle-Plains Museum, Canyon, Texas.*

Scout Billy Dixon's telescope. As a buffalo hunter he used a pair of field glasses. Billy is seated at left in the photograph, which will be more closely examined in Chapter Thirteen. *Courtesy Hutchinson County Museum, Borger.*

that flowed north to south past the post, thus assuring a water supply. Indeed, a dugout ice house was built on the fort's west side, closer to the creek. When the stream froze in winter, ice was cut and stored in the dugout beneath hay-covered tarpaulins, ready for use in summer drinks.[16]

Within a few months, in June 1875, Major Biddle and his men were replaced by Maj. H.C. Bankhead and 263 men from units of the Fourth Cavalry and the Nineteenth Infantry. The following month picket stables and storehouses began to be erected with adobe and cottonwood posts, and the corral attached to the stables featured tall adobe walls. A large parade ground was laid out, measuring 650 feet by 450 feet. Lumber and other building materials were freighted in nearly 200 miles from Dodge City. Six sets of officer's quarters and the commanding officer's residence were erected across the north side of the parade ground, facing south. Across the parade were five company barracks. There was a twelve-bed hospital, a bakery, a guard house, a headquarters building and an adjutant's office, a combined chapel and school, laundresses' quarters, and a sutler's store.

The buildings were all single-story frame structures. The colors flew from a fifty-foot flagpole on the parade ground.[17]

In 1876 the now-substantial Cantonment on the Sweetwater was designated Fort Elliott, named after Maj. Joel Elliott who died, along with seventeen of his Seventh Cavalry troopers, at the Battle of the Washita in 1868.

Fort Elliott became the home of Billy Dixon. He was twenty-four when he first encamped at the cantonment, and he was thirty-two when he finally departed Fort Elliott. That eight-year period was the longest Billy had stayed in any one place since he struck out on his own at the age of thirteen. Fort Elliott usually was garrisoned by less than 200 soldiers, so there was plenty of space to quarter a few scouts. Three times a day meals were served at the company mess halls. Like the rest of the garrison, he was paid every other month with the arrival of the paymaster. As with his other government jobs, he was provided with guns and ammunition. Dixon received a Springfield Model 1873 Officer's Rifle which suited him so well that he kept it when he left Fort Elliott. (Olive later donated the weapon to the Panhandle-Plains Museum, where it is on display.)

Another part of Dixon's life at Fort Elliott was the wolf howl of a community that grew up a mile south of the post. Although

Fort Elliott was erected east of Sweetwater Creek, the last frontier outpost established in Texas. Designed to accommodate five companies, Fort Elliott was built around a parade ground that measured 650 feet by 450 feet. *Courtesy National Archives.*

An infantry company, with about sixty men present, is arrayed in dress uniforms - complete with white gloves and plumed dress helmets — on the Fort Elliott parade ground. The company captain is at front center, while the other two officers, the first lieutenant and second lieutenant, stand with drawn sabers in front of their respective platoons. *Courtesy Weldon Walser of Canadian.*

most of the construction work at Fort Elliott was carried out by soldiers, some civilian craftsman were employed. So were teamsters, and the fort offered a steady market for nearby farmers and ranchers. Off-duty troopers wanted such recreational options as drinking and gambling and women. A trading post near the fort opened by Dodge City merchants Robert Wright and Charles Rath utilized green buffalo hides to cover the crude structure and led to the name Hide Town. Hide Town soon was changed to Sweetwater, after the nearby creek. But in 1879, when Wheeler County was organized with Sweetwater as county seat, a request for the required post office was denied because there already was a Sweetwater, Texas. A local resident suggested asking a scout at Fort Elliott for a Native American translation of "Sweetwater." Soon Billy Dixon and two Indians came down from the fort. With Dixon serving as interpreter, the Indians were asked their word for "sweet water," and the reply, "mobeetie," was written on the post office application. The post office was approved on September 4, 1879, and the oldest permanent community in the Panhandle received its historic name.[18]

In the Census of 1880 Mobeetie was credited with 150 residents. Of a total of 1,379 citizens in the Panhandle in 1880, 512 — almost forty per cent — resided in Wheeler County. The soldiers at Fort Elliott were listed, and so was "William Dixon," whose occupation was listed as "post guide."[19]

Mobeetie had saloons and a dance hall and soiled doves and a rough reputation. The most notable gunfight in Mobeetie involved Billy Dixon's friend, Bat Masterson. Masterson left Lt. Frank Baldwin's scouting company on October 12, 1874. More than a year later, with hostile Indians now confined to reservations, Bat returned to the Texas Panhandle as a buffalo hunter. With other hunters he gravitated to the Rath and Wright trading post, and to the rowdy night life of Mobeetie.[20] Bat Masterson and Billy Dixon must have had a rambunctious reunion in

The authorized strength of a cavalry company was 100 men, larger than an infantry troop, but all frontier units were chronically understrength. A mounted platoon seems about to leave on patrol from Fort Elliott. These thirty-seven men brandish drawn carbines, and they wear miscellaneous headgear, from campaign hats to kepis. The officer in command is front and center. The fourth man from the right appears to be an Indian scout. Is scout Billy Dixon among this command? Features simply could not be made out under my strongest magnifying glass. *Courtesy Weldon Walser of Canadian.*

A company barracks at Fort Elliott, with separate rooms for each platoon and a mess hall in the rear. *Courtesy Weldon Walser of Canadian.*

Sweetwater. But there is no mention of Billy's presence on the evening of January 24, 1876.

Bat was in a saloon in the company of Mollie Brennan when confronted by an off-duty soldier, Cpl. Ed King of the Fourth Cavalry. Apparently there was a conflict over Mollie. Corporal King drew his service revolver and fired a round which passed through Mollie's abdomen. That round, or perhaps a second bullet, struck Bat, lodging in his pelvis. But Bat palmed his revolver and gunned down King. Both Mollie and King died, while Bat was taken to the post for treatment by the military surgeon.[21]

During Billy Dixon's years at Fort Elliott, Mobeetie grew to a population of nearly 300, with a hotel and boarding houses, a drugstore, a Chinese laundry, a blacksmith shop, livery stable, wagon yards, and, of course, saloons and dives. In 1882, the year before Dixon left town, a newspaper began publication, the *Texas Panhandle*. Mobeetie was a raw but bustling frontier community, and it was just as congenial to the tastes of Billy Dixon as Dodge City and Hays City and Adobe Walls and other pioneer towns had been to him. He liked the company of buffalo hunters and frontier settlers. He enjoyed spending time in saloons. He still did not gamble or dance, but he liked having a drink and listening to the loud talk of other saloon denizens. And instead of merely overhearing and enjoying the tales of other men of the West, Billy Dixon now was a frontier celebrity — a sharpshooting hero of Adobe Walls and of the Buffalo Wallow. The Medal of Honor he was presented earned Dixon considerable respect and admiration in the military community of Fort Elliott, where he lived and served.

There was a spirited social life at the fort. Officers were permitted to bring their families to their stations, and wives arranged dinner parties, dances, and entertainments. As a civilian — a civilian hero of Indian battles, a civilian entitled to wear the Medal of Honor — Dixon may have been invited to some of these events. Surely he was welcomed by bachelor officers, sometimes at their mess and any time at a saloon gathering in Mobeetie. At some point Billy began to upgrade his wardrobe. He acquired a Prince Albert coat, a vest, a dress shirt, nice pants, and with his long hair and sweeping moustache he cut a striking figure. He could, if he chose, pin his Medal of Honor to his coat, as officers did to their dress uniforms.

Billy Dixon's fame extended beyond the Texas Panhandle, as he learned in 1875. A letter was forwarded to Dixon from the

A barracks interior, with cots, foot lockers, and a heating stove. *Courtesy Weldon Walser of Canadian.*

U.S. Consul of Manchester, England, who had contacted Colonel Miles on behalf of an English widow named Dixon. Mrs. Dixon had read an account of the Buffalo Wallow Fight initially printed in a Chicago newspaper and reprinted in England. Her son, William Dixon, who was about thirty-years of age and a blacksmith by trade, had emigrated to the United States about twelve years earlier. Mrs. Dixon was hopeful that the heroic scout of the Indian fight was her son, and Billy was requested to furnish "the information whether he is the person whose identification is desired."[22] The exploits of Scout Dixon were being written about in newspapers across the United States and in England.

In 1879 the post headquarters building burned. It was the only fire of consequence in the fifteen-year history of the fort, and the frame structure soon was rebuilt.

Also in 1879 a troop of the Tenth Cavalry Regiment was stationed at Fort Elliott. There were ten cavalry regiments during the Indian Wars, and the Ninth and Tenth were comprised of "Buffalo Soldiers." Of the twenty-five infantry regiments, the Twenty-Fourth and Twenty-Fifth were Buffalo Soldier units. During the 1880s companies of the Ninth Cavalry and the Twenty-Fourth Infantry served at Fort Elliott, and from November 1881 until February 1884 all of the soldiers at the post were black.

The officers of these regiments were white, except for Lt. Henry O. Flipper, who was the first black graduate of West Point. Born into slavery in Georgia, Flipper attended Atlanta University after the Civil War, and in 1877 became the first African American to graduate from the U.S. Military Academy. Flipper endured racial harassment at West Point and after receiving his commission. Assigned to the Tenth Cavalry, Lieutenant Flipper served in Texas at Forts Concho, Elliot, Quitman, and Davis. At Fort Elliott Lieutenant Flipper and Billy Dixon were acquainted with each other. And when Dixon left the post early in 1883,

Among the officers with whom Dixon was acquainted during his long stay at Fort Elliott was Lt. Henry O. Flipper. In 1877 Flipper became the first African American to graduate from West Point. Assigned to the 10th Cavalry Regiment of Buffalo Soldiers, Flipper served in Texas at Forts Elliott, Concho, Quitman, and Davis. *Courtesy National Archives.*

the entire complement of enlisted men were Buffalo Soldiers.

The principal field activity of the garrison was to patrol the border area of the Texas Panhandle and Indian Territory, and to pursue bands that slipped away from their reservations into their old Panhandle hunting grounds. But buffaloes virtually disappeared within a few years — 1878 was the last year for commercial hunters in Texas. With buffalo herds gone from the range, along with horseback warriors whose old way of life no longer was possible, cattlemen promptly filled the gap.

Within a year of Col. Ranald Mackenzie's assault on Palo Duro Canyon, Charles Goodnight drove 1,600 head of cattle into the sheltered, well-watered Palo Duro. And within a few more years Goodnight's riders were herding 100,000 cattle on 1.3 million acres of Panhandle range. During this same period other ranchers were establishing large Panhandle spreads. The army primarily tried to keep Panhandle livestock away from the reservations and to supervise the routes of trail herds across agency lands. With few military duties to perform, Fort Elliott was closed in 1890.

By that time Billy Dixon had established a new home. With

After Fort Elliott was abandoned in 1890, the post buildings were sold or were hauled away as part of the frontier custom of "midnight requisitioning." These young people were photographed at the adobe corrals. *Courtesy Weldon Walser of Canadian.*

scant likelihood of hostilities around Fort Elliott, scouts no lon-ger were needed, and Billy Dixon's position was terminated on February 10, 1883. "I was the last scout to be relieved of duty at that post," he pointed out with a touch of pride.[24] After more than eight years as an army scout at Fort Elliott, Billy needed a new occupation and a new home. He knew just where he want-ed to go.

Chapter Eleven
Back to Adobe Walls

It was the land of my boyhood dreams . . .

Billy Dixon

When Billy Dixon left Fort Elliott he went in search of another home. He was in his thirties now, and after being settled for years on the army post, he did not want to resume the nomadic wanderings that had seemed so adventurous during his teens and early twenties. Dixon gravitated to the scenic location where he had found fame. He rode north to the Canadian, then west along the river to Adobe Walls. "Everything was to my liking — pure air, good water, fruitful soil, game, and room enough for a man to turn round without stepping on some fellow's toes."[1]

But cattlemen, with the absence of buffalo herds and hostile war parties, already had begun ranching in the area Billy coveted. Late in 1876 Thomas S. Bugbee brought his family, several trail hands, and 1,800 head of cattle from Kansas into the Panhandle. A dugout was built for the family in what became Hutchinson County, and the ranch became known after its brand, the Quarter Circle T. By 1878 there was a complex of headquarters buildings, some erected by Portuguese stonemasons. Bugbee's cattle numbered 12,500 in 1882, when he sold out to the Hansford Land and Cattle Company for $350,000.[2]

The second ranch in Hutchinson County was founded in 1878 east of the Quarter Circle T and on the site of Adobe Walls. The Scissors Ranch was organized by William E. Anderson and was a small operation which, like the nearby Quarter Circle T, was purchased by the Hansford Land and Cattle Company.[3]

Nearby and just north of the Scissors Ranch was the Turkey Track Ranch, which originated in 1878 when Richard McNalty drove a herd of cattle into the Panhandle from Colorado. In 1882 McNalty sold his herd and Turkey Track brand to Charles Word and Jack Snider, who sold the ranch in January 1883 — to the Hansford Land and Cattle Company. The company's cattle now would be branded with the Turkey Track, and the range covered the northern half of Hutchinson County and the southern half of Hansford County.[4]

The Hansford Land and Cattle Company was a Scottish syndicate organized by Kansas City banker James M. Coburn.

Cape Willingham was friends with Billy Dixon in Mobeetie. Cape and Billy later were neighbors, when Dixon created a home at Adobe Walls and Willingham served as longtime manager of the adjacent Turkey Track Ranch. *Author's collection.*

Coburn was an immigrant from Scotland who saw opportunity in the Texas Panhandle during the "Beef Bonanza" ranching boom in the West. To operate the expanded Turkey Track Ranch in a lawless Panhandle, Coburn offered a handsome salary to a thirty-year-old frontiersman, Cape Willingham.[5]

Willingham had become friends with Billy Dixon in Mobeetie. Cape had ridden for legendary cattleman Charles Goodnight at his Colorado and Palo Duro Canyon ranches. For the best part of a year, Willingham and Marion Armstrong operated the "Star Route," also known as the "Lightning Express," a stagecoach and mail line from Fort Elliott to Las Vegas, New Mexico. In 1880, when Oldham County was organized, Cape was elected sheriff, and he killed troublemaker Fred Leigh in Tascosa's first shootout. By then Cape and his wife Mary had five children, and in 1882 he moved back to Mobeetie, where he ran the Cattle Exchange Saloon. Billy Dixon surely patronized his friend's establishment.[6] In 1883 both Dixon and Willingham found themselves together on the Turkey Track Ranch.

One of the reasons James M. Coburn hired Cape Willingham was because several Turkey Track cowboys were appropriating their own cattle from the big ranch they tended. Coburn vigorously opposed this theft, common on the open range, and Cape Willingham was a gunman who could straighten out the crew. And when Billy Dixon showed up, recently detached from Fort Elliott, he was a calming addition to the contentious crew of the Tracks. Dixon was employed by the ranch, but soon he was encouraged to acquire title to land at the Adobe Walls site.

In 1883, therefore, "I filed on two sections of land on Bent Creek, taking in the site of the original Adobe Walls ruins. I built my house right at the west edge of the old sod building which by that time stock had rubbed to the ground. In the front yard, . . . when the south wind swept the dirt clear, could still be seen the foundations of the old ruins."[7]

Billy's log home was built beside Bent Creek, and it stood just two miles south of Turkey Track headquarters. His 1,280 acres were adjacent to the south range of the rapidly expanding Turkey Track Ranch. Within a few years the Hansford Land and Cattle Company owned 85,000 acres of land and leased another 350,000 acres, with as many as 30,000 head of cattle bearing the Turkey Track brand. For twenty years James M. Coburn and Cape Willingham operated the big ranch, and during their long tenure Billy Dixon was their most prominent and contented neighbor.

Dixon's little spread was the first property ownership ex-

Billy began his new home at Adobe Walls with a one-room log cabin (shown here in disrepair in later years). Several additions produced a spacious residence, for the time and place. *Courtesy Panhandle-Plains Historical Museum, Canyon, Texas.*

perience of his life, and he responded with a determination to develop and improve the place he regarded as a garden spot of the Panhandle. He built a cottonwood log cabin that measured fourteen feet square with the door facing east. About one hundred yards north of the cabin he fashioned a low check dam to divert "the course of Bent Creek until its clear, swift waters flowed almost at my doorstep, and I was able to undertake extensive irrigation." With the eager help of a nursery salesman, "I planted 200 carefully selected trees, consisting of apples, peaches, pears, plums, apricots and cherries, together with a small vineyard." West of the orchard he planted thirty acres in alfalfa, which yielded three or four cuttings a year. He thus had plenty of hay for his own livestock, while selling the rest to the Turkey Track. The orchard and the alfalfa field were the first in the area. "In my yard I set out a number of cottonwoods which grew rapidly and became big, strong [shade] trees."[8]

The check dam created a small lake which teemed with catfish and perch, and each winter ducks and geese used the pond.

Billy set out salt along Bent Creek for the deer that habitually nibbled on green alfalfa. When he needed meat he slipped out among the trees early in the morning and shot a buck. One rifle shot, one deer, and the next day the animals would be back in his alfalfa field. To aid his frequent outings as a hunter he trained hunting dogs, including Fly and Dutch. Billy owned their mother, trained then as pointers "from puppyhood," and when Olive moved to Adobe Walls as a bride she learned that Fly and Dutch were part of the family.

The bird hunting was excellent. "During a greater part of the year wild ducks and geese frequented the Canadian and its tributaries, literally by thousands, and deer and turkey were commonly found along the creeks." A favorite dish of this came after hunting wild turkeys and stewing "a pot full of gizzards, hearts and livers. This was best of all, a dish fit for a king . . ."[9]

"Mine was a happy life in my cabin at Adobe Walls, without fret or worry, and with abundance of everything for my simple needs," reflected Billy. "It was the land of my boyhood dreams, and I was satisfied."[10]

Billy opened a little store at his cabin, stocking small items

Billy planted and irrigated a large orchard of 200 fruit trees. *Through permission from Virginia Irwin Maynard.*

that would appeal to passing cowboys. The two most popular articles that he carried were candy and chewing gum. "No schoolgirl could be as foolish as a cowboy about candy and chewing gum," he remarked. "The boys seemed to crave such things, and bought more candy and chewing gum than they did tobacco."[11]

There was plenty of space in his cabin for a small supply of hard candy and chewing gum and tobacco, but the fourteen-foot-square room became crowded when it was designated a post office. In 1887 the Turkey Track headquarters was visited by L.B. Miller, District Attorney of the vast 35th Judicial District. (Centered in Mobeetie, this district for a few years encompassed fifteen unorganized Panhandle counties.) Miller was appalled to learn how inaccessible the U.S. Mail was to the big ranch, and he offered to make arrangements for an "Adobe Walls Post Office" if Dixon would serve as postmaster. There would be three deliveries a week by mail wagon from Miami, and Billy readily agreed. "I received my commission," he reported, and "Billy Dickinson" was listed as postmaster on August 3, 1887. Soon the Adobe Walls Post Office was moved a couple of miles south, from the ranch to the Dixon cabin. "William M. Dixon" was reappointed on April 23, 1888. Billy served fourteen years, until September 10, 1901.[12]

With the little log cabin now serving as a combination store and post office, Billy added a lean-to onto the west side to use as his bedroom. Later he agreed to serve as a justice of the peace for Hutchinson, Gray, and Roberts counties, as well as a state land commissioner for the area. The enterprising Dixon thus busied himself as a postmaster, storekeeper, justice of the peace, and land commissioner.

His prominence as an area hero made him a natural for appointments, but none of these tasks required much of his time. Cowboys dropped by the Dixon cabin occasionally to pick up mail and purchase sundries. A few scattered settlers also made mail stops now and then. Once in awhile he had to process land title paperwork, or perform a justice of the peace function in the absence of other officials. Judge Dixon despised stumbling through marriage ceremonies. Otherwise, his miscellaneous duties were not onerous nor very time-consuming. He received small fees for his services, and he visited with men — and a few women and children — who enjoyed his company. And Billy still had plenty of time for hunting with his rifle and dogs and favorite saddle horse.

He continued to add to his Adobe Walls home. Two small frame structures fell out of use at the Turkey Track. Billy purchased the frame buildings and skidded them to his home site. Soon he located a log cabin that had been abandoned by a failed settler. Billy took the cabin apart and hauled the logs to Adobe Walls. He reassembled the logs into a room about sixteen by eighteen feet, locating it six or eight feet behind his lean-to bedroom. Dixon topped the room with a "heavy sod roof," and used it for a kitchen and living area. The Dixon home may have been cobbled together, but there was the original log cabin, the lean-to bedroom, the log kitchen, and two frame rooms. Billy had put together one of the most spacious homes in the entire pioneer Panhandle.[13]

Billy Dixon turned forty in 1890. By 1893 a decade had passed since he left Fort Elliott and began creating a home at Adobe Walls. "Everything was to my liking — " he insisted. "Mine was a happy life in my cabin at Adobe Walls . . ." Billy was almost overwhelmed by his new circumstances; "It was the land of my boyhood dreams, and I was satisfied." But he was no longer a boy, and he was not satisfied. Despite his seemingly idyllic existence, Billy increasingly sensed that something was missing. By the time he was in his forties, Billy Dixon wanted and needed a wife and children. And even though he lived in a land of few men and fewer women, just the right young woman for Billy Dixon soon would journey to the lonely Texas Panhandle.

Chapter Twelve

The Hero of Adobe Walls
Meets a New Schoolmarm

*The first time I saw you, Little Girl, I thought to myself
that an angel would likely look the way you do.*

Billy Dixon to Olive King

Olive King was twenty-years-old in 1893 when she set out on the adventure of her life. Born into a noted Virginia family, Olive lost her father when she was seven. She spent the next nine years in Decatur, Alabama, growing up in the home of a prosperous older cousin. When Olive moved back to Virginia she lived with a married sister for a time. Returning to her mother's home, she became restless in a household comprised of sisters and a little brother and a venerable grandmother.

Therefore she welcomed a letter which arrived from the Panhandle of Texas in November 1892. During the 1880s two older brothers, Archie and Albert, adventurously left Virginia and made their way to the Texas frontier to become cowboys. Olive had not seen her cowboy brothers since she was a little girl, but now she had an invitation from Archie to visit the Wild West. Archie had married, and he and his wife Sena now had a baby boy. There were few women in the Panhandle, and Archie knew that Olive would provide welcome company for his wife. When Olive expressed interest, Archie sent money for train fare.[1]

Archie's invitation appealed to Olive's own sense of adventure. The opportunity to see the West of cowboys and big ranches and vast open spaces came at just the right time in Olive's life. No suitor in Virginia offered marital appeal. Olive had completed high school in Decatur, but her widowed mother had no money for college, and career opportunities were scarce for women during the 1890s. Plans began to be made to visit the Texas Panhandle ranch country.

The long journey offered Olive an opportunity to pay a visit to Decatur. Her cousin, Dora King Wade, had welcomed her into her home in 1880. Dora and Miles Wade, a successful building contractor, were the parents of two sons. For nearly a decade Dora lavished upon Olive all of the love and motherly attention she would have bestowed upon a daughter. Clothes, schooling, a social life, a loving family home, all were generously dispensed to Olive by Dora and Miles and their sons, Henry and Alva, who were a few years older than their cousin. Sadly, Henry died of typhoid fever in the summer of 1888. But by 1893 Alva and his bride were living in the family home with their baby.

In Decatur early in 1893 Olive enjoyed an affectionate reunion with the Wades, visited old friends, sewed and gardened with Dora. Before Olive departed Decatur for Virginia in 1889, Dora and Miles had offered to send her to college, at least to a normal school for teachers. Now Dora renewed the offer for Olivia to resume her education. But Olive had not wanted to be further "beholden" to Dora and Miles when she was sixteen, and she felt the same way as a twenty-year-old. Besides, she was excited at the prospect of seeing the West.

Olive studied train schedules and wrote Archie when to expect her to arrive in Canadian, the nearest town to his home. Early in April she offered her farewells and boarded a train for Texas. The westbound train steamed 215 miles to Memphis. Crossing the Mississippi River, Olive continued to ride westward 140 miles to Little Rock, capital of Arkansas. The train angled southwestward 145 miles to Texarkana, then west 175 miles across northeast Texas to Dallas, a growing city of nearly 40,000. Thirty-five more miles and the train reached Fort Worth, formerly a frontier town but now boasting a population approaching 25,000.[2]

The Fort Worth and Denver City Railway led northwest, past ramshackle villages that were born when railroad tracks were laid. The landscape became flat, with almost endless vistas in every direction. The open country seemed nearly empty. At Washburn, a whistle stop community twenty miles east of Amarillo, a spur line led north to the little town of Panhandle. From there the Southern Kansas and Panhandle Railroad headed northeast to Canadian and on to Kansas.

And so, from Decatur, Alabama, through a network of changing lines, Olive King finally reached the objective of an 1,100-mile rail journey. Canadian, named for the river that flowed just north of town, boasted saloons and false-front commercial buildings along the little main street. A hotel hack driver picked up Olive and her baggage, and during the short trip to the hotel he learned that she was looking for her brother, Archie King of the Bar CC Ranch. Escorting Olive into the hotel lobby, the driver explained her situation to the clerk.

The hotel clerk had seen Archie earlier in the day, and the cowboy soon was summoned to the hotel. The brother and sister had not seen each other in more than a decade, when Olive was nine and Archie was not far past boyhood. But they instantly recognized each other, and Archie was proud to introduce his sister to every man they encountered. Soon he had his team of bays hitched to his buckboard, and they headed west out of Canadian.

Archie told Olive that his sod house was fifty miles from Canadian and the railroad. The King home stood beside John's Creek just north of the Canadian River. Archie explained that he had brought his wife and baby as far as the home of Dave Lard and his family. Indeed, the wives of Archie and Dave were sisters. The Lard place was about twenty miles from Canadian, but if Archie and Olive arrived in time to spend the night, the King soddy could be reached by the next evening. At the

Lard home Olive met Dave, Sena, her sister, and toddler Woods King, named after her father. The three young women soon were engaged in a lively conversation about the latest fashions from back East.

The next day Archie drove the wagon alongside the Canadian River toward the King home on John's Creek. During the ride Olive began to realize that she was falling in love with the wide-open countryside. She "could see so far that her imagination had difficulty in matching the horizons that filled her sight."[3] That night Olive stood outside the sod house with Archie and Sena, gazing at the countless stars in the clear skies. The memory remained vivid six decades later, when Olive was in her eighties. Indeed, she told her biographer, John L. McCarty, that on that brilliant night she "knew that she had found her country."[4]

John's Creek ran north to south near the King soddy. The stream was filled with fish, and Olive and Sena — and little Woods — often took fishing poles and bait and angled for supper meat. A more elaborate fishing expedition was launched during the summer, as part of a camping trip with Sena's family. Olive had met Sena's sister in her first night in the Panhandle. But plans were formed for Olive to visit more of the Walstads, who were among the first settlers of Ochiltree County.

Archie took time to deliver his wife and son and Olive to the Walsteads. But on the first day of the trip north Archie stopped beside Home Ranch Creek at the headquarters of the vast Bar CC Ranch, which everyone called the "Barcees." Grazing cattle across more than one million acres in Ochiltree and adjoining Roberts and Hemphill counties, the Bar CC had been Archie's employer since the 1880s. Archie introduced Olive to ranch manager W.J. Todd and to his lovely wife, Laura.

The founder and longtime superintendent of the Bar CC, Henry W. Cresswell, had encouraged his ranch hands to start their own herds. Archie King and Dave Lard were among those who took advantage of Cresswell's benevolent policy, building their own little spreads while earning cowboy wages — twenty-five dollars a month — on the Bar CC. Although Cresswell was popular with his cowboys and neighboring ranchers, by 1889 he sold out to a syndicate and moved on to found another operation.[5]

When the Todds arrived at the Bar CC, Laura had to live in a tent with her baby while a frame ranch house was erected. But Laura had furniture freighted in, and she placed potted flowers around her yard. She staged a Christmas celebration featuring wild turkey and a layer cake with candles, along with a holiday dance. Archie King and Dave Lard were two of a half dozen veteran Barr CC employees who aided Laura with the Christmas preparations.

Laura Todd was a native of Virginia, so she was especially delighted to meet Olive. The travelers visited overnight, then proceeded on to the Walstad home. Archie headed back to work, while the Walstads prepared for a camping trip. Bedding and camp equipment were loaded into a wagon, along with fishing gear and the camping crew: Olive, Sena, and little Woods King; Mrs. Walstad, her son George, and two younger Walstad daughters. The party camped beside Wolf Creek, even setting out baited lines at night. More than a week passed before camp was broken, and when two weeks had passed Archie drove up in the family buckboard.

While Archie, Sena, and Woods headed back in the buckboard, Olive rode alongside on a fire mount. At the Walstads she was introduced to a man named Dick Kattal, who let Olive use a horse that he had ridden to victory in various races. Kattal had observed that Olive was comfortable around horses, and she was an experienced rider. During the trip from the Walstad home to the King spread Kattal and Olive rode beside the buckboard, and long afterward she described feeling "an exaltation in the beauty of the country and in the pleasure of riding a good horse into the summer wind."[6]

At about this time a Bar CC cowboy, Billy Bell, began showing up at the King soddy, usually late in the day. Billy and Archie were old friends, and they enjoyed swapping tall tales. After supper, the four young adults could sit around the kitchen table and play dominoes or cards. When word spread that there would be a Fourth of July dance, Billy Bell eagerly volunteered to be Olive's escort.

July Fourth was a favorite holiday across the West. The celebration would be held at Parnell in Roberts County. When the county was organized in 1889, Miami won election as seat of government. But Miami was in the southeastern corner of Roberts County, and even though it was located on the railroad line from Washburn to Canadian, the powerful Bar CC wanted the county seat closer to ranch headquarters. The election was disputed, and soon the county seat was moved twenty-five miles northwest to a hamlet first called Oran, then Parnell. A two-story frame court house was erected in Parnell, and in the absence of similar structures anywhere in Hutchinson or Gray counties, the Parnell court house served as the seat of government for those adjacent counties. It also served as the site for the July Fourth dance of 1893.[7]

Olive sewed a new dress for the occasion, but she designed a big skirt so that she could ride sidesaddle alongside Billy Bell. It was twenty-five miles from the King home to Parnell, and Archie, Sena, and little Woods rode in the family buckboard. Late in the day as vehicles and saddle horses arrived in Parnell, an 1893 version of modern tailgate parties took place as everyone ate picnic meals. Ladies donned their party dresses, and small children were put to bed. A few travelers stayed at the Hansford, Parnell's dugout hotel.

The lead musician at country dances always was a fiddler, and Jake Walstad — Sena's brother — came with his fiddle from Kansas to provide dance tunes. Jake brought a guitarist with him, and there almost certainly were a couple of other musicians, probably someone with a guitar, or a banjo player. Billy Bell claimed Olive for the first dance, but later she danced with one partner after another. There were far more males than ladies, and twenty-year-old Olive King was an attractive single woman with blue eyes and brown hair — and a new dress.

At midnight the ladies put together the customary late supper, after which the dancing went on until dawn. Olive had a grand time, and so did everyone else, but as the sun came up the temporary population of Parnell went into decline as weary dancers began to head in every direction for their scattered homes.[8]

Romance did not blossom between Olive and Billy Bell. No feelings developed with any other of the men Olive danced with, or with anyone else she met during the spring and summer. The Panhandle was sparsely settled, but more than twice as many men as women lived in the High Plains of Texas. Olive was only twenty and understood that romantic involvement was likely in this remote land. But how long could she stay in the Panhandle? Archie drew merely twenty-five dollars a month from the Bar CC, and he and Sena were expecting another baby in the fall. Olive no more intended to be beholden to her brother than to Cousin Dora, and she began planning a return to Virginia.

But before the summer ended a settler named J.A. Whittenburg invited Olive to teach at Garden Creek School, a one-room log structure that served the Whittenburg and Newby families. George Whittenburg would be the oldest pupil, and four Newby children would complete the five-student roster. This little school was located south of the Canadian River on a flat between Reynolds and Tallahone creeks in western Roberts County. The monthly salary was modest but enough for Olive to remain in Texas.

The King soddy was only five miles north of the school, but

Olive would have to cross the treacherous Canadian River twice daily on horseback, which would have been dangerous and sometimes impossible during the winter months. The Whittenburg and Newby families had no extra room in their modest homes. But arrangements for room and board were made with another neighborhood family. The Lewises were natives of Portugal. John Lewis had fashioned a three-room picket house with a dirt roof. One room was a kitchen and living area, and there was one bed in each of the other two rooms. Five-year-old John Lewis shared one bed with his Uncle Joe, John's brother, while Mr. and Mrs. Lewis were in the more spacious bedroom. But a corner was found for a cot in the Lewis bedroom, and a curtain was rigged that could be drawn at night to provide Olive a modicum of privacy.

Olive rode fifty miles to the courthouse in Parnell to take the required teacher certification examination.[9] The written exam proved to be no problem for a high school graduate of 1889. According to the census of 1890, fewer than seven percent of Americans between the ages of fourteen and seventeen (high school consisted of grades eight through eleven) were still attending school. Indeed, in 1890 there were no more than 2,500 public high schools in the entire United States. With fewer than one in ten teenagers attending high school annually, Olive King was well qualified to teach five elementary pupils.

The school house had been built of cottonwood logs and was about twelve feet square. There was a sod roof, and an outhouse completed the little campus. Inside there were benches for the scholars, a table and chair for the teacher, a blackboard hung on a wall, and a pot-bellied, wood-burning stove for heating. Each week a barrel of drinking water was hauled to the school; kept outside, the water barrel was covered with an old sack. "We had no thought of microbes or germs," reminisced the former schoolmarm, "all drank from the same 'dipper' that lay on top of the sack until needed."[10]

At the Lewis place on school days a substantial lunch was prepared by Mrs. Lewis for Olive ("I can't remember a single day that it did not contain a half of a quail") while her horse was being bridled and saddled. Part of the way down the two-and-a-half mile trail to school George Whittenburg was waiting for his teacher, and they rode on to school together. George took care of her borrowed horse while Olive swept out the schoolroom and in cold weather, started the stove. As winter arrived Olive led her pupils in chinking the spaces between the logs. At noon the Newby children went to their nearby home for lunch, so Olive began the treat of permitting one child to stay each day and share the meal with the teacher. "I look back on this year as the happiest year of my life."[11]

During the fall term a cowboy named John Cunningham tried to court the schoolmarm, but again there was no romantic spark. Little did Olive realize that by this time Mrs. Lewis was at work behind the scenes as a matchmaker. She had become quite close to the polite, plucky young woman who now shared her home. And Mrs. Lewis already was a friend of the most famous man in the Panhandle.

Olive was to learn that Billy Dixon was a sharpshooting buffalo hunter who became a hero of the 1874 Battle of Adobe Walls, especially because of an epic shot at a far distant warrior. Shortly afterward he became an army scout and promptly fought in another desperate battle. The Buffalo Wallow Fight, like the Battle of Adobe Walls, took place at a nearby location, and his courageous performance against deadly odds earned Dixon a Congressional Medal of Honor. During most of his years as an army scout Dixon was stationed at Fort Elliott near Mobeetie — in the Texas Panhandle. After leaving the army in 1883 Dixon worked for the big Turkey Track Ranch and he acquired his own spread - at Adobe Walls. As small as the population was in Hutchinson and surrounding counties, everyone knew or knew of the renowned Billy Dixon. And Billy certainly had heard of Olive King, who was visiting her cowboy brothers and teaching school only a few miles east of Adobe Walls.

But Billy was notoriously shy around females. "I had always been rather bashful in the presence of women," he admitted. "Merely the sight of a good-looking woman coming in my direction made me feel like leaving the trail."[12]

So unlike Billy Bell and John Cunningham, Billy Dixon did not take the trail to become acquainted with Olive King, nor did he even attend the Fourth of July dance at Parnell. But Mrs. Lewis felt certain that Billy and Olive would be a good match. "Mrs. Lewis was a cultivated woman," said Billy, with his usual admiration of the fairer sex. "Mrs. Lewis had been a good friend of mine for several years," he added, "and I suspect that it was largely through her influence that I got the girl I so greatly admired."[13]

One reason Billy responded to the "influence" generated to nudge him toward Olive related back to a previous disappointment. For years Billy Dixon served as a justice of the peace of Hutchinson County, and since ministers were rarely in the area, couples seeking marriage had to find a justice of the peace or a county judge. "The hardest job I ever tackled was to perform a marriage ceremony," reminisced Judge Dixon. "My usual embarrassment in marrying a couple was once increased beyond measure. I had grown to be very fond of a young lady who lived with Mrs. [Cape] Willingham on the Turkey Track, but had never been able to muster courage to tell her how much I thought of her and to ask her to marry me."[14]

Eligible young ladies did not long remain single in the Panhandle. While Billy Dixon struggled with his bashfulness, "a pesky cowboy" wooed and won the young lady's affections. One day the couple unexpectedly turned up at Billy Dixon's Adobe Walls home/office and asked to be married. Judge Dixon always found wedding ceremonies to be uncomfortable, and he had silently watched others win girls he admired from afar, but to the tasked with marrying another man to a young lady he had become smitten with was exquisitely painful.[15] Perhaps it was this torturous experience that made him receptive to the matchmaking of Mrs. Lewis. Dixon was in his forties now and had spent his life in a man's world, and the need for a wife and family he had so long repressed at last was exerting itself.

Late in November 1893 Olive returned to the Lewis house from school. Dismounting, she noticed Mrs. Lewis talking in the front yard with a stranger who held a bundle of laundry. Mrs. Lewis often took in laundry from cowboys, although Olive had never before seen this man. But she had heard of him. Mrs. Lewis eagerly introduced her to "Mister William Dixon" — the famous Billy Dixon.

Dixon was a handsome men with rugged features, thick black hair, and a strong physique. But Olive noticed that he blushed fiercely as he made a formal reply. "I am pleased to meet you, madam."[16]

In turn Olive remarked that she had heard a great deal about him, primarily from Mrs. Lewis and from her brother, Archie. Mrs. Lewis opened a conversation about the weather, and Olive soon retreated into the house. After Dixon rode off, carrying his laundry bag and followed by two hunting dogs, the Lewises talked about him all evening. They not only reiterated the combat exploits that had brought him fame — they also told Olive about his nearby home on the site of the original Adobe Walls trading post, about his irrigated orchard and alfalfa field, about his services to the neighborhood as a justice of the peace and a notary public and postmaster. Dixon operated the Adobe Walls post office out of his residence, as well as a small store. One reason that Archie King knew Billy Dixon so well is because he visited the post office on a regular basis.

Less than a week after Olive met Billy Dixon, he and his hunting dogs turned up at the school one afternoon shortly after class was dismissed. Dixon remarked that he happened to be hunting, and he asked to ride along with George and the schoolmarm. George soon turned off to ride to the Whittenburg place, while Billy accompanied "Miss King" — which he habitually called her — to the Lewis home. The family insisted that Billy stay for supper. During and after the evening meal Dixon was asked about events of his life, and Olive began to hear firsthand the adventures she would one day record and publish.

The following week there was another coincidental encounter after school, with Dixon muttering something about picking up another bag of laundry. Again he agreed to stay for supper, and again he was questioned about his past as a frontiersman. While describing these events Dixon steadfastly avoided talking about his personal exploits. One night when asked to describe the Buffalo Wallow Fight, he offered such bloody details that he later apologized to the ladies.[17]

Dixon's hunting trips in the vicinity of the Garden Creek School became a weekly event. When the school term ended in the spring, Mrs. Lewis asked Olive to continue her stay. The two ladies had developed a real attachment, and Mrs. Lewis wanted continued help from Olive in improving her broken English. Besides, it was obvious that her efforts as a matchmaker were working.

Billy Dixon continued to ride to the Lewis home, usually on Sundays, and he did not come empty-handed. From his orchard he brought cherries or plums or other fruits. And he led an extra mount so that the couple could continue to ride together. Dixon always had kept good saddle horses, and every week he brought her favorite mount. By now Billy and "Miss King" had learned of similar childhood experiences. Both were born in the mountains of Virginia (Billy's Ohio County birthplace became part of West Virginia when that state was formed in 1862.) Olive lost her father when she was a little girl, and she and Billy each had been sent to live during childhood with relatives. As adults both Billy and Olive shared a passionate love for the

Now a frontier celebrity, Billy Dixon upgraded his wardrobe, and he could cut an impressive figure. Olive King certainly thought he did. *Courtesy Roberts County Museum, Miami.*

High Plains of the Texas Panhandle — and for each other.[18]

"Mr. Dixon was quiet and bashful — a bachelor — and although he was more than twenty-years older than I, I liked him from the first," admitted Olive, adding meaningfully: "The admiration was mutual . . ."[19]

During a Sunday afternoon ride in July, Billy and Olive — and the two hunting dogs — took the familiar trail toward the school. They stopped at a lovely spot dominated by the Garden Creek Spring. Olive always remembered the emotionally charged conversation that followed:[20]

"This is the most beautiful place I ever saw," began Olive.

"Would you like to live all your days on these plains?" asked Billy.

"I want to live here forever!"

"I love you, Miss King. Will you marry me?"

"Yes."

Billy began to describe his house, the store, the orchard, his garden, his livestock — her future home. He spoke of his mother, and compared her kindness and sweet disposition to Olive's temperament.

"The first time I saw you, Little Girl, I thought to myself that an angel would likely look the way you do," he said with a once-in-a-lifetime poetic flair. "I thought your eyes were star-blue and your hair was colored like the prairie grass after frost time." Perhaps Olive improved a little of the poetic expression when she described the moment to her biographer.

"I have always insisted that she did the proposing," reminisced Billy in permanent disbelief that he could actually propose marriage, "but could say no more when she reminded me of the time we were riding together and watered our horses at Garden Springs . . ."[21]

Soon they decided to ride back to the Lewis home and tell of their engagement. A couple of days later Archie King drove his buckboard to the Adobe Walls post office to check his mail. Dixon, "sweating and spitting," nervously informed Archie that he was going to marry his sister. "The most words in a string that I ever heard that man say," laughed Archie.[22]

Having spoken to Olive's brother, Dixon now wrote a letter to her mother, as we have seen. Meanwhile, Olive and Mrs. Lewis were creating a wedding dress and a trousseau, while planning the marriage ceremony and a wedding supper. The previous year the Lewis family had invited everyone in the county — "all thirty of them," observed Olive — to a Thanksgiving dinner. "In the room that served as the kitchen and dining room, we took turns at the table that had been made by smoothing logs to a semblance of levelness." The area teemed with wildlife, and Mrs. Lewis was a fine cook. Olive described a "bountiful feast of deer, wild turkey, quail, cakes, and pies that were placed on the table in such prodigal quantities."[23]

The wedding supper must have been planned along these same lines. Another "bountiful feast" of wild game, pies, and a cake would have been arrayed on the smooth log table. Of course, both the supper as well as the wedding ceremony were delayed because of the tourist inclinations of Rev. C.V. Bailey. At least, in a land where preachers were scarce, Olive's wedding was presided over by a fellow Methodist. The groom had acquired a new blue suit, and Billy and Olive made a handsome couple. They were married on the evening of October 18, 1894, amid a company of friends and relatives — cowboy brother Archie King and his wife and two little children. Following the ceremony and supper, Billy and Olive departed for their home at Adobe Walls.

Chapter Thirteen

Mr. and Mrs. Billy Dixon

Whither, thou goest, I will go.

Ruth (and Olive)

On his first morning as a married man, Billy Dixon arose early and — as he did every day — cooked breakfast. As his marriage approached, Billy had worked to repair and clean his house, and he ordered new sheets for his bed from Montgomery Ward. Now he served a fried chicken breakfast to his bride. Olive donned the second-day dress from her trousseau, and the Dixons set out to visit the nearby Turkey Track Ranch.[1]

They drove first to a remote line camp so that Billy could introduce Olive to an aging bachelor cowboy known as Uncle Jake Quick. Charmed by Billy's pretty bride, Uncle Jake gave her a sorrel pony as a wedding gift. The next stop was at the home of Turkey Track wagon boss Woods Coffee, who had a wife and two children. Mrs. Coffee was delighted to have a new female neighbor, and the "second day" climaxed with a supper with the family.[2]

"Sometimes on Sunday my husband would take me to spend the day in a line camp," recalled Olive. "There we would eat wild turkey or a pot full of stewed wild duck. On the outside of the dugout we could see a quarter of beef. These were red-letter days for me." Olive observed that life in these line camps, "was simplicity itself — almost no housekeeping, bathing and laundry took place in a near-by creek. The cooking was done in the fireplace over the open fire or in dutchovens."[3]

The young housewife took careful note of the "menu" at line camps: "bacon, ham, dried fruit, coffee parched in a frying pan and ground as needed, rice, beans, occasionally [sic] potatoes, and always 'lick' (molasses) . . ." Molasses was used on sour dough biscuits, a staple which Olive mastered as a cook. "These biscuits were light and flaky and no modern bakery can boast of better bread than we had." She carefully described the ingredients and baking process, but expressed her curiosity that in cow country no butter was available. "It always seemed strange to me that while there were thousands of cows on the range, none were milked. The cowboys preferred bacon grease to butter."[4]

Sometimes during the summer "a party of women" would visit Turkey Track headquarters just north of Adobe Walls, "but only for a short stay." Once each year Olive and Billy traveled "into Roberts County to visit the Lards, Ledricks, Walstads and my brother's family twenty-five miles away." These same families would come to Adobe Walls every year. "Often we took a camping outfit and went up on Moore's Creek over night to kill wild turkeys which were then plentiful and roosted in the tall cottonwood trees along that stream."[5]

Although there were no churches in the vicinity when Olive and Billy married, there was an annual celebration of religion. "Settlers twenty-five miles southeast of my home at Adobe Walls gathered once a year on Tallahone Creek in Roberts County for a series of revival meetings. People came in wagons, buggies and horseback and camped on the ground. Nearby ranchers furnished beeves and the women brought bread, pies and cakes. There was always black coffee." In this isolated land one other spiritual expression could be expected: "Always there was a religious service at a burial."[6]

During their first Christmas season together, Billy and Olive journeyed by buckboard on Christmas Eve north to Hansford for the annual dance at the frame courthouse. Although Billy did not dance, he spent the evening swapping stories with friends. There were more men than women, and Olive happily danced every waltz and square dance. Festivities broke up about four o'clock Christmas morning. A local doctor offered the Dixons the use of his office, and Billy and Olive slept on the bedrolls they had brought. About ten o'clock they roused, ate breakfast, and spent the rest of Christmas driving thirty miles back to Adobe Walls.

Early in their marriage Billy returned from a supply trip to Canadian with a new bedroom suite from Gerlach's, a big main street mercantile. Other wedding gifts came from Gerlach's, including a set of dishes and small items of furniture. On Cape Willingham's first visit to the post office, he told the couple that a milk cow and calf awaited them at ranch headquarters. Periodically Turkey Track cowboys would drop off a quarter of beef, and someone brought a baby pig.[8]

Billy Dixon had equipped his bachelor kitchen with a homemade table and five chairs and a cupboard that held fifty pounds of flour and heavy cooking utensils. Before the first year of their marriage was over, Olive had acquired a set of granite cooking utensils, two new steel skillets, a white cloth for the dining table, a Majestic cook stove, and a sewing machine.

Soon the sewing machine was seeing heavy use. Olive was pregnant, and she used her new machine to produce a complete layette: eight long baby dresses, four wool slips with embroidered stitching, six muslin slips with crocheted edgings, four outing nightdresses, four undershirts, half a dozen head bands, several bibs, two crocheted caps, half a dozen small blankets, and a supply of diapers.[9]

Olive decided that the log kitchen was far warmer and more suitable for a baby than the lean-to bedroom. Billy went to work enclosing the open space between these two rooms, and the new kitchen was complete with a fireplace. A wall-to-wall carpet was ordered from Montgomery Ward for the converted nursery/bedroom.

A little more than a year after Billy and Olive were married, their first baby was born at their Adobe Walls home. Dora Miles

Dixon — named for Olivia's cousin Dora and for Gen. Nelson A. Miles — was born on December 29, 1895. Fortunately Olive and little Dora did not need special medical care. "Everyone was healthy in those days and it was a good thing that they were," reminisced Olive, "for the nearest doctor was over a hundred miles away at Fort Elliott and he didn't leave the Fort unless one were really sick."[10]

Olive had written to her mother asking for her help at the birth and sending money for train fare. About two months before the expected arrival, however, Mrs. King decided that she was not up to the long trip. Billy and Olive wrote to Grandma Lard, an experienced midwife who lived on Chicken Creek. Two weeks before the expected birth date, Billy went after Grandma Lard in his buckboard. Shortly before dawn on December 29, Grandma Lard supervised the birth of a baby girl. On Billy's next supply trip to Canadian, he brought back a rocking chair from Gerlach's for his wife and baby.

James Coburn periodically brought his large family from Kansas City when he visited the Turkey Track Ranch. At Christmas 1896 the Coburns entertained Billy, Olive, and little Dora. Several months later, on September 26, 1897, another Dixon daughter was born. She was named Mary Lou Cindy, but when Dora tried to say "Baby" it sounded like "Bobbie," and the little girl would be called Bobbie by everyone. Mrs. Coburn came for a visit when Bobbie was just a few days old. Mrs. Coburn, immediately recognizing Olive's need for assistance with a newborn and another daughter who was not even two, sent over her family nanny to help out for the next several days.[11]

On another family visit to the Turkey Track one of the Coburn sons fell ill. A doctor was sent for, but the Canadian River flooded and crossing was impossible. Sadly, the little boy died. A burial service was held at the small ranch cemetery, and in the absence of clergy James Coburn read the Episcopalian funeral service. Because the river was flooded, the only mourn-

Turkey Track cowboys were neighbors and friends of Billy and Olive Dixon, and they were customers at his little store. *Courtesy National Archives.*

ers who could attend were Turkey Track ranch hands and Billy and Olive Dixon and their children. At the first opportunity, the little Coburn boy was disinterred and shipped to Kansas City, where he was laid to final rest in the family burial plot.[12]

In 1898 Billy and Olive had a son, William Drew, born on September 13. Also in 1898 Billy was summoned to participate in a federal court case pertaining to the Battle of Adobe Walls. Frederick J. Leonard and A.C. Myers filed suit against Kiowa, Comanche, and Cheyenne Indians for destruction of their merchandise as a result of their attack on Adobe Walls. Similar suits were filed by Charles Rath & Company and by buffalo hunters James H. and Arthur Cator. Since thinly-settled Hutchinson County was not yet organized, Billy Dixon was asked to submit a deposition in Carson County, immediately to the south. Arrangements were made with M.K. Callison, Carson County Clerk, to submit a set of questions.

Billy Dixon appeared in Callison's office at the courthouse in Panhandle on August 4, 1898. After being sworn in, Dixon carefully answered questions about Adobe Walls, the battle, and events after the fighting. Myers and Leonard had meticulously listed lost merchandise, from 6,000 buffalo hides to 60,000 pounds of corn, from 18,000 pounds of lead to 35,000 primers, from a $600 hide press to $3,600 for their buildings and stockade. They claimed a total loss for eleven items as $33,375. But Billy Dixon swore that battle damage was only a fraction of this amount, that the Myers and Leonard structures were not destroyed during or shortly after the battle, and that the only property that was stolen by the warriors was the horse herd that was grazing when the attack was launched. Billy Dixon's testimony did little to support the claims of Myers and Leonard.[13]

The 1890 Census revealed that Hutchinson County had nine ranches — principally the Turkey Track — and only fifty-eight people. Forty acres in the county were planted in corn, but there was little other farming activity (Billy Dixon, of course, was working a small alfalfa field). Most of the county was unfenced. The next census, in 1900, listed sixty-three ranches and farms, and a population increase to 303. Most of the ranches were small. Billy Dixon ran perhaps 100 head of cattle out of nearly 30,000 head in the county. Aside from small acreages planted in corn and cotton, there still was little farming. The Turkey Track hosted the only school, a dugout classroom opened in 1900.[14]

The population growth — from 58 to 303 in ten years — was stimulated by the Four-Section Act, which allowed the sale or lease of four sections, or 2,560 acres, of school, asylum, or public lands in Texas. In 1887 the Legislature had advanced an act for settlers to buy four sections of pastureland from the public domain. A few "nesters" came to Hutchinson County as a result of the 1887 act, but most were not successful. (Billy Dixon appropriated the logs from a deserted nester cabin.) But there was more response from the 1895 version for these 2,560-acre parcels.

"I was State Land Commissioner for Hutchinson County and did a thriving business," reminisced Dixon, happily recalling his fees. The nesters "settled first along the creeks and then spread to the uplands. The Turkey Track began buying out some of the small operators. Other nesters wanted their own piece of Texas. As with all big open range ranches, the Turkey Track lost cattle to stock theft. Hard feelings grew between small operators and large ranchers and the cowboys who rode for the brand. James Coburn received threats, and hay stacks on Turkey Track pastures were set on fire. A detail of Texas Rangers came to the county, but they used blunt measures that were resented by some.[15]

This photograph features Billy Dixon, seated at left, and an unidentified group. But standing behind Billy is Olive, and this pose apparently was snapped early in their marriage. Billy appears to be in his forties, and Olive in her early twenties (compare this photo with Olive at eighteen, in Chapter One) *Courtesy Haley Memorial Museum Library, JEH-H-40.2.*

In this tense atmosphere, the population growth encouraged a movement to organize Hutchinson County and establish a county seat. The county was created in 1876 but the lack of people or a town rendered county organization impossible. In 1900, however, organizers began to collect signatures for the required petition, which was to be submitted to the Texas State Legislature with the names of as many adult males as possible.

(Women, of course, could not yet vote.) Although there were 179 signatures on the petition, one of the election judges claimed that there were only 85 legally qualified voters in the county. But the Legislature approved the petition, and an election was scheduled for April 25, 1901, to determine county officials and the location of the county seat.[16]

The Turkey Track and other big ranches that ran cattle in part of Hutchinson County — mostly in the north and west — favored a location named Bugbee for county seat. But J.A. Whittenburg (father of George Whittenburg, Olive's student at her rural school in 1893) had built a dugout overlooking a crossing of the Canadian River. The location was set in the central part of the county, a prime consideration for the Legislature. There was talk of naming the county seat Dixon, but there already was a Texas post office by that name. The community was dubbed Plemons, after Barney Plemons, who had filed on land at the site. Barney was the son of Judge William B. Plemons of Amarillo, a former state legislator. The county seat village of Plemons began to take shape in the spring of 1901.[17]

The first slate of Hutchinson County officials was headed by County Judge W.H. Ingerton and Sheriff Billy Dixon. Dixon, one of the county's first residents and long famous as a hero of the Indian Wars, already had been appointed to several official positions, but he was no politician. "I was elected sheriff, not because I sought the office, but because I had lived in the country so long that I was widely known," he explained. "I was ignorant of politics and the ways of politicians."[18]

"When a man gets mixed up in politics he is soon traveling a rocky road," discovered Sheriff Dixon. When the newly elected officials gathered there was acrimony from the start. In addition to policy disputes, enemies of Judge Ingerton and Sheriff Dixon accused them of excessive drinking. Ingerton and Dixon had agreed to serve so that they could help form the county where they lived, but neither man intended to put up with pub-

Panhandle history buffs examine the long-abandoned Dixon home site at Adobe Walls. Olive is behind the second man from the left. *Courtesy Panhandle-Plains Historical Museum, Canyon, Texas.*

lic abuse. "I became disgusted and resigned my office," stated Dixon, "rather than be forced into strife that was not to my liking." Judge Ingerton also resigned.[19]

Dixon was sworn in as Hutchinson County's first sheriff on April 25, 1901, but he resigned within less than two weeks. His successor was appointed on May 6, 1901. Dixon gratefully "went back to the quietude of Adobe Walls." But the level of "quietude" he always had treasured at Adobe Walls was rapidly declining. [20]

During the troubled year of 1901 a baby girl was born, the fourth Dixon child and third daughter. But the baby died when only a few days old, and she was buried in a small grave at Adobe Walls.[21]

Not long after Dixon resigned as sheriff, James Coburn and Cape Willingham came to the Adobe Walls store for a visit. The three men walked out to the corral and had a "long talk" that Olive, who was watching from the house, said featured "some kind of proposition" about buying the Adobe Walls property. Olive was certain that Billy replied with a "firm" no. Billy did not discuss the conversation, but the family stayed at their home and began to plan for an expanded operation and for a new and larger house. For the Turkey Track management, however, the matter of acquiring the Adobe Walls property was not closed.[22]

Billy Dixon and Olive owned about 100 head of cattle. Olive, who had accumulated savings since her day as a teacher, had invested in some of these cattle, registering a D Bar brand for her livestock. Learning of a herd of 400 cattle for sale in Miami, the Dixons and Marion Drumm, a former Turkey Track cowboy who had started a spread in Carson County, combined their resources. Drumm brought his half of the herd to his little ranch, while 200 head were driven to Adobe Walls. Now there were 300 cattle on Billy's three sections, a strain on the Dixon grass. Of course, Billy had alfalfa hay to supplement his grazing, and the unfenced range offered another supplement that

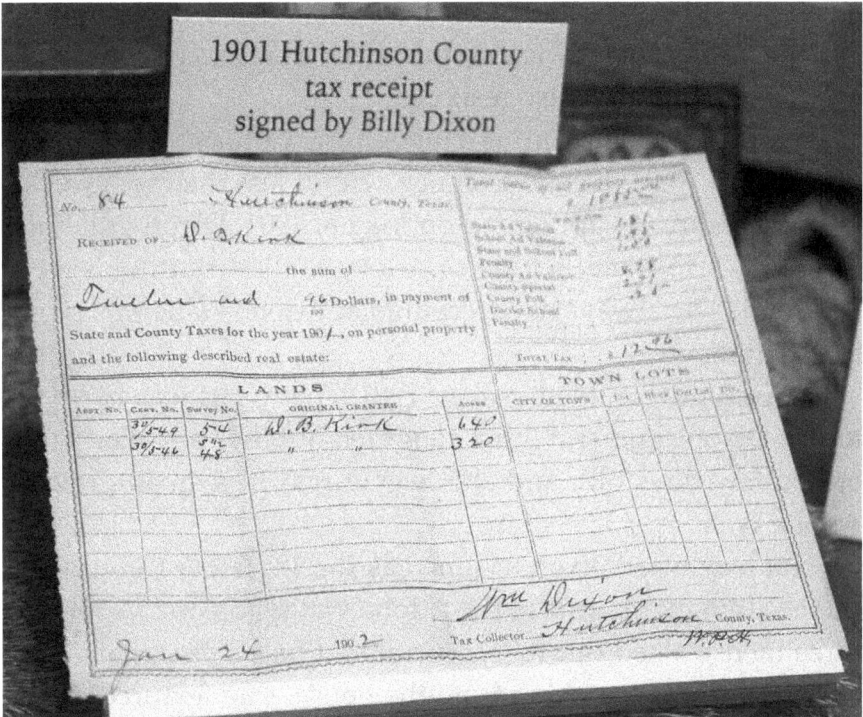

A tax receipt signed by Billy Dixon, who was functioning as tax collector for Hutchinson County. *Courtesy Hutchinson County Museum, Borger.*

the adjacent Turkey Track did not appreciate. But the winter of 1903-04 was the worst in memory, with snowfall of more than two feet. Billy suffered heavy livestock losses and, of course, he was operating on borrowed money.[23]

James Coburn sold off a great part of his herd and sent the remainder to range along the Pecos River in New Mexico. Mart Cunningham, a veteran Turkey Track employee, purchased 7,280 acres of the ranch land for three dollars per acre, plus another $5,000 for the headquarters complex. Shortly after this transaction, in 1903, a new partnership — Price, Patten, and Hyde from Kansas — bought out Mart Cunningham and Billy Dixon.[24]

"When Patten, Price & Hyde, the Kansas cattlemen, bought the Turkey Track range and stock," stated Dixon in plain terms, "I sold my place at Adobe Walls to them."[25]

Olive elaborated on the sale, pointing out that Billy was "offered five dollars an acre for the home section, and less for the other two sections. He was aware this was a far more attractive offer than the ranchers had made other settlers . . ." Besides, the sale would alleviate Billy's indebtedness. But Olive could not help reflecting on her years at Adobe Walls: "My older children were born there. I spent the happiest days of my life there."[26]

Before the property transfer was made, a fifth Dixon child was born. Edna Lee Dixon made her appearance on June 11, 1903. By that time Dora, the oldest child, had started school at the primitive facility on the Turkey Track. Wayne Hedgecoke, the teacher, boarded with the Dixons. Bobbie was seven and ready to begin her schooling, and five-year-old Drew was not far behind. Olive certainly had every hope of placing her children in a stronger school.[27]

Olive also wanted a more substantial house for her growing family. Billy freighted in lumber and other building materials from Channing to the west. Performing most of the carpentry work himself, Billy put together of a two-story house. Soon afterward Billy agreed to sell the Dixon property but Olive insistently asked about the house. The ranchers immediately replied: "You can just have it. And the old one too. We'll close the deal." The ranch partners got Billy Dixon's land, and Olive got her house. The two-story structure was jacked up and hauled fourteen miles to Plemons.[28]

During this period of transition, Olive decided to visit her mother in Virginia. Olive had not seen her mother and Virginia siblings since 1893, when she left on a trip to the Texas Panhandle. More than a decade had passed, and Olive wanted to introduce daughters Dora, Bobbie, and Baby Edna. It was decided that five-year-old Drew would stay at home with his father. But when the ladies decided to leave Virginia, Billy and Drew would meet them in St. Louis, where the Dixon family would attend the spectacular World's Fair.

Olive and her daughters boarded an eastbound train in Miami. At the old home place in Virginia, the household had changed with the passage of time. Grandma Blankenship was dead, Olive's mother had gone blind, and the woman of the house now was Olive's youngest sister, Ida. Ida had married a young man named Kyle Wickham, but the couple had no children yet. Olive noticed "that her children made a startling amount of noise in the old home." Olive and her mother, Mary Jane King, talked endlessly about Billy and the children. Olive was able to tell Mary Jane about Archie and Sena, who now had five children. She also explained to Mary Jane that her other cowboy son, Albert, had become a successful rancher in Lipscomb County. [29]

After a two-week stay, Olive said her goodbyes and she and the girls took a train to St. Louis, meeting up with Billy and Drew. The Louisiana Purchase Exposition, popularly known as the St. Louis World's Fair, ran from April 20 to December 1, 1904. Almost 20 million visitors attended the extravaganza. There were more than 1,500 buildings, connected by seventy-five miles of roads and walkways on a 1,200-acre site. The Palace of Agriculture covered twenty acres. The St. Louis World's Fair hosted the 1904 Summer Olympics, the first Olympic games held in the United States. John Philip Sousa's popular band performed on several occasions at the Fair, and Ragtime music was played throughout the event. Geronimo, the former Apache war chief, was exhibited in a tipi at the Ethnology Exhibit. The St. Louis World's Fair must have been an unforgettable experience for the Dixon family.

The Dixons were among the first fifteen families to settle in Plemons. One of the initial structures at the new county seat was a small courthouse, fourteen feet by twenty feet, erected in 1901. Immediately a two-story courthouse was approved and built, and when it was occupied the original structure became the town's first school. The single street ran north to south through the village to the Canadian River. The two-story courthouse was the first building on the west side of the street about 100 yards north of the river. The Plemons post office opened on May 29, 1901, at the boarding house of Joe and Mattie Sams; Mattie was designated postmistress. There was a doctor's office near the courthouse, a wagonyard on the east side of the street, a general store, a drugstore, and a barber shop.[30]

When the Dixon home finished its fourteen-mile journey from Adobe Walls, it was the only building in Plemons, aside from the courthouse, that was two stories tall. The second floor featured two rooms with two double beds each, and Olive operated her home as a boarding house. Overnight guests were charged fifty cents each, while meals were twenty-five cents. Billy's services were needed: "He cut up the meat, helped with the cooking and housework, visited with the guests and helped to care for the children." These were not activities characteristic of the famous buffalo hunter and scout. Granted that he was an experienced cook and butcher, and he was caring for his own children. But visiting with the guests was hardly his strong suit.

Guests would have wanted to converse with the famed Billy Dixon, but Billy was a far better listener than a lead conversationalist. Domestic chores. Nanny duties. Socializer. Little wonder that Billy was quoted that he "found living in town worse than it could have been in jail."[31]

The Dixon cattle herd had been sold, so the family income was dependent on the boarding house. Attorneys, the district judge, and other legal officials stayed with the Dixons when court was in session in Plemons. Although there was no church in Plemons, there were camp meetings and religious services held by circuit riders in the school or courthouse. Such ministers as Dr. J.W. Hunt and Rev. J.E. Eldredge, a Methodist evangelist who brought along a young song leader, were warmly welcomed by Olive. Overall, however, there were not enough customers in little Plemons to produce a prosperous boarding house.

But Olive dug into her savings to order a piano from a New York firm. Shipped to Galveston by boat, the piano went by rail to Panhandle, then overland by freight wagon to Plemons. Everyone in town gathered to see the shiny new instrument. There was plenty of help to unload the piano and carry it into the living room. It was the first piano in the county seat, and one of the first in the Texas Panhandle.[32]

At some point during this period Billy apparently visited the Plemons barber shop. The shoulder length hair he had worn throughout his life was trimmed into a modern haircut, although he maintained a bushy moustache. There is a photo of him with his contemporary tonsorial appearance. He is attired in a suit with a Masonic pin in the lapel.

In September 1903 Billy Dixon submitted a single-page "Petition" to join the newly-organized Plemons Lodge of Free and Accepted Masons. The Dixon family had not yet moved into Plemons — Billy's petition stated that he was still farming ten miles northeast of town. But the Masonic fraternity was estab-

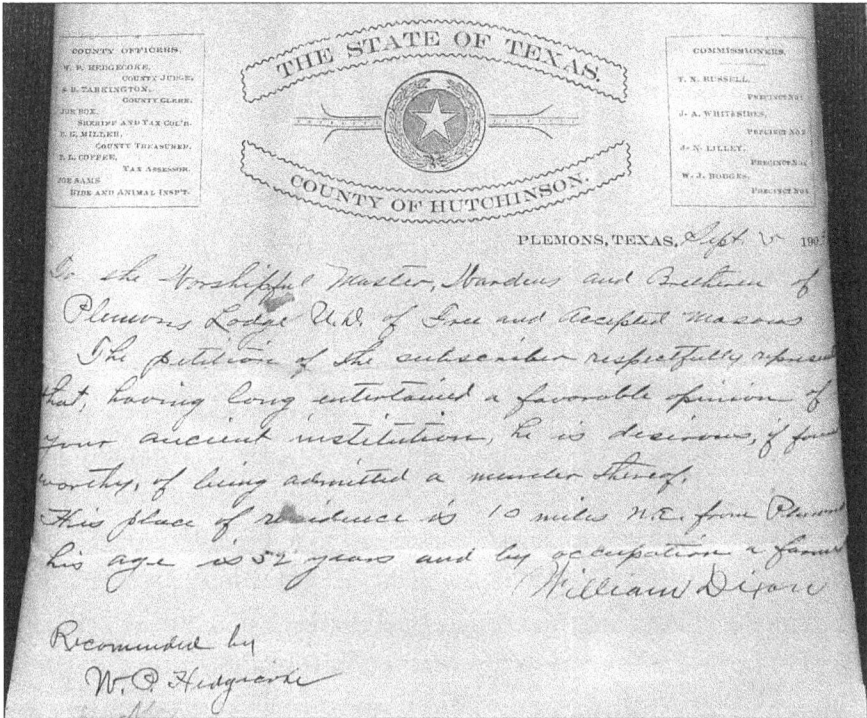

Billy Dixon's petition to join the Masonic Lodge. *Courtesy Grand Lodge of Texas, Waco.*

lished in Texas by such notable pioneers as Stephen F. Austin and Sam Houston, and most prominent men in Texas communities and in statewide politics were Masons. Billy was initiated into the fraternity on October 3, 1903; he passed his memory work on October 31 and was "Raised" into membership on November 28. He served as treasurer in 1904 and 1905. But the next year he moved from Plemons to a homestead in the Oklahoma Panhandle, and in 1910 he was suspended for non-payment of dues.[33]

In Plemons another Dixon baby boy was born on June 22, 1906. He was named Archie King Dixon, after the cowboy brother who had brought Olive to the Panhandle. The three oldest children attended school in Plemons. A cosmopolitan element enriched their education, because the principal street of Plemons intersected with one of the best river crossings on the Canadian, and a parade of miscellaneous travelers passed through the

In 1957 the Masons of Fritch named their lodge after Billy Dixon. *Photo by the author.*

little village. In many ways the Canadian River was one of the most important geographic features of the Texas Panhandle.

Billy and Olive Dixon had a long association with the Canadian River, both separately and as a married couple. In 1874 Billy hunted buffalo along the Canadian River Valley, and only a short distance north of the river, at Adobe Walls, he earned fame for his performance in battle. Beginning in 1883 Billy created a home beside Bent Creek, a tributary of the nearby Canadian. To this home he welcomed his bride, Olive, in 1894, and here she bore their first children. In 1904 Billy and Olive moved their growing family to the new county seat town, Plemons, located on the north bank of the Canadian.

When Olive first came to the Panhandle in 1893 she stepped off the train in Canadian, before traveling with her brother to his sod house just north of the river. When she was offered a teaching position at a rural school a short distance south of the Canadian, she had to move because she could not count on crossing the treacherous river throughout the winter. And it was at her new lodgings with the Lewis family south of the river that she met Billy Dixon.

At the end of a chapter on the Canadian in *Texas Rivers*, the gifted writer John Graves briefly described activities of nearby dwellers from earliest Native Americans to Spanish-speaking pastores to Anglo pioneers. His summation could have been written specifically about Billy and Olive Dixon: "And you know it was a good life — isolated, yes, tough in the Panhandle winters and during drouths and other troubles, but full of meaningful work and love and satisfaction."[34]

But by 1906 Billy Dixon's restless pioneer spirit was about to propel him away from the Canadian — more to the point, away from Plemons — in a desperate search for one last frontier home. The Homestead Act of 1862 was extended to the Oklahoma Panhandle, and Billy was one of several men in and around Plemons who wanted to investigate.

From 1886 until 1890 the future panhandle of Oklahoma was a separate jurisdiction known as Cimarron Territory. In 1890 Cimarron Territory became part of Oklahoma Territory, with the designation of Beaver County. Beaver County, named because of the Beaver River, comprised the entire panhandle until 1907. Billy Dixon filed on a quarter-section claim in southwestern Beaver County. A ten-dollar filing fee was required, and so was the erection of a dwelling, and after five years the land would belong to Billy. The southern border of Dixon's 160 acres was the Texas-Oklahoma line. Indeed, Billy's homestead adjoined the northernmost division of the gigantic XIT Ranch, the Buffalo Springs Division.

From his homestead Billy could see the grove of trees where the Buffalo Springs headquarters stood. An old hand at building dugouts, Billy fashioned a half-dugout with a canvas roof to house his family until he could build a more permanent dwelling.

In the spirit of "whither thou goest," Olive agreed to the move. She was a strong woman, but she was devoted to Billy and followed him — away from schools and churches and next-door neighbors. The big house in Plemons was sold, along with all the furnishings. Olive kept her piano, but she admitted to weeping over the loss of her Majestic stove. For the trip to Oklahoma, the Dixon family was loaded into a Spaulding hack pulled by a span of mules. Billy herded six milk cows to their new home. There was a shepherd dog named Watch, and two saddle horses.[35]

Within days after arriving at the homestead, Billy brought in lumber and began building a house. The older children helped, and Billy erected a three-room dwelling in the shape of a T, with a hall between the rooms. Meanwhile, water was hauled from a neighbor's place until Billy had time to dig a well by hand into the shallow water table. Next he put up a new windmill to water the live-

Billy Dixon in middle age, proudly wearing his Masonic pin in the lapel of his suit coat. *Courtesy Hutchinson County Museum, Borger.*

stock and to irrigate a vegetable garden. With a water supply that could be controlled, Billy built an adobe milk house. Then he began fencing in his little claim, before breaking forty acres of land for feed with a steel plow and a mule. The fatiguing physical labor of establishing a new home would prove to be an unrelenting feature of Billy's life as a homesteader.[36]

Later he built an adobe corral and stable. Hoping to duplicate the big irrigated orchard at Adobe Walls, Billy planted seventy-five fruit trees west of the house. Despite his herculean efforts, however, the 160-acre farm was too small to support more than a few head of livestock, and he could produce little in the way of cash crops. It soon became evident that the Oklahoma homestead at best would serve the Dixon family as a subsistence farm. The most Billy could hope for was to feed his growing family and provide for their basic needs.

Olive, of course, was constantly busy with their children. She sewed undergarments and night clothes out of flour sacks.[37] Preparing three meals a day was a constant chore, especially since she no longer had her prized Majestic cook stove. Supplies were brought in from Texline, a railroad town on the Texas and New Mexico line fourteen miles southwest of the homestead.

But there were other nearby homesteaders. Neighbors included the Thaxtons, Reeds, Smiths, the Rices, and several families from Hutchinson County. Shelly Rice, only daughter of the Rice neighbors, was engaged to teach piano to the Dixon daughters. A rural school was organized just three miles from the Dixon home. The three oldest children, Dora, Bobbie and Drew, drove to and from school in a buggy pulled by a gentle horse. And soon enough there were two more children. Olive Virginia Dixon, named after her mother and the native state of both parents, was born on October 9, 1908. Two years later, on November 18, 1910, Ernest Hugh — who came to be called by his middle name — became the final Dixon child.[38]

During a fifteen-year period, from December 29, 1895 until November 18, 1910, Olive had given birth to eight children. A baby girl had died in 1901, so there were four daughters and three sons in the little three-room house. Olive was thirty-seven when Hugh was born, and for a decade and a half she almost constantly was pregnant or nursing, with a baby or a toddler - or both — to tend.

Billy was sixty when his last child was born. His daughter Edna described her father as "kind and gentle" with his children, adding that Billy "loved animals."[39] Billy did not become a father until he was forty-five, and he cherished his children. But as he entered his sixties, Billy found it harder and harder to support his beloved family on a hardscrabble Oklahoma homestead claim.

Chapter Fourteen

Widow and Mother

*In changing that wild and barbaric country to peaceful
civil settlement, [Billy Dixon] was like the
Daniel Boones and Kit Carsons of a former period . . .*

General Nelson A. Miles

By 1912 Olive was worried about her husband. "He had acquired a backward-looking habit," she explained to her biographer. "Partly because people were always asking him about his Indian-fighting days, Billy Dixon had begun to live more and more in the past." Olive was quick to praise "the detailed accuracy of his memory" and the clarity of Billy's mind.[1]

She was deeply concerned about winter attacks of the "grippe" that her sixty-something husband was having a hard time throwing off. The grippe was a catch-all term of the age referring to everything from winter colds to influenza. *Webster's Dictionary* defines the grippe as "characterized by fever, bronchial inflammation, catarrhal discharge, and intestinal disorder."

Billy Dixon had spent his life outdoors, and most of his winters were in plains country with freezing temperatures and high winds and snow. He was blessed with an iron constitution and a strong, muscular physique, but during nearly seven years on his Oklahoma homestead the aging plainsman wore himself down with grinding physical exertions around the farm. Billy thus became more susceptible than at any other time in his life to the harsh weather of the Oklahoma Panhandle.

Acclaimed author John Erickson spent more than four years during the 1970s ranching in the Oklahoma Panhandle, an experience he wrote about in *Panhandle Cowboy*. Erickson is a na-

tive of Perryton in the northern Texas Panhandle, so he is accustomed to the region's weather. But he found the Oklahoma
Panhandle winters to be especially vicious. "In the winter, we
were thrashed by north winds which produced a brutal form of
cold that was reflected in the chill factor. It was not uncommon
for the chill factor to reach thirty or forty degrees below zero in
January. In March, a day of northerly gales was often followed
by a day of southerly gales like slaps delivered to both sides of
the face."

"We dressed for warmth," wrote Olive. "We always wore
heavy, woolen underwear in the winter and several petticoats,
one at least being a heavy woolen one . . . Out on the range in a
big wagon or spring wagon with nothing to break the wind was
a different thing from riding in an airtight, heated car." Little
wonder that Billy began to suffer illness during the Oklahoma
winters.[2]

In 1908 writer Edward Campbell Little published a lengthy
article in *Pearson's Magazine*, "The Battle of Adobe Walls." Olive
and Billy both were impressed by this fine article. The Dixons
wrote Little, asking if he might write the story of Billy's adventures in a book. Little responded eagerly, but the fee he requested seemed impossible the the Dixons, who dropped the idea of
a book project.

But friends and old-timers from the early days continually
urged Billy to record his frontier exploits. With her instincts as a
historian, Olive knew that she had married a genuinely important historical figure, and from time to time she had asked her
taciturn husband about his colorful past. At last, late in 1912,
Billy agreed to talk systematically and in detail about his youthful adventures to his wife.

"I kept notebooks in every room," related Olive, "and sometimes carried them to the corral, that I might be in readiness
to set down what my husband might say . . ." Billy "became
greatly interested in the undertaking," and he recounted "the
past with ease and accuracy." As his pioneer friends learned of

what Billy and Olive were doing, they "encouraged him to persevere," and the dictated pages piled up. "The material grew until there was an armful of manuscript," Olive recalled, "and the ground had been fairly covered."[3]

The ground was covered just in time. Early in 1913 Billy ignored a vicious winter storm and continued the necessary outdoor chores. But one day Billy "went unwillingly and complainingly to his bed . . ." Although Billy had been sick with the "grippe" in recent years, he had never before given in to illness. But now he was feverish and could not pull himself out of bed, and pneumonia developed.[4]

The two oldest daughters, Dora and Bobbie, had been staying on the Roberts County ranch of Archie King. Archie had persuaded the Dixons to let the girls live at his ranch so that he could start a rural school. The five children of Archie and Sena were of school age, and so was a nephew of Sena's. Dora and Bobbie would add up to eight pupils, which "would make a strong school." One of the rooms in the ranch house was converted into a school room and Archie employed a teacher. Archie asked only that Dora and Bobbie help their first cousins with chores around the house; there was no charge for schooling or board.[5]

But now a worried Olive contacted Archie and her two daughters, by letter and telephone, that Billy was gravely ill. Billy's sickbed was the double bed normally used by Dora and Bobbie. When Olive suggested sending for a doctor, Billy insisted that, "I'll be all right in a few days." Instead he grew visibly weaker. On Saturday, March 8, neighbors came over to visit with Billy and Olive. But that night she declined their offers to relieve her from nursing duties so that she could get some sleep. They left after midnight and Olive lay down beside her husband.

Olive cooked breakfast the next morning, before going outside to milk the cows. Meanwhile, Archie King was driving Dora and Bobbie toward their home in his Studebaker automobile. At noon Olive noticed that Billy's condition had worsened, and she telephoned Dr. J.M. Winchester of Clayton, New Mexico, frantically expressing her deepest fears. Clayton is only eleven miles northwest of Texline, and about twenty-two miles from the Dixon farm. but most of the roads were mere trails, and it was four o'clock before the doctor arrived at the farm in his car.[6]

Dr. Winchester felt of Billy's pulse and turned him over. Billy gasped for breath, then died within seconds. Billy Dixon passed away on Sunday afternoon, March 9, 1913, at the age of sixty-two. A little later in the day Archie King's Studebaker passed the homestead of a neighboring family named Davis. Bobbie called out to the neighbor children in the yard, asking for news about her father. "He's dead," came the answer with childlike honesty.

Archie King was of immediate help and comfort to his grief-stricken sister. It was decided that Billy would be buried in Texline, site of the nearest Texas cemetery. But since the Texline cemetery was adjacent to the state border, Archie agreed to make certain that the grave was on Texas soil. Because Billy was a Mason, arrangements were made with the lodge in Clayton to bury him with Masonic rites. Billy's body was washed,

Following funeral services at the Methodist Church in Texline, Billy Dixon was buried with Masonic rites at the Texline Cemetery. *Courtesy Hutchinson County Museum, Borger.*

dressed in a suit, and otherwise prepared for burial at home. A casket was acquired in Clayton. The funeral was conducted at the Methodist Church in Texline, four days after Billy's death, on March 13.[7]

The widowed Olive now was responsible for seven children, from two-year-old Hugh to seventeen-year-old Dora. Archie King offered to bring up his namesake, six-year-old Archie King Dixon, on his ranch. But Olive, who was seven when she was sent off to Cousin Dora in Alabama, adamantly insisted that she would keep her children together. Since the homestead produced little income, Olive's children would have to be of help. The oldest, Dora, attended a summer "Normal" for teachers at newly-opened West Texas Normal College in Canyon. Through these summer training programs, aspiring teachers could obtain entry-level certificates.

Dora's Uncle Archie had introduced her to Roberts County rancher Charley Cowan, a school trustee at Miami. Cowan not only promised Dora a teaching position — he offered her room and board at his home if she would instruct his two small daughters in music.

Olive and Dora signed a note for a fifty-dollar bank loan. With this money Dora attended West Texas Normal College in the summer of 1913, and that fall she began teaching, paying on her note and sharing part of her salary with her family.[8]

There was another bank note in 1913, far larger and more onerous that the fifty dollars that launched Dora's teaching career. Olive hoped that the pile of pages she had copied from Billy's reminiscences might be converted into a book that would provide a windfall for the family. Several years earlier, she and Billy had tried to enlist Edward Campbell Little in a book project, but the writer's price was too great for the homesteaders. Nevertheless, Olive felt incapable of transforming her stack of dictated pages into a book. And if she had a book-length manuscript, she had no idea whatever of how to deal with a publisher. So she wrote to another writer, Frederick Barde, the "Dean of

Oklahoma Journalism." Barde freelanced for the *Oklahoma City Times-Journal*, the *New York Sun*, and the *Philadelphia Ledger*. He also was an avid naturalist, and a Guthrie lawyer encouraged him to use a wilderness stone retreat of his which was named "Doby Walls."[9]

Barde visited Olive and, after inspecting her lively, colorful manuscript, offered to edit it and find a publisher for a fee of $500. Olive had faith in Billy's story, and apparently in Barde's background as a professional writer. She borrowed $500 from a bank in Clayton at twelve percent interest. Barde was as good as his word. *The Life of "Billy" Dixon: Plainsman, Scout and Pioneer* was released in the fall of 1914 by The Southwest Press of Dallas and became a frontier classic. The initial run was 1,000 copies, at a retail price of $1.50 per volume. Her share as author was miniscule, and she would be unable to finish payment on the $500 note — at twelve percent — until 1925. Olive was immensely proud of the book, but it only added to her financial burdens.[10]

During the summer of 1913 several neighboring men came to the Dixon homestead and, in the pioneer spirit of log rollings and barn raisings, planted forty acres of feed crops. The wives of these men brought chicken, bread, pies and cakes, and aided Olive in preparing lunch. At the end of the summer Bobbie, now sixteen, arranged to attend high school in Texline, and she found work in town to supplement the family income.

Meanwhile, fourteen-year-old Drew helped his mother with work on the farm. In October Olive and Drew began harvesting maize, their principal feed crop. But a few days of constant stooping to pull the clustered heads of grain from the stalks sent Olive to her bed. When she noticed a swelling in her side, Olive visited Dr. Winchester in Clayton. He initiated a surgical procedure which corrected an abscessed gall bladder.[11]

While Olive was recuperating, Archie came for an important visit. He insisted that Olive move with her children from the farm into Texline. She objected that it was impossible for her to buy or build a house in town, but Archie made rental arrangements in Texline.

Texline originated in 1888 when a townsite was purchased from the Capitol Land and Investment Company (parent company of the XIT Ranch) by the Fort Worth and Denver City Railway, which built a division point. Railroad shops were erected, along with a hotel and post office. Texline served as county seat of Dallam County from 1891 to 1903, when the government center was transferred to Dalhart.

The first school in the county was opened in Texline in 1892, and in 1912 a new two-story school building was erected. The Dixon children therefore would have a good school to attend, and also there was a Methodist church in town. Furthermore, it was of some comfort that the grave of the family's father and husband could be visited.

Drew, now assuming the role of man of the family, took a job in a grocery store. And before work he could be seen patrolling the railroad yards while pulling a child's wagon, looking for chunks of coal to use for fuel. There was nothing to use for fuel on the prairie surrounding Texline, and the railroad sold coal to citizens, but the Dixon family was strapped for cash.

Billy had died intestate. With no will, an estate hearing was scheduled for August 24, 1914, in Boise City, the seat of Cimarron County, Oklahoma. There are sixty-one pages contained in the estate file for William Dixon, and Olive Dixon is listed as the petitioner. At the hearing, which took place at eleven o'clock in the courthouse at Boise City (north of the Dixon homestead), Olive was appointed Administratrix of the estate, which consisted entirely of the 160-acre homestead, valued at $700. She posted a bond of fifty dollars (apparently provided by two family friends, H.B. Lawrence and C.S. Bingham) and signed an oath as Administratrix.[12]

One week after this hearing, on September 1, 1914, County Judge M.W. Pugh responded to a Petition for Family Allowance by Olive and her seven children. An Order Fixing Family

Allowance was issued, providing the Dixon family fifty dollars per month. This monthly allowance was secured by the Dixon property, and was issued for a period of twelve months. Olive therefore had a badly needed transfusion of fifty dollars in cash each month, although the money eventually would have to be paid back.[13]

Meanwhile, Bobbie finished Texline High School in the spring of 1914, and in September she began teaching at a rural school in Gray County, immediately south of Roberts County.

Periodically the family would stay at the farm for chores and to maintain a semblance of residence in Cimarron County. But by March 1915 Olive had decided to sell the Oklahoma homestead, and she submitted a Petition to Sell Real Estate — "For the payment of debts and family allowance and for the best interests of the Estate." Following a hearing of this petition, Notice of a Sale of Real Estate was posted, announcing a "private sale to the highest bidder" on April 28, 1915, at two o'clock in Boise City. Results of the sale finally were determined in August 1915. T.J. Cochran was the highest bidder, purchasing the property for $650. An Order for Hearing the Return of the Sale was held on September 13, 1915. From the proceeds of the sale, Olive would have to surrender to Cimarron County $600 for family allowance payments that had been made, along with $35.28 in back taxes and $29.60 in probate costs. The total owed by the estate was $665.18 — $15.18 more than the sale proceeds. Apparently the $15.18 was waived by the county.[14]

By the time the sale of the estate was settled, Olive had moved her family to Canyon. Both Dora and Bobbie needed to work on further teacher certification in the summer of 1915. Olive partially supported the Canyon household by taking in two boarders. In September 1916 Dora married Emmett Coble in her mother's home. Emmett was the only child of ranchers in the Miami area, and he had courted Dora since she had begun teaching nearly three years earlier. Emmett owned an automobile, still a comparative rarity in the Texas Panhandle, and the newlyweds motored off to Colorado on their honeymoon. In 1918 Dora and Emmett presented Olive with her first grandchild, William Emmett Coble, born in St. Anthony's Hospital in Amarillo.

After two years in Canyon, Olive decided to move to Miami in 1917. She had a number of longtime friends in Roberts County. Her new in-laws, the Cobles, ranched nearby, and Bobbie was teaching across the county line to the south. Somehow Olive managed to buy a house, the former residence of Clarence Pursley. There was a three-story brick school on a hill in the south part of town. A Methodist church stood just south of downtown, and during Olive's twelve-year stay in Miami a new sanctuary was erected.

Miami became the seat of Roberts County in 1891, and in 1913 a new brick courthouse was erected atop a hill in the east part of town. Arrival of a railroad in 1888 resulted in the rapid creation of a town complete with hotels, livery stables, stores, saloons, churches, the *Miami Weekly Herald*, grocery stores, a post office, a depot.

The Turkey Track, the Bar CC, the Laurel Leaf, and other ranches used Miami as a shipping point, resulting in the label "the last cowtown in the Panhandle." When Olive moved to Miami, the population exceeded 700.[16]

At the time of the move Drew Dixon, now seventeen, was working in Moore County, just west of Hutchinson County. Drew was not inclined to move to Miami, but an old family friend advised Olive that a job with the Santa Fe Railroad was Drew's for the asking. Drew came to Miami and asked, and he became a longtime railroad employee.[17]

In 1920 Olive hosted another wedding in her home. Bobbie, who had spent the past three years teaching, married Glenn McKee of Plainview. The younger members of the family attended school in Miami, and Andy and Hugh participated in sports at Miami High School. The boys also found jobs in downtown stores while going to school.

The Roberts County Courthouse was built in Miami in 1913, only four years before Olive moved to town. *Photo by the author.*

This handsome Methodist church was erected in Miami while Olive and her children were members of the congregation. *Photo by the author.*

Olive's younger children attended Miami's big brick school. *Courtesy Roberts County Museum, Miami.*

The Miami railroad depot was built in 1888 and still is in use today, as a museum. *Photo by the author.*

A view of Miami while Olive and her children lived there. *Courtesy Roberts County Museum, Miami.*

By the early 1920s Dora and Emmett Coble had moved to Clayton, New Mexico, where she taught school and he became chief of police. Edna ventured to Clayton, where she lived for a time with Dora and Emmett and held a job in the business district. Olive Virginia, the youngest daughter, took a four-year course in nursing at Northwest Texas Hospital in Amarillo.[18]

The highlight of Olive's years at Miami came in 1923. She decided to visit her mother for the first time in two decades. Thanks to Drew, Olive had access to railroad passes on the Santa Fe system. Olive's mother, Mary Jane Blankenship King, was eighty-nine and blind. Olive and twelve-year-old Hugh traveled by rail to Virginia.

Olive told her mother detail after detail about her seven children and the sons-in-law who had married into the family and the grandchildren who were starting to arrive. And from her mother Olive heard about her siblings who lived nearby. It was a timely visit, because Mary Jane passed away the next year.[19]

Before leaving the East, Olive and Hugh visited Washington, D.C. Olive wanted her son to see the nation's capitol, but she had another purpose. She wanted to meet and interview Lt. Gen. Nelson A. Miles, Billy Dixon's commander during the Red River War and the man responsible for Billy's Medal of Honor.

Following a magnificent, although sometimes controversial, military career that began with Civil War combat, Lieutenant

General Miles reached the mandatory retirement age of sixty-four in 1903. By 1923, when Olive visited his apartment at the Rochambeau Hotel, General Miles was eighty-three. He was widowed, but he was physically and mentally active.[20]

Olive had arranged to stay with a friend from Texas, Mrs. Alice Cunningham. On the day that Olive visited General Miles, she was accompanied by Hugh and by a daughter of Mrs. Cunningham. General Miles was an impressive

In 1923 Olive and Hugh traveled by rail from Miami to her old home in Virginia. *Courtesy Roberts County Museum, Miami.*

Olive with Jim and Edith Cator. The Cator brothers, Jim and Bob, traced back with Billy Dixon to buffalo hunting days around Adobe Walls. *Courtesy Panhandle-Plains Historical Museum, Canyon, Texas*

man and one of the most important American military figures who was still alive. He greeted Olive with great courtesy, and he gave her a copy of his autobiographical *Personal Recollections*, which included his account of the Red River War. General Miles also composed in longhand generous remarks about Billy Dixon:

Washington, D.C.
July 10, 1923
My dear Mrs. Dixon:

I take pleasure in stating that your husband, Mr. William Dixon, was one of the heroes of the serious and very important engagements at the Adobe Walls, June 27, 1874, and the Buffalo Wallow fight of Sept. 12, 1874. That he was one of the leaders of those engagements and his heroic acts most commendable.

In changing wild and barbaric country to peaceful civil settlement, he was like the Daniel Boones and Kit Carsons of a former period, and whose surroundings were even more desperate and whose deeds of valor more conspicuous.

Very sincerely,
Nelson A. Miles
Lt. General U.S. Army[22]

Billy Dixon could have received no higher personal compliment than to be compared by General Miles to Daniel Boone and Kit Carson.

Olive's visit with General Miles was a key inspiration in her development as an important, produc-

During her trip to the East, Olive visited Gen. Nelson A. Miles in Washington, D.C. *Courtesy National Archives.*

tive historian. By the time of their of their meeting, Olive already had made significant strides as a chronicler of the past of the Texas Panhandle. Somehow she had managed to raise her children, despite straitened circumstances, and now she could focus on the activity that would become her passion. Olive Dixon was en route to becoming a foremost historian of the Texas Panhandle.

Chapter Fifteen

Panhandle Historian

*The one woman who seemed to make it her business
to keep alive public interest in the past was Mrs. Olive K. Dixon . . .*

Joseph A. Hill
Founder of the Panhandle-Plains
Historical Society

Dr. C.L. Somnichsen came to Texas in 1931 as an English professor at the Texas College of Mines and Metallurgy, later the University of Texas at El Paso. Doc, as his friends and colleagues called him, had an Ivy League education, earning M.A. and Ph.D. degrees from Harvard. But in Texas he became an avid researcher and writer on blood feuds. With every project he was helped by locals who knew a great deal and shared it with him. They were grassroots historians, and with his classical education Doc whimsically coined a Latin phrase to classify them: *genus historianus herbidus.*[1]

Olive Dixon was a resourceful and determined grassroots historian, a distinguished member of *genus historianus herbidus.* Olive was not a college-trained historian. But when she came to Texas as a young woman, the lonely, windswept Panhandle was one of the few remaining frontiers in the American West. She married an authentic and widely recognized hero of the Panhandle. Olive and Billy raised their family at historic Adobe Walls, at a newly-created county seat town, and at one of the 160-acre homesteads that created more than one million farms throughout the West. At each of these three homes Olive conducted her household work under the primitive conditions experienced by every pioneer wife and mother.

Even though Olive was perpetually busy and hard-working, she embraced the opportunity to systematically record the adventures of Billy Dixon. A sense of history had been instilled during her childhood, and now she had a project worthy of any grassroots historian. She put together a fascinating account of the life of a frontier hero, and in the wake of Billy's death she was determined to produce a book. Despite a $500 fee that was daunting to a widow with seven children and almost no income, Olive borrowed the money at high interest. In 1914 the *Life of "Billy" Dixon* was published — an enormous achievement for a budding grassroots historian.

Olive received widespread praise for the book from aging Panhandle pioneers, from history professors, from editors. Professor James B. Thoburn of the University of Oklahoma wrote a lengthy evaluation to Olive. "Posterity will always owe you a debt of gratitude for your persistence in persuading your husband to tell his life story for publication," he emphasized. "So much valuable historical material of this class has been lost in the West because the story of a man's life was permitted to die with him."

A Chicago editor, William M. Camp, wrote an echo of this praise: "Permit me to say that your husband and yourself have written a book that your posterity may be proud of." The fame of the book spread, and in 1927 P.L. Turner Company of Dallas published a "revised edition." An excellent preface is proudly signed by Olive as "The Author." Professor Thoburn provided an introduction with the conclusion: "It is a plain story, simply told, with no effort at embellishment, though such a story needs no embellishment. The historical literature of the Great Plains is enriched by such a contribution."[2]

Olive did not wait on the publication of the revised edition to continue her activities as *historianus herbidus*. With a growing set of acquaintances among men and women who shared her passion for the Texas Panhandle, Olive was among the founders of the Panhandle-Plains Historical Society and the Panhandle-Plains Historical Museum. This highly important historical development had its beginning early in 1921 on the campus of West Texas Normal School for teachers in Canyon. Joseph A. Hill was the first chair of the WTNSC history department, before serving as president of the college for thirty years, 1918 - 1948. On February 21, 1921, on the campus of WTNSC, President Hill led nine faculty members and thirty students in organizing the Panhandle-Plains Historical Society. The first president was Lester F. Sheffy, who had succeeded President Hill as chair of the history department.[3]

There was considerable interest among members of the Panhandle Old Settlers Association as well as non-members from the not-so-distant pioneer period. Olive Dixon was one of the most enthusiastic of those who wanted to expand membership of the Panhandle-Plains Historical Society beyond the WTNSC campus. One year after the organizational meeting, on February 24, 1922, the Society met to enlist new members and elect a new slate of officers. Olive Dixon was elected second vice president. A year later, the Panhandle-Plains Historical Society incorporated. Olive was re-elected second vice president and she was elected to the board, positions she would retain for the next several years. After his first meeting with her, President Hill reported that "Mrs. Olive K. Dixon of Miami had expressed interest in what the Society was trying to do and provided help" — an understatement, as her actions soon proved.[4]

For years Olive had dreamed of placing monuments at the Adobe Walls Battlefield and at the site of the Buffalo Wallow Fight, and she recognized the Panhandle-Plains Historical Society as an organization through which these goals could be achieved. At the 1922 Society meeting a member suggested that a fiftieth anniversary celebration of the Battle of Adobe Walls should be staged on June 27, 1924.

The 1923 meeting of the Society was held at the Turkey Track Ranch headquarters, just over a mile from the battlefield. Olive, recently returned from her visit to see her mother and General Miles, was disappointed to learn that little had been done toward organizing the celebration, now only one year away. But Olive already had brought to the Society "quite a collection of their own relics." She was able to report that citizens in "Pampa, Panhandle, Canadian, and Spearman were greatly interested" in the project. Inevitably, President Hill was able to report that "Mrs. Dixon was appointed chairman of a committee to work out a program for the anticipated celebration at Adobe Walls . . ."[5]

Olive also was unanimously appointed treasurer of the finance committee to raise money for a suitable monument at Adobe Walls. Pampa Mayor F.P. Reid, Mrs. Tom Coble of the Turkey Track Panch, and Judge Thomas Turner of Amarillo, now the Society president, were other members of the committee. Seventy-five dollars was donated at the meeting.

At Canadian Olive raised eighty-five dollars; at Higgins thirty-five dollars was collected; at Perryton two hundred dollars was donated. She was stopped on the street in Miami and a rancher handed her five dollars. Area newspapers solicited contributions of "any amount from fifty-cents up, to the monument fund."

Donations were mailed in from New York City and Los Angeles and points in between. The account Olive opened at the First National Bank of Miami soon

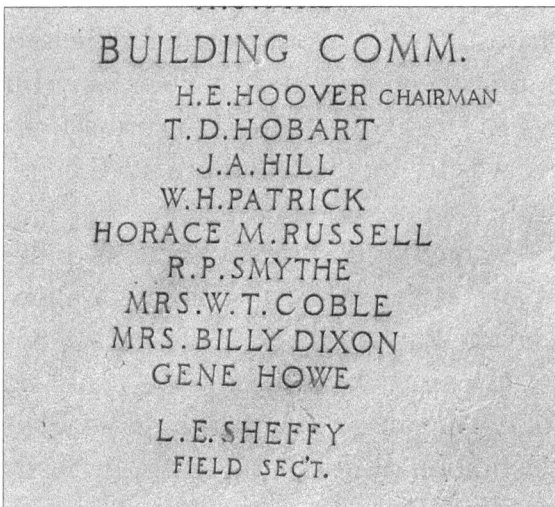

BUILDING COMM.
H.E.HOOVER CHAIRMAN
T.D.HOBART
J.A.HILL
W.H.PATRICK
HORACE M.RUSSELL
R.P.SMYTHE
MRS.W.T.COBLE
MRS.BILLY DIXON
GENE HOWE

L.E.SHEFFY
FIELD SEC'T.

The list of Building Committee Members, engraved beside the Museum entrance, includes "Mrs. Billy Dixon." *Photo by the author.*

reached one thousand dollars. Another key contribution was announced by Mrs. Tom Coble, who with her husband agreed that the Turkey Track would donate to the Society a five-acre tract centered on the old Adobe Walls community.[6]

On June 27, 1924, a great many men, women, and children gathered at Adobe Walls. A large number of them arrived the previous day. There was a picnic supper and barbecue, featuring several barbecued beeves. Turkey Track bunkhouses were filled, and multiple campfires marked the campsites of other celebrants. The next day the big red granite monument was unveiled, with names of the defenders engraved in the order in which Billy Dixon had dictated them to Olive. Provided by the Osgood Monument Company of Amarillo, the handsome marker was placed at the north end of the site of the Rath and Company Store, which was the southernmost building at Adobe Walls.[7]

Following the success of the Adobe Walls monument cel-

The 50th Anniversary of the Battle of Adobe Walls, June 27, 1924, was a major historical activity of the Texas Panhandle. Attendees have gathered around the new monument. *Courtesy Panhandle-Plains Historical Museum, Canyon, Texas.*

Closeup of the Adobe Walls marker, photographed during a 2015 field trip of 200 members of the Wild West History Association. *Photo by the author.*

ebration, the Panhandle-Plains Historical Society soon launched a campaign to memorialize the Buffalo Wallow Fight. Olive, of course, played a leading role, but there was widespread assistance. The precise site of the battle was determined, and one acre of land was deeded to the Society by the owner.

The Canadian Chamber of Commerce pressed a case for placing the monument in their town rather than at the remote site twenty-two miles to the south. Olive was offended, along with other members of the Society, and the idea was dropped. The effort took three years, but in time $600 was deposited in

Olive Dixon at the unveiling of the Buffalo Wallow monument. *Courtesy Haley Memorial Library, JEH-H-40.1.*

the Miami bank account. The Osgood Monument Company went to work on another granite marker. An additional $200 was needed to set the marker in concrete. Society President T.O. Hobart, a land dealer from Pampa, invited Olive to come over from Miami with the assurance that she could raise the money in one day. On that day Hobart wrote a check for twenty-five dollars, then sent an employee around town with Olive. By the end of the day the $200 goal was met.[8]

The crowd at the Buffalo Wallow monument unveiling was not large. A few people made short remarks, and Olive offered words of thanks. The marker and the base were just over five feet in height:

> BUFFALO WALLOW BATTLEGROUND
> Here on September 12th, 1874, two scouts and four sol-
> diers defeated 125 Kiowa and Comanche Indians.
> Scouts:
> > William Dixon
> > Amos Chapman
> Soldiers:
> > Sergeant H.D. Woodall, Co. I
> > Peter Rath, Co. A
> > John Harrington, Co. H
> > George W. Smith, Co. M 6th Cavalry
> > Stand Silent! Heroes Here Have Been
> > Who Cleared the Way for Other Men
> Erected by the Panhandle-Plains Historical
> Society, September 12th, 1925
> This site marker under direction of
> J.J. Long, Mobeetie, Texas
> Mrs. William Dixon, Miami, Texas

Olive wrote a lengthy newspaper article about the Buffalo Wallow Fight and the commemoration, and she titled the piece after the sentiment on the marker: "Stand Silent! Heroes Here

Have Been."[9]

When Joseph A. Hill, founder of the Panhandle-Plains Historical Society, wrote a history of the Society in 1955, early in the
book he paid tribute to Olive. "The one woman who seemed to
make it her business to keep alive public interest in the past was
Mrs. Olive K. Dixon, widow of Billy Dixon, hero of the Adobe
Walls fight of 1874 and also a participant in the Buffalo Wallow
skirmish a few months later. Working with old settlers at Canadian, Miami, Pampa, Amarillo, and other places, Mrs. Dixon
determined . . . that both these battlegrounds . . . should be giv-
en appropriate permanent markers. Later she saw her dreams
come true under the sponsorship of the Panhandle-Plains Historical Society . . ."[10]

As her skill at accomplishing historical projects became ap-
parent, Olive began to be encouraged — especially by citizens
of Hutchinson County — to rebury Billy at Adobe Walls. Ulti-
mately it was offered to remove him from the Texline Cemetery,
transport him to Adobe Walls, and rebury him at no expense to
the family. Olive gave her consent, and plans began to be made

The gravestone marking the site of the 1929 reburial of "William Dixon." *Photo by the author.*

for a reburial ceremony for "Col. Billy Dixon" (an honorary title
— he was never a colonel of anything) on June 27, 1929. Military honors would be part of the reburial, which would involve
a steel vault. The grave would be marked with a monument
that read simply: "William Dixon, 1850 - 1913" with a Masonic
emblem engraved between the dates. Borger Scoutmaster J.D.
Miller planned to bring a large contingent of Boy Scouts. On
Thursday, June 27, a police escort led a long caravan of auto-
mobiles and Billy's remains. Along the way through Dalhart
and Dumas and Stinnett men stood and removed their hats.
Judge H.E. Hoover of Canadian presided at the gravesite. As
airplanes flew above Adobe Walls, a volley was fired into the
air and "Taps" was played as a flag was raised. A large crowd
included old-timers from the Panhandle's pioneer days. Scoutmaster Miller remarked on "what the historic importance will
mean [to the Scouts] in their development as loyal Texans and
as good citizens generally."

Sixty-three years later, in 1992, Billy's gravesite was en-
hanced by a marker with a Medal of Honor plaque. Below the
Medal of Honor symbol, the plaque reads:

WILLIAM DIXON
MEDAL OF HONOR
INDIAN SCOUT 6 US CAV
INDIAN WARS
SEP 25 1850   MARCH 9 1913

Billy's Medal long has been on display in the Panhandle-Plains Historical Society Museum in Canyon.

With her historical instincts unleashed, Olive began traveling to appealing events. In 1926 she went to Montana for the
fiftieth anniversary at the Custer Battlefield. During the 1920s
she was an attendee at the Indian Fair at Craterville Park near
Lawton, Oklahoma, where she met venerable warriors who
claimed to have fought at Adobe Walls. Olive visited Dodge

In 1992 a Medal of Honor marker was added to Billy Dixon's gravesite. *Photo by the author.*

City on several occasions, most notably at the 1947 Diamond Jubilee of the famous cattle town. Also in Kansas in 1947 she participated in the eightieth anniversary of the Medicine Lodge Treaty, which young Billy Dixon had witnessed as a military teamster. A highlight of 1947 was the twenty-first anniversary of Borger, a prosperous Hutchinson County oil boomtown. Olive was recognized as the earliest settler of the county and she was asked to deliver the keynote address of the event. She also helped write the script for a radio drama about the Battle of Adobe Walls.[12]

Olive found herself in demand as a public speaker because she was an authority on Panhandle history. The Texas Folklore Society, meeting in Austin in 1927, featured a program by Mrs. Billy Dixon on "The Legend of Adobe Walls." During this trip she was introduced to Governor Dan Moody.

In 1938, during the Golden Anniversary celebration of Amarillo, she was presented to a crowd alongside the First Lady of the United States, Eleanor Roosevelt. In earlier years Olive met Quanah Parker, General Nelson Miles, and Charles Good-

Olive on one of her historical trips to Dodge City.
Courtesy Panhandle-Plains Historical Museum, Canyon, Texas.

night. Indeed, one of her first tasks with the Panhandle-Plains Historical Society was to interview legendary cattleman Charles Goodnight. In company with Fay Lockhart, secretary of WTNSC President J.A. Hill, Olive visited Goodnight and began asking historical questions. But when the irascible old rancher saw Fay Lockhart taking notes, he growled at her to "Put up that damn paper and pencil or I won't say a word."

Olive realized that she could not bring out the best in Goodnight, and she recommended that a man should handle his interview. J. Evetts Haley agreed to work with Goodnight, who responded with numerous donations of artifacts to the society, and the two men collaborated on a classic biography, *Charles Goodnight, Cowman and Plainsman.*[13]

A large part of Olive's reputation as a historian stemmed from her biography of Billy Dixon. Although she never wrote another book, Olive penned a great many historical articles and stories for newspapers and magazines. While living in Miami she began writing historical pieces for the local newspaper, the *Miami Chief.* The *Canadian Record* picked up some of her articles, and so did the *Paducah Post.* In time the *Fort Worth Star Tele-*

gram ran her work, and so did the *Lubbock Avalanche*, the *Kansas City Star*, the *Amarillo Globe*, the *Amarillo News* and *Hutchinson County Herald*. Olive sold her writing at space rates — so much per column inch — and she sent items to the Associated Press. The popular magazine *Ranch Romances* twice bought historical stories from Olive.

Late in 1929, not long after the reburial of Billy at Adobe Walls, Olive moved from Miami to Amarillo. Her children all had finished school, and she would be much closer to Canyon, home of the Panhandle-Plains Historical Society. Amarillo began to develop in the late 1880s, and by 1900 it was one of the largest cattle shipping points in the nation.

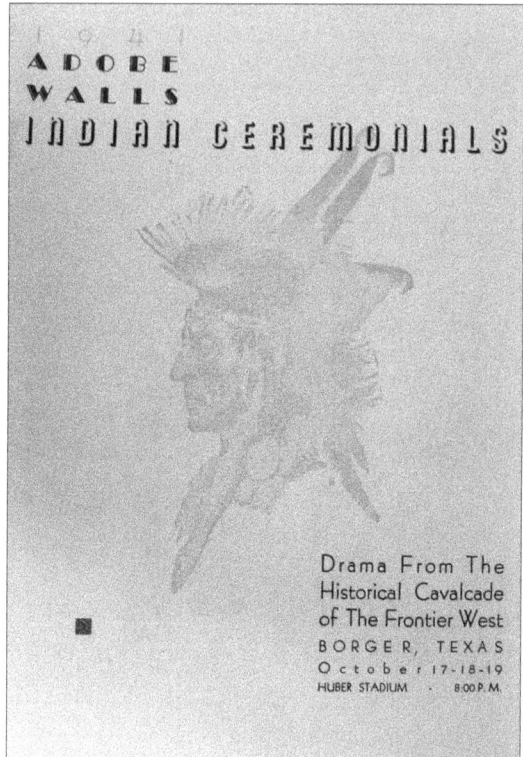

Program for the 1941 "Indian Ceremonials" at Adobe Walls, which featured the placement of a large marker honoring warrior casualties. *Courtesy Panhandle-Plains Historical Museum, Canyon, Texas.*

Oil, natural gas and helium were discovered in the region. The Amarillo Helium Plant was the only commercial producer of helium in the world. There was a major stockyard complex, soaring downtown hotels, and a growing population of more than 43,000.[14]

Shortly after settling in Amarillo, Olive secured a part-time position as a staff writer at the *Globe-News*. In 1937 she was promoted to a salaried position, complete with a desk and a typewriter. The following year Olive was given major responsibili-

The marker commemorating the Indian participation at Adobe Walls. *Photo by the author*

ties in producing the big *Golden Anniversary Edition* of the *Globe-News*, which featured the history and heritage of the city and the region. She also wrote short social pieces, describing children's play parties and birthday celebrations.[15]

On April 10, 1931, at the annual meeting of the Panhandle-Plains Historical Society, the principal topic of business was the construction of a permanent museum facility. A great many artifacts had been donated to the society, including important collections from Charles Goodnight and Olive Dixon. L.F. Sheffy had been busy for years as field secretary, soliciting items from pioneer families throughout the Panhandle. Olive was one of nine members appointed to the Building Committee; the only other female member was Mrs. W.T. Coble.

Despite the onset of the Great Depression, progress was rapid and the structure began to take shape on the southwest corner of the WTNSC campus. On Texas Independence Day, March 2, 1932, Olive attended the meeting for the final fund drive. The building was completed before the year was out, and the official opening was on April 13, 1933. Olive's name is engraved beside the entrance with the other committee members.[16]

The new public facility advertised itself as the "Museum of the Pioneer." This theme was at the heart of Olive's historical

Board meeting of the Panhandle-Plains Historical Society. Olive is seated in the rear, fourth from left. *Courtesy Panhandle-Plains Historical Museum, Canyon, Texas.*

The Panhandle-Plains Historical Museum opened in 1933. *Photo by the author.*

work. Her book, *Life of "Billy" Dixon: Plainsman, Scout and Pioneer*, related the adventures, deeds of valor, and daily hardships of perhaps the most notable hero of the Panhandle frontier. Olive's newspaper articles relived Billy's exploits and those of other pioneers who had performed bold and courageous deeds. Her outstanding work on behalf of the Panhandle-Plains Historical Society and its "Museum of the Pioneer" was a reflection of her personal interests and experiences - not only did he marry a renowned pioneer, Olive herself was a pioneer woman, and so were the men and women and children that she interacted with during the 1890s and the early 1900s.

The talks and programs that she was called on to present centered on the same frontier themes. In the spring of 1942 she enrolled in a Wednesday evening class taught by Dr. L.R. Sheffy on the campus of what was now called West Texas State Teach-

Olive at her typewriter in the office of the *Amarillo Globe-News. Courtesy Panhandle-Plains Historical Museum, Canyon, Texas.*

ers College. It was the first college work she had ever taken. Of
course, Dr. Sheffy realized that in Olive Dixon he had an incomparable classroom asset, and he assigned her to deliver "talks"
to the other students, while submitting typescripts of her pre-
sentations. "Talk No. 1" was on "Adobe Walls," and "Talk No.
2" was about "Thanksgiving on the Panhandle Plains 1893."
Olive was taped talking about the "Adobe Walls Battle"; she
speaks with quiet command of the subject, and her voice and
enunciation still carry the distinctive lilt of Virginia. There is
a typescript on "Pioneer Churches," as well as a fifteen-page
manuscript entitled "Reminiscences of a Pioneer."[17]

In the final paragraph of "Reminiscences of a Pioneer," Olive
indirectly stated her basic theme as an historian. "Many hardships and experiences have been endured and mastered since I
came to this country but never for a day have I regretted that I
came. I am thankful to a kind Providence that has allowed me
to have had the experiences I have had in this part of the state
that has been my home for forty-five years. I do not look upon
my life on the frontier as a hardship but a blessed privilege of
having some small part in the building of the glorious Panhandle Country that we have today."[18]

Throughout her historical work, Olive honored the pioneer
spirit that conquered a wilderness — the Panhandle country of
her young adulthood, and the larger Plains area of Billy's youth
and early manhood. In a number of ways — a fine biography,
a great many newspaper articles, numerous public addresses,
an excellent historical society, and an outstanding museum —
Olive Dixon celebrated the men and women who mastered a
hostile environment and who played their part in the Westward
Expansion of America. It was a story of violence and triumph,
of hardship and sacrifice. It was the story of Billy and Olive
Dixon, and for the latter half of her life she endeavored to tell it,
to present it by every means at her disposal.

During World War II the descendants of Billy and Olive

Two of the four German sisters, who were captured by a Cheyenne war party in 1874 and later were rescued by the army, returned to the Texas Panhandle in 1928. Adelaide German Andrews and Sophia German Feldman, both seated, were en route to California to visit another sister when they stopped at the Hemphill County ranch of T.D. Hobart. Hobart stands third from right, while Olive Dixon stands at far right. *Courtesy Haley Memorial Library, JEH-H-51.1.*

Olive pictured with the two German sisters in 1928. *Courtesy Haley Memorial Library, JEH-H-51.07.*

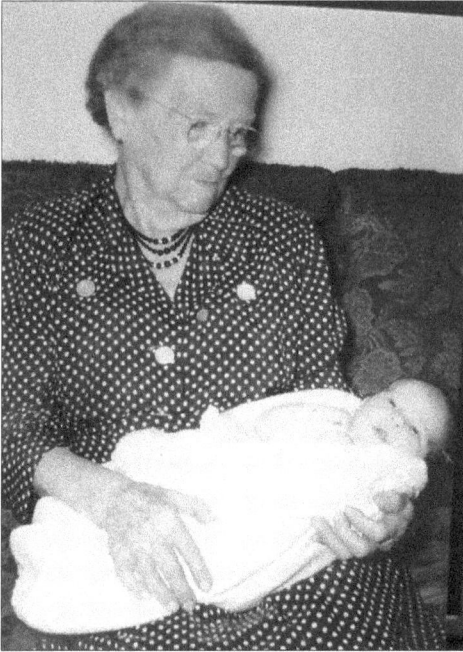

Olive with her first great-grandchild, Michael
Glenn McKee. *Courtesy Virginia Irwin Maynard.*

Dixon carried on the family military tradition. Sons Archie and Hugh Dixon entered the army and navy, respectively. Archie fought in the European theater, while Hugh served on a destroyer. Grandson Clifford Coble became an Air Force captain and later graduated from West Point. Another grandson, William Drew Dixon, Jr., enlisted in the army as a teenager, quickly earned sergeant's stripes, and remained in the service as a career man. Three other grandsons, Harold and Lloyd McKee and Bill Irwin, each entered naval officer training programs, were commissioned as ensigns, and won promotion to lieutenant junior grade.[19]

Two sons and five grandsons. Billy Dixon, army scout of the Indian Wars, would have been proud, and so would Olive's great-great-grandfather, Gen. Andrew Lewis. Olive took deep pride in her sons and grandsons, and, of course, she was relieved that all of these young men survived the war. It should be mentioned that her first grandson, William Emmett Coble, died in 1931 at the age of thirteen of Rocky Mountain fever. In 1947 Olive's first great-grandson, Michael Glenn McKee, was born.[20] The baby's grandmother was Bobbie Dixon McKee, Olive's second-born.

Edna Dixon Irwin's husband, Walter, was the general claim agent for the Santa Fe Railroad in Amarillo. The Irwins had three children, Bill, Olive Virginia, and Kathryn. Olive Virginia, like her aunt, was named after her grandmother and her grandmother's native state (which also was Billy's native state at the time of his birth, in 1850). Olive Virginia, always known as Virginia, called her grandmother "Ama." Ama was deeply pleased when Virginia named her third child, a boy, Thomas Dixon.[21]

Living in Amarillo, Edna conscientiously attended her mother. Olive went out to eat with the Irwin family, she went to church with them, and she was visited by Edna. Olive lived in apartment houses close to downtown, and she walked daily to the newspaper office. Shortly after moving to Amarillo, Olive became a member of the Polk Street Methodist Church. The congregation had recently moved into a large, impressive new sanctuary, and Olive — a lifelong Methodist — enjoyed a rich church life at Polk Street Methodist for more than a quarter of a century.[22]

Bobbie Dixon McKee and her family also lived in Amarillo, and so did brother Drew, following a period in California. Archie wound up in Amarillo, but Olive Virginia Dixon Ragan spent her life nursing in San Angelo, and Hugh lived in Ore-

Olive joined the Polk Street Methodist Church soon after moving to Amarillo. *Photo by the author.*

gon. During Thanksgiving in 1934, Olive requested that every-one spend the holiday with her. On Thursday, November 29, a family photo was taken, Olive standing with all seven of her handsome, well-dressed children. Another photo was snapped of Olive with nine fine-looking grandchildren of all ages. Clifford Dixon Coble of Clayton is proudly wearing his "C" letter sweater.

Olive was an active member of the Panhandle Penwomen's Association, the Eastern Star, the Daughters of the American Revolution, the United Daughters of the Confederacy, and the Methodist Missionary Society.[23] At the newspaper office she socialized with other journalists, most notably John L. McCarty, who was editor of the *Amarillo Globe-News*. McCarty also was a director of the Panhandle-Plains Historical Society, and he eagerly interviewed early Panhandle settlers, including Ol-

Olive and her biographer, John L. McCarty, signing copies of *Adobe Walls Bride* in 1947. *Courtesy Panhandle-Plains Historical Museum, Canyon, Texas.*

ive Dixon. A member of the Texas Institute of Letters, his books included *Maverick Town*, a highly enjoyable account of old Tascosa.

McCarty and Olive began to develop a biography that would be titled *Adobe Walls Bride, The Story of Billy and Olive Dixon*. McCarty began interviewing Olive in the 1940s. He worked hard on his chapter outlines, and *Adobe Walls Bride* was published by The Naylor Company of San Antonio in 1955. The first printing was released in September 1955, and a second printing came out just four months later, in January 1956. Olive was in her eighty-third year, but she happily autographed books at signings. *Adobe Walls Bride* was illustrated by a gifted native of the Panhandle, Harold Dow Bugbee, and it is an especially rich source about Olive's life.[24]

In a newspaper article about Olive entitled "Scout's Wife," she modestly — too modestly — summed up her accomplishments: "Mrs. Dixon declares that all she ever did worth mentioning was to marry Billy Dixon, rear [seven] of his children (one dying in infancy) and try to keep a record of his bravery and service to his country."[25]

She certainly achieved the goal of keeping a record of Billy's bravery and service to his country. He hardly would be as well-known to subsequent generations without her efforts on his behalf — Olive was the same perpetuating force to Billy Dixon's reputation as Libby Custer was to her husband. But Olive's efforts as a grassroots historian went far beyond the life of her husband or of herself. She was a most productive *historianus herbidus* from 1913, when she began recording Billy's adventures, until the end of her life in 1956 — more than four decades of prolific activities in her beloved Texas Panhandle.

On Saturday evening, March 17, 1956, Olive went out with Edna and Walter Irwin to eat barbecue. "Ama loved ice cream," related her granddaughter, Virginia Irwin Maynard. So the group visited Heap o' Cream, a popular ice cream parlor. Afterward, while driving back to Olive's apartment, she sighed and her head dropped onto Edna's shoulder. Walter raced to the hospital, but Olive had died of a heart attack.[26] She was eighty-three. Olive Dixon had been a widow for forty-three years, and she had resided in Amarillo for twenty-seven years — the longest she ever had lived anywhere. On March 20 she was interred in Amarillo's Llano Cemetery, where Edna and Walter later were buried beside her.

A "Tribute to a Lady" appeared in the *Amarillo Daily News* shortly after Olive passed away. "There are so few left who can really remember when the whir of wild turkey wings was a hum on the river breaks," the *Tribute* began. "There are so few left who really knew the awesome wildness of the range country, and the little communities of men and women who were pioneering a wide and not too friendly country, who could remember the thrill of the first piano in the first parlor of a brand new town . . ."

Finally, the writer pointed out that such a woman was Olive Dixon. "She was typical of the women who really brought civilization to the frontier . . . She raised children to sturdy manhood and womanhood. She taught school. She planted trees and flowers. She added to the stream of culture by laboriously gathering the stories of the men who were there at the beginning, the folklore as well as the fact, and set them down for others to read."[27]

The *Tribute* connected Olive's beginnings to her presence in the newsroom. "She remained to the last breath of her life exactly what she was at the beginning — a Virginia gentlewoman whose business was womanly business: making a home; raising a family; paying decent homage to the continuity of human affairs by keeping the records of her generation for those who come a little after; jerking up the younger generation from time to time on their manners and morals. (You see, we were under her somewhat strict eye here in *The Daily News* city room, and

At Thanksgiving in 1934 Olive posed with her seven children. Back row, L to R: Archie, Olive, Hugh, Drew. Front row, L to R: Edna Irwin, Bobbie McKee, Olive Virginia Ragan, Dora Coble. *Through permission of Virginia Irwin Maynard.*

we toed the mark of certain civilities that Virginia gentlewomen take for granted.)"

The *Tribute* made it clear that for Mrs. Dixon "every day [was] a blessing and source of sheer enjoyment. She was making plans on the day of her death for the annual luncheon attended by Spelling Bee champions of the Golden Spread, where as usual she would tell the youth of that first schoolhouse where she taught in what is now Hutchinson County."

During her first important historical project, the recording of Billy's frontier adventures, Olive copied down a conclusive statement he made that was placed on the final page of their book. "Gladly would I live it all over again, such is my cast of mind and my hunger for the freedom of the big wide places. I would run the risks and endure all the hardships . . . just for the contentment and freedom to be found in such an outdoor life.

Olive was interred at Amarillo's Llano Cemetery. *Photo by the author.*

I should be unspeakably happy once more to feast on buffalo meat and other wild game cooked on a camp-fire, to eat sour dough biscuit and drink black coffee from a quart tin cup."[28]

"Gladly would I live it all over again," said Billy. During the long years of her widowhood Olive recounted Billy's early exploits to readers of history and biography, to newspaper readers, to audiences interested in listening to history topics. Such audiences and readers sometimes were exposed to Olive's own pioneer life, and so were schoolchildren who heard about her days teaching five students in a one-room log school. And as the years passed she adopted the same view as her husband. Despite the hardships and struggles of her life, Olive emphatically stated to an audience:[29]

"Gladly would I live it all over again."

Endnotes

I wanted to use as many quotes as possible from Billy and Olive Dixon, in order to achieve an immediacy that is difficult to obtain from a nineteenth-century subject. The principal source of first-person statements from Billy Dixon is the book on which he and Olive collaborated: *Life of "Billy" Dixon, Plainsman, Scout and Pioneer*. Although published in 1914, a revised edition was released in 1927, with various minor changes. I decided to use the 1927 edition, because copies are more readily available. In the Endnotes the abbreviated reference is to *"Billy" Dixon*, from the *Frontier Classics Library*. Regarding Olive Dixon, there is a biography by John L. McCarty, *Adobe Walls Bride, The Story of Billy and Olive Dixon*, published in 1955. Olive also wrote a first-person Preface to Billy's biography, and she penned a great many newspaper articles.

Notes to Chapter 1

1. Dixon, *Reminiscences of a Pioneer*, 1,2,4; and McCarty, *Adobe Walls Bride*, 109.

2. McCarty, *Adobe Walls Bride*, 136-138.

3. *Ibid*, 152-158.

4. *Ibid*, 152-158.

5. *Ibid*, 168-170.

6. Dixon, *Reminiscences of a Pioneer*, 4, 8.

7. Dixon, *Reminiscences of a Pioneer*, 22; and Dixon, *"Billy" Dixon*, 250.

8. Dixon, *Reminiscences of a Pioneer*, 12.

9. Dixon, *Adobe Walls*, 2.

10. McCarty, File, Outline p. 2

Notes to Chapter 2

1. Dixon, *Life and Adventures of "Billy" Dixon*, 7.

2. William R. Dixon, Ancestry; and Nancy Privett Dixon, Ancestry.

3. William R. Dixon, Ancestry.

4. Dixon, *"Billy" Dixon*, 8.

5. O'Neal, *Fighting Men of the Indian Wars*, 51-53, 76.

6. Dixon, *"Billy" Dixon*, 8.

7. *Ibid*, 8.

8. *Ibid*, *"Billy" Dixon*, 9.

9. McCarty, *Adobe Walls Bride*, 146.

10. Dixon, *"Billy" Dixon*, 9.

11. *Ibid*, 9-10.

12. Nevin, *The Expressmen*, 53.

13. Dixon, *"Billy" Dixon*, 11.

14. *Ibid*, 15.

15. *Ibid*, 15-16.

16. *Ibid*, 16-17.

17. *Ibid*, 17-18.

18. *Ibid*, 20-21.

19. *Ibid*, 22.

20. *Ibid*, 23-24.

21. *Ibid*, 26-27.

22. *Ibid*, 24-25.

23. *Ibid*, 26-27.

24. Collins, *Jim Lane: Scoundrel, Statesman, Kansan*, 275; and *Dixon, "Billy" Dixon*, 28-29.

25. Dixon, *"Billy" Dixon*, 28.

26. *Ibid*, 30.

27. *Ibid*, 30-31.

Notes to Chapter 3

1. Dixon, *"Billy" Dixon*, 32.

2. *Ibid*, 32.

3. *Ibid*, 33.

4. Nevin, *The Expressmen*, 59-60.

5. Dixon, *"Billy" Dixon*, 34-35.

6. Yost, *Medicine Lodge*, 22-35.

7. Dixon, *"Billy" Dixon*, 36.

8. Yost, *Medicine Lodge*, 25-26.

9. Dixon, *"Billy" Dixon*, 37-38.

10. *Ibid*, 51.

11. Billington, *Westward Expansion*, 661-662. Also see Utley, *Frontier Regulars*, 135-144.

12. Dixon, *"Billy" Dixon*, 51-52.

13. *Ibid*, 53.

14. *Ibid*, 53-55.

15. *Ibid*, 54.

16. *Ibid*, 55.

17. *Ibid*, 56.

18. *Ibid*, 57-58.

19. *Ibid*, 58.

20. Hart, *Old Forts of the Southwest*, 152-154.

21. O'Neal, *Fighting Men of the Indian Wars*, 104-105.

22. Dixon, *"Billy" Dixon*, 59.

23. *Ibid*, 59-60.

24. *Ibid*, 60.

Notes to Chapter 4

1. "Lewis, Andrew." *Dictionary of American Biography*; Jeter, "Andrew Lewis." *The West Virginia Encyclopedia*, December 7, 2015; Heitman, *Historical Register and Dictionary of the U.S. Army, Vol. I*, 630.

2. McCarty, *Adobe Walls Bride*, 76.

3. Olive Dixon, Interview by McCarty, July 10, 1946.

4. Olive Dixon, Interview by McCarty, July 10, 1946.

5. McCarty, *Adobe Walls Bride*, 79-80.

6. *Ibid*, 80.

7. *Ibid*, 81.

8. *Ibid*, 82-86.

9. Olive Dixon, Interview by McCarty, July 10, 1946.

10. McCarty, *Adobe Walls Bride*, 93-94.

11. "International Cotton Exposition," Wikipedia; "Piedmont Exposition," Wikipedia; "Cotton States and International Exposition," Wikipedia.

12. McCarty, *Adobe Walls Bride*, 95-96.

13. Olive Dixon, "Pioneer Churches," Typescript. Panhandle-Plains Museum Research Center.

14. McCarty, *Adobe Walls Bride*, 96.

15. *Ibid*, 97-98.

16. Olive Dixon, Interview by McCarty, July 10, 1946.

17. McCarty, *Adobe Walls Bride*, 103-104.

18. *Ibid*, 104-105.

19. *Ibid*, 105-106.

Notes to Chapter 5

1. Dixon, *"Billy" Dixon*, 60.

2. *Ibid*, 60-61.

3. *Ibid*, 61.

4. Capps, *The Indians*, 62, 74-75, 112-113, 167.

5. Dixon, *"Billy" Dixon*, 62.

6. *Ibid*, 62-63.

7. *Ibid*, 63-64.

8. *Ibid*, 64.

9. *Ibid*, 64-65.

10. *Ibid*, 69-70.

11. *Ibid*, 70.

12. *Ibid*, 71.

13. *Ibid*, 72.

14. *Ibid*, 73-74.

15. *New York Times*, October 30, 1867, cited in Carlson, *West Texas*, 4.

16. Dixon, *"Billy" Dixon*, 74-75.

17. Caravaglia and Worman, *Firearms of the American West*, 141-158; Worman, *Gunsmoke and Saddle Leather*, 277-299; Boorman, *Guns of the Old West*, 44-49; Walter, *Guns That Won the West*, 11, 17, 264, 265-276; Peace, "Sharps Buffalo Rifle," *Handbook of Texas, Vol. 5*, 996-997.

18. Mooar, *Buffalo Days*, 79.

19. Caravaglia and Worman, *Firearms of the American West*, 143-145.

20. Dixon, *"Billy" Dixon*, 33.

21. Mooar, *Buffalo Days*, 70-71.

22. Dixon, *"Billy" Dixon*, 81.

23. *Ibid*, 88-91.

24. *Ibid*, 13-14, 79-80.

25. *Ibid*, 92-93.

26. *Ibid*, 93-94.

27. *Ibid*, 95-96.

28. *Ibid*, 99-106.

29. *Ibid*, 106-109.

30. *Ibid*, 110.

Notes to Chapter 6

1. Dixon, *"Billy" Dixon*, 110.

2. *Ibid*, 110-111.

3. Dixon, "Billy" Dixon, 115-116. An excellent study of this expedition was compiled by Lowell H. Harrison, "Adobe Walls, Frontier Enterprise," *West Texas Historical Association Year Book*, 46 (1970), 14-24. The most meticulous study was made by T. Lindsay Baker and Billy R. Harrison, *Adobe Walls, The History and Archaeology of the 1874 Trading Post*.

4. Dixon, *"Billy" Dixon*, 132.

5. The measurements and other construction details of Adobe Walls which follow are contained in Baker and Harrison, *Adobe Walls*, in the chapter "Structures," 137-173.

6. Dixon, *"Billy" Dixon*, 137.

7. Baker and Harrison, *Adobe Walls*, 154-155.

8. Dixon, *"Billy" Dixon*, 135

9. *Ibid*, 135-137.

10. *Ibid*, 141.

11. *Ibid*, 141.

12. *Ibid*, 143.

13. *Ibid*, 143-145.

14. Dixon, *"Billy" Dixon*, 145-146; Baker and Harrison, *Adobe Walls*, 32-33.

15. Baker and Harrison, *Adobe Walls*, 33-35.

16. Mooar, *Buffalo Days*, 42-45.

17. *Ibid*, 48-49.

18. Dixon, *"Billy" Dixon*, 145-149.

19. *Ibid*, 149.

20. *Ibid*, 152-153.

21. *Ibid*, 154.

22. *Ibid*, 155.

Notes to Chapter 7

1. The most authoritative study is by Alvin Lynn, *Kit Carson and the First Battle of Adobe Walls: A Tale of Two Journeys* (Lubbock: Texas Tech University Press, 2014). Alvin hiked the entire route from Fort Bascom to Adobe Walls.

2. The most modest estimates of the war party indicate a force of 200 or 250 braves, an eight to one advantage. Billy Dixon, who saw the

entire force charge and who was accustomed to estimating numbers of buffaloes in the distance, reported 300 to 500 warriors. In an 1898 court deposition, Dixon stated that there were 450 to 500 warriors. (But when Olive's book was revised in 1927, fourteen years after Billy's death, she and the editor expanded the number to 700 up to 1,000.) James Langston, Andy Johnson, and other 1874 defenders estimated 400 to 600 attackers. Three young Comanche warriors, Yellow Fish, *Tim-bo*, and *Tahan*, were interviewed as old men by the *Amarillo Globe-News*. *Tahan* said there were 700 warriors, while the other two estimated 500. See Baker and Harrison, *Adobe Walls*, 69-70.

3. Mooar, *Buffalo Days*, 49.

4. The two best accounts of the Comanche decline and the Adobe Walls strike are T.R. Fehrenbach's insightful *Comanches, The Destruction of a People*, 521-539, and S.G. Gwynne's award-winning *Empire of the Summer Moon*, 258-278. Also see Haley, *The Buffalo War*; Richardson, *The Comanche Barrier*; Baker and Harrison, *Adobe Walls*.

5. Riddle, "Indian Survivors of Adobe Walls Visit Site 65 Years After Fight." *Amarillo Globe News*, April 28, 1939.

6. Dixon, *"Billy" Dixon*, 156.

7. Mooar, *Buffalo Days*, 50-51.

8. Dixon, *"Billy" Dixon*, 157.

9. *Ibid*, 158-159.

10. *Ibid*, 159.

11. *Ibid*, 160.

12. Sargent, "War Paint Off . . .," *Amarillo Globe-News*, n.d., 1939.

13. Dixon, *"Billy" Dixon*, 161-162, 166-167; Lyttle, "The Battle of Adobe Walls," *Pearson's Magazine*, 1907, 79.

14. Sargent, "War Paint Off . . . ," *Amarillo Globe-News*, n.d. 1939; Dixon, *"Billy" Dixon*, 161; Baker and Harrison, *Adobe Walls*, 65.

15. Dixon, *"Billy" Dixon*, 165.

16. Baker and Harrison, *Adobe Walls*, 53, 63.

17. Sargent, "War Paint Off . . . ," *Amarillo Globe-News*, n.d. 1939.

18. Dixon, *"Billy" Dixon*, 165-166.

19. Dixon, *"Billy" Dixon*, 178; DeArmant, *Bat Masterson*, 44.

20. Dixon, *"Billy" Dixon*, 165-166.

21. *Ibid*, 167-168.

22. *Ibid*, 169-170.

23. *Ibid*, 170.

24. Little, "The Battle of Adobe Walls," *Pearson's Magazine*, 80-81.

25. Dixon, *"Billy" Dixon*, 171-172, 183.

26. *Ibid*, 175-176.

27. *Ibid*, 167.

28. *Ibid*, 175.

29. *Ibid*, 177.

30. *Ibid*, 158-159.

31. *Ibid*, 178-179.

32. *Ibid*, 179.

33. Little, "The Battle of Adobe Walls," *Pearson's Magazine*, 81.

34. Little, "The Battle of Adobe Walls," *Pearson's Magazine*, 84; Dixon, "Billy" Dixon, 179-180.

35. Dixon, *"Billy" Dixon*, 180.

Notes to Chapter 8

1. Riddle, "Indian Survivors of Adobe Wall . . . ," *Amarillo Globe News*, April 28, 1939.

2. Baker and Harrison, *Adobe Walls*, 66.

3. Dixon, *"Billy" Dixon*, 170; Little, "The Battle of Adobe Walls," *Pearson's Magazine*, 81.

4. Dixon, *"Billy" Dixon*, 180-181.

5. *Ibid*, 121.

6. When preparing for the chapters on buffalo hunting and Adobe Walls, I examined buffalo guns in the Panhandle-Plains Museum in Canyon, Texas; the Scurry County Museum in Snyder; the NRA Museum in Springfield, Missouri; the Frontier Texas! displays in Abilene, Texas; the Hutchinson County Museum in Borger. I consulted books in my personal library: Walter, *The Guns That Won the West*; Garavaglia and Worman, *Firearms of the American West, 1866-1894*; Boorman, *Guns of the Old West*; Worman, *Gunsmoke and Saddle Leather*. Also see the article by Elmer Keith, "The 'Big Fifty' Sharps Rifle." *The American Rifleman*, June 1940.

7. There is a varied and highly useful collection of articles on the internet about Sharps rifles, Adobe Walls, Billy Dixon's shot, and related subjects. All are well-illustrated and many have video clips, most of a few minutes' duration. Google the subject Sharps Big Fifty Rifles to find: "Sharps Big 50 Buffalo Rifle - NRA Museums"; ".50-90 Sharps - Wikipedia"; "Sharps Rifle-Wikipedia"; "Big Fifty Sharps Rifle-The Wild West"; "Guns Stories: The Sharps Rifle";

"Sharps Big 50: The Gun That Changed the History of the West"; "The Big Fifty Sharps Rifle"; "National Firearms Museum Treasure Gun - Sharps Big 50 Buffalo Rifle"; "Adobe Walls - History of the Sharps Rifle"; "Adobe Walls"; "Adobe Walls, Texas." Google Billy Dixon's Famous Shot at Adobe Walls to find: "Billy Dixon's One Mile Shot - Rifle Shooter"; "Billy Dixon's Famous Shot at Adobe Walls"; "Re-creating the Billy Dixon Shot at Adobe Walls"; "Billy Dixon's Lucky Shot"; "Billy Dixon & Adobe Walls Long Range Shot"; "The Greatest Long-Range Shot Ever Made"; "The Shot that Changed a War: The Billy Dixon Story."

8. Dixon, *"Billy" Dixon*, 180-181; Baker and Harrison, *Adobe Walls*, 67-68, 315-316, note 62.

9. Thornton and Shirokawa, "A Trajectory Analysis of Billy Dixon's Long Shot," *Journal of Forensic Sciences*, Vol 34, No. 4, 1989, 1037-1041; Minita, "The Greatest Long-Range Shot Ever Made; "Billy Dixon & Adobe Walls Long Range Shot."

10. Dixon, *"Billy" Dixon*, 181-182.

11. *Ibid*, 182.

12. *Ibid*, 182-183.

13. DeArment, *Bat Masterson*, 46-48; Dixon, *"Billy" Dixon*, 188.

14. Dixon, , 188-189.

15. Billy Dixon described the trip to Dodge City, including the discovery of Charley Sharp's mutilated body. Dixon, *"Billy" Dixon*, 189-190.

16. Dixon, *"Billy" Dixon*, 190.

17. Dixon, *Ibid*, 190-191.

18. Dixon, *Ibid*, 190.

19. Dixon, *Ibid*, 193-194.

20. Baker and Harrison, *Adobe Walls*, 107.

21. *Ibid*, 107.

22. Dixon, *"Billy" Dixon*, 196-197.

Notes to Chapter 9

1. Dixon, *"Billy" Dixon*, 190.

2. *Ibid*, 191-192.

3. Miles, *Personal Recollections*, 163.

4. *Ibid*, 164.

5. Haley, *Buffalo War*, 128.

6. Dixon, *"Billy" Dixon*, 192.

7. DeArment, *Bat Masterson*, 50, 402 fn. The civilian scouts were David

Campbell, A.C. Coburn, J.G. Dewalt, Billy Dixon, J.C. Frederick, C.E. Jones, John Kirley, J.D. Leach, J.T. Marshall, A.J. Martin, Bat Masterson, Thompson McFadden, J.A. McGinty, C.B. Nichols, J.H. Plummer, W.F. Schmasle, David Shulz.

8. Informative overviews are available in Haley, *Buffalo War*, and Utley, *Frontier Regulars*, 225-241.

9. Dixon, *"Billy" Dixon*, 192-193.

10. *Ibid*, 196.

11. Miles, *Personal Recollections*, 167-168.

12. Miles, *Ibid*, 168.

13. Haley, *Buffalo War*, 153-157.

14. Dixon, *"Billy" Dixon*, 199-200.

15. *Ibid*, 200.

16. Dixon, *"Billy" Dixon*, 204; Miles to Adjutant General, U.S.A., Sept.24, 1874.

17. Dixon, *"Billy" Dixon*, 200-201.

18. *Ibid*, 201-202

19. *Ibid*, 203-204.

20. *Ibid*, 205-206.

21. *Ibid*, 206-207.

22. *Ibid*, 209-210.

23. *Ibid*, 211-212.

24. *Ibid*, 213.

25. *Ibid*, 214.

26. I obtained photocopies of the Medal of Honor Correspondence at the Panhandle-Plains Museum Library in Canyon, Texas. Much of this correspondence also is reproduced in Billy Dixon's book on pages 215-220.

27. O'Neal, *Fighting Men of the Indian Wars*, 20-35.

28. Townsend to Miles, November 6, 1874; Townsend to Dixon, November 19, 1874.

29. Miles to Dixon, December 24, 1874; Dixon, *"Billy" Dixon*, 218.

30. General Orders No. 28 from Miles, January 24, 1874.

31. Baldwin to Dixon, July 14, 1875; Baldwin to Dixon, September 27, 1875.

32. Dixon, *"Billy" Dixon*, 200.

33. Congressional Medal of Honor File of Civilian Scout William Dixon.

Notes to Chapter 10

1. Miles, *Personal Recollections*, 174.

2. Dixon, *"Billy" Dixon*, 196.

3. *Ibid*, 196-197.

4. *Ibid*, 174, 197-198.

5. Miles, *Personal Recollections*, 174-175.

6. Olive Dixon, "Rescue of Four German Sisters . . . ," *Fort Worth Star Telegram*, August 14, 1938.

7. Dixon, *"Billy" Dixon*, 233.

8. Baldwin, *Memoirs*, 74-75.

9. O'Neal, *Fighting Men of the Indian Wars*, 23.

10. Dixon, *"Billy" Dixon*, 233.

11. Baldwin, *Memoirs*, 76; Miles, *Personal Recollections*, 175-176; Dixon, *"Billy" Dixon*, 234.

12. Miles, *Personal Recollections*, 181.

13. Utley, *Frontier Regulars*, 234.

14. Baldwin to Dixon, September 27, 1875.

15. Miles, *Personal Recollections*, 179.

16. Weldon Walser, owner of the site of Fort Elliott, pointed out to me the location of the post ice house and the way it functioned.

17. Kyvig, "Fort Elliott," *Handbook of Texas, Vol. 2*, 1099-1100.

18. Baker, *Ghost Towns of Texas*, 96-99.

19. U.S. Census of 1880; Wheeler County, Texas.

20. DeArment, *Bat Masterson*, 55-66.

21. O'Neal, *Encyclopedia of Western Gunfighters*, 221.

22. Craine to Miles, January 11, 1875.

23. Kyvig, "Fort Elliott," *Handbook of Texas, Vol. 2*, 1099-1100.

24. Dixon, *"Billy" Dixon*, 191-192-233.

Notes to Chapter 11

1. Dixon, *"Billy" Dixon*, 241.

2. Anderson, "Quarter Circle T Ranch," *Handbook of Texas, Vol.5*, 382.

3. Anderson, "Scissors Ranch," *Handbook of Texas, Vol. 5*, 933.

4. Anderson, "Turkey Track Ranch," *Handbook of Texas, Vol. 5*, 382.

5. Anderson, "Coburn, James M.," *Handbook of Texas, Vol. 2*, 179-180.

6. Anderson, "Willingham, Caleb Berg [Cape]," *Handbook of Texas*, O'Neal, *Henry Brown*, 78-81, 83, n. 84.

7. *Dixon, "Billy" Dixon*, 214.

8. *Dixon, "Billy" Dixon*, 241-242; McCarty, *Adobe Walls Bride*, 178-179.

9. Dixon, *"Billy" Dixon*, 243.

10. *Ibid*, 64.

11. *Ibid*, 64.

12. Dixon, *"Billy" Dixon*, 64., 242; Hecht, *Postal History in the Panhandle*, 32.

13. McCarty, *Adobe Walls Bride*, 174.

Notes to Chapter 12

1. Dixon, Interview by McCarty, July 10, 1846.

2. McCarty, *Adobe Walls Bride*, 103-107.

3. *Ibid*, 109.

4. *Ibid*, 111.

5. Robertsons, *Cowman's Country*, 78-79.

6. McCarty, *Adobe Walls Bride*, 118-119.

7. Anderson, "Parnell, Texas," *Handbook of Texas, Vol. 5*, 68-69.

8. McCarty, *Adobe Walls Bride*, 120-122; Dixon, "Reminiscences of a Pioneer, "Typescript, 5-6.

9. Dixon, "Reminiscences of a Pioneer," Typescript, 3.

10. *Ibid*, 3.

11. *Ibid*, 5.

12. Dixon, *"Billy" Dixon*, 249.

13. *Ibid*, 249-250.

14. *Ibid*, 246.

15. *Ibid*, 247.

16. McCarty, *Adobe Walls Bride*, 136-37.

17. *Ibid*, 140-148.

18. *Ibid*, 150-152.

19. Dixon, "Reminiscences of a Pioneer," Typescript, 11.

20. The proposal conversation was related by Olive to John L. McCarty, *Adobe Walls Bride*, 153-154.

21. Dixon, *"Billy" Dixon*, 249.

22. McCarty, *Adobe Walls Bride*, 156.

23. Dixon, "Reminiscences of a Pioneer," Typescript, 5.

Notes to Chapter 13

1. McCarty, *Adobe Walls Bride*, 176-177.

2. *Ibid*, 177.

3. Dixon, "Reminiscences of a Pioneer," Typescript , 2.

4. *Ibid*, 2-3.

5. Dixon, "Pioneer Tells of Early Days in Hutchinson," *Hutchinson County Herald*, [1927].

6. Dixon, "Pioneer Churches," Typescript, 2.

7. McCarty, *Adobe Walls Bride*, 183-185.

8. *Ibid*, 181-182.

9. *Ibid*, 190.

10. Dixon, "Reminiscences of a Pioneer," Typescript, 12.

11. McCarty, *Adobe Walls Bride*, 201, 203.

12. Anderson, "Coburn, James M." *Handbook of Texas, Vol. 2*, 179-180.

13. William Dixon Deposition, Aug. 4, 1898, *Myers & Leonard vs. The United States*.

14. Anderson, "Hutchinson County," *Handbook of Texas, Vol. 3*, 805-806.

15. Dixon, *"Billy" Dixon*, 27; McCarty, *Adobe Walls Bride*, 205.

16. McCarty, *Adobe Walls Bride*, 204-205.

17. Anderson, "Plemons, Texas," *Handbook of Texas, Vol. 5*, 240.

18. Dixon, *"Billy" Dixon*, 248.

19. McCarty, *Adobe Walls Bride*, 206-207; Dixon, *"Billy" Dixon*, 248.

20. Tise, *Texas County Sheriffs*, 275; Dixon, *"Billy" Dixon*, 248.

21. McCarty, *Adobe Walls Bride*, 213.

22. *Ibid*, 206.

23. *Ibid*, 208.

24. Anderson, "Turkey Track Ranch," *Handbook of Texas, Vol. 6*, 591.

25. Dixon, *"Billy" Dixon*, 250.

26. McCarty, *Adobe Walls Bride*, 209; Dixon, "Adobe Walls," address, Jan.14, 1942.

27. McCarty, *Adobe Walls Bride*, 209.

28. *Ibid*, 210.

29. *Ibid*, 210-213.

30. Anderson, "Plemons, Texas," *Handbook of Texas, Vol.5*, 240; McCarty, *Adobe Walls Bride*, 217-219; Hecht, *Postal History in the Texas Panhandle*, 34.

31. McCarty, *Adobe Walls Bride*, 219; Anderson, "Plemons, Texas," *Handbook of Texas, Vol. 5*, 240

32. McCarty, *Adobe Walls Bride*, 219-220.

33. Masonic Lodge of Texas, file of William Dixon.

34. Graves, *Texas Rivers*, 17

35. McCarty, *Adobe Walls Bride*, 221-222.

36. *Ibid*, 222-223.

37. Olive Dixon, interview with McCarty, July 10, 1946.

38. McCarty, *Adobe Walls Bride*, 223.

39. Virginia Maynard, interview by O'Neal, September 7, 2018.

Notes to Chapter 14

1. McCarty, *Adobe Walls Bride*, 223-224.

2. Erickson, *Panhandle Cowboy*, 9; Dixon, "Reminiscences of a Pioneer," 13.

3. Dixon, *"Billy" Dixon*, viii.

4. *Ibid*, viii.

5. McCarty, *Adobe Walls Bride*, 229-230.

6. *Ibid*, 232.

7. *Ibid*, 233.

8. *Ibid*, 236-237.

9. Wilson, "Barde, Frederick Samuel," Oklahoma Historical Society.

10. McCarty, *Adobe Walls Bride*, 238-239.

11. *Ibid*, 237-238.

12. Dixon, Order for Hearing Petition for Letters of Petition, August 24, 1914; Order Appointing Administrator, August 24, 1914; County Judge M.W. Pugh to Olive Dixon, August 24, 1914; Administrator's or Executor's Bond, September 1, 1914.

13. Petition for Family Allowance, September 1, 1914; Order Fixing Family Allowance, September 1, 1914; General Inventory and Appraisement, Estate of William Dixon, September 1, 1914.

14. Petition to Sell Real Estate, March 5, 1915; Order for Hearing Petition to Sell Real Estate, March 6, 1915; County Judge M.W. Pugh to Olive Dixon, April 5, 1915; Dixon, Decree of Sale, April 5, 1915; Notice of Sale of Real Estate, April 7, 1915; Notice of Sale of Real Estate, April 12, 1915; Return of Sale of Real Estate, August 28, 1915; Order for Hearing Return of Sale, September 13, 1915; Notice of Hearing Return of Sale of Real Estate, September 15, 1915; Order Confirming Sale, October 5, 1915; Decree of Settlement of Final Account, March 15, 1918.

15. McCarty, *Adobe Walls Bride*, 239-241.

16. Anderson, "Miami, Texas." *Handbook of Texas,*

17. McCarty, *Adobe Walls Bride*, 240.

18. *Ibid*, 241, 243, 244.

19. *Ibid*, 241.

20. McCarty, *Adobe Walls Bride*, 242-243; O'Neal, *Fighting Men of the Indian Wars*, 167-170.

21. Johnson, *The Unregimented Generals.*

22. McCarty, *Adobe Walls Bride*, 242-243.

Notes to Chapter 15

1. Sonnichsen, *Ten Texas Feuds*, Foreword by Dale Waller, x and xii. During the 1980s I worked on three projects with Doc, and from him I heard a great deal about grassroots historians.

2. McCarty, *Adobe Walls Bride*, 247-248; Dixon, *"Billy" Dixon*, v-ix and xv-xvi.

3. Hill, The Panhandle-Plains Historical Society, 123-124.

4. Hill, The Panhandle-Plains Historical Society, 12, 123.

5. Hill, The Panhandle-Plains Historical Society, 17, 18; McCarty, *Adobe Walls Bride*, 250-251.

6. McCarty, *Adobe Walls Bride*, 251; Hill, The Panhandle-Plains Historical Society, 23; *Lubbock Morning Avalanche*, n.d., 1924, from an undated article in the *Paduch Post*.

7. *Lubbock Morning Avalanche*, n.d., 1924; Hill, The Panhandle-Plains Historical Society, 28-29; McCarty, *Adobe Walls Bride*, 252-253.

8. "Monument is Unveiled at Battleground," *Canyon News*, November 17, 1927; Dixon, "'Stand Silent! Heroes Here Have Been', Two Scouts, Four Troopers Immortalized at Buffalo Wallow," *Amarillo Sunday News-Globe*, August 14, 1938; McCarty, *Adobe Walls Bride*, 254-256; Hill, The Panhandle-Plains Historical Society, 29-30.

9. Dixon, "'Stand Silent!" Heroes Here Have Been," *Amarillo Sunday News-Globe*, August 14, 1938.

10. Hill, The Panhandle-Plains Historical Society, 9.

11. "Adobe Walls Ceremony Plans June 27 Completed," *Miami Chief*, June 13, 1929; McCarty, *Adobe Walls Bride*, 252-254.

12. *Ibid*, 256-258.

13. *Ibid*, 249, 257.

14. See Carlson, *Amarillo*, the first comprehensive history of the city.

15. Newspaper clipping scrapbook of Olive Dixon articles, compiled by

Edna Dixon Irwin, and shared with the author by Olive's granddaughter, Olive Virginia Irwin Maynard.

16. Hill, *The Panhandle-Plains Historical Society and Its Museum*, 66, 68. Today the greatly expanded museum boasts more than three million artifacts.

17. Dixon, "Adobe Walls," January 14, 1942, and Dixon, "Thanksgiving on the Panhandle Plains, 1893," January 14, 1942. Dixon, undated transcripts: "Pioneer Churches" and "Reminiscences of a Pioneer." On July 10, 1946, Panhandle journalist and author John L. McCarty interviewed Olive (who was his colleague at the *Amarillo Globe-News*): "Interview with Mrs. Olive King Dixon at our home, July 10, 1946." All of these typescripts are on file at the Panhandle-Plains Historical Museum Library. Olive's taped interview about "Adobe Walls Battle" was copied onto a DVD by the Hutchinson County Museum in Borger.

18. Dixon, "Reminiscences of a Pioneer," Typescript, 14-15.

19. McCarty, *Adobe Walls Bride*, 244-245.

20. *Ibid*, 241, 244.

21. Interview by the author with Virginia Irwin Maynard, September 7, 2018.

22. Polk Street United Methodist Church, Amarillo, membership records.

23. Berry, "Scout's Wife," *Amarillo Sunday News-Globe*, Golden Anniversary Edition, August 14, 1938.

24. McCarty, *Adobe Walls Bride*, second printing, 1956.

25. Berry, "Scout's Wife," *Amarillo Sunday News-Globe*, Golden Anniversary Edition, August 14, 1938.

26. Interview by the author with Virginia Irwin Maynard, September 7, 2018.

27. "Tribute to a Lady," *Amarillo Daily News*, n.d., 1956.

28. Dixon, *"Billy" Dixon*, 251.

29. Dixon, "Reminiscences of a Pioneer," 15.

Bibliography

Government Records and Correspondence

Baldwin, Lt. Frank D., to William Dixon. Fort Leavenworth, Kansas. September 27, 1875.

Congressional Medal of Honor File of Civilian Scout William Dixon. National Archives Catalog, 1805-1889. U.S. National Archives & Records Administration.

Dixon, William. Oklahoma, Wills and Probate Records, 1801-2008. Ancestry.com, 61 pages of estate documents.

Foster, L.L. Commissioner. Forgotten Texas Census: First Annual Report of the Agricultural Bureau of the Department of Agriculture, Insurance, Statistics, and History, 1887-88.

Austin: State Printing Office, 1889. Reprint by Texas State Historical Association, Austin, 2001.

Heitman, Frances B., comp. Historical Register and Dictionary of the United States Army. 2 volumes. Washington, D.C.: Government Printing Office, 1903.

Hutchinson County, Texas, Survey Files. Field Notes of Survey made for William Dixon. File B, 2. Filed: July 12, 1904.

Miles, Nelson A., Bvt. Genl., to Adjutant General USA, September 24, 1874. Townsend, E.D. U.S. Consul, to Gen. N.A. Miles, Fort Leavenworth, Kansas, March 1, 1875.

Townsend, E.D., Adjutant General War Department, to Scout William Dixon,   November 19, 1874.

Townsend, E.D. Adjutant General, War Department, to the Commanding General Military Division of the Missouri, St. Louis, Mo., 1874.

Miles, Bvt. Maj. Genl N.A. General Orders No. 28, Headquarters Indt. Terry Expedition, Camp near Fort Sill, I.T., September 24, 1875.

Wheeler County, Texas: Marriage Book I and 1880 Census of Wheeler County. Amarillo: TapRoots Research and Publications, n.d.

Woodall, Z.T. to Billy Dixon. Fort Wingate, N.M., January 4, 1889.

Books

Atlas of Texas Surface Waters: Maps of the Classified Segments of Texas Rivers and Coastal Bays. Texas Commission on Environmental Quality, 2004.

Baker, T. Lindsay, and Billy R. Harrison. *Adobe Walls: The History and Archaeology of the 1874 Trading Post*. College Station: Texas A&M University Press, 1986.

Baldwin, Alice Blackwood. Memoirs of the Late Frank D. Baldwin, Major General, U.S.A. Los Angeles: Wetzel Publishing Co., 1929.

Billington, Ray Allen. *Westward Expansion, A History of the American Frontier*, Second Edition. New York: The Macmillan Company, 1960.

Billy Dixon and Adobe Walls. Dixon, Billy. *Life and Adventures of "Billy" Dixon: Scout, Plainsman & Buffalo Hunter*. Little, Edward Campbell. The Battle of Adobe Walls (*Pearson's Magazine*). Leonaur, 2010.

Branch, Douglas. *The Hunting of the Buffalo*. Lincoln: University of Nebraska Press, 1962.

Capps, Benjamin. *The Indians*. New York: Time-Life Books, 1973.

Carlson, Paul H. *Amarillo, The Story of a Western Town*. Lubbock: Texas Tech University Press, 2006.

Carlson, Paul H. *The Buffalo Soldier Tragedy of 1877*. College Station: Texas A&M University Press, 2003.

Carlson, Paul H., and Bruce A. Glasrud *West Texas, A History of the Giant Side of the State*. Norman: University of Oklahoma Press, 2007.

Collins, Robert. *Jim Lane: Scoundrel, Statesman, Kansan*. Gretna: Pelican Publishing Company, 2007.

Dictionary of American History, Revised Edition. New York: Charles Scribner's Sons.

Dixon, Olive K. *Life of "Billy" Dixon: Plainsman, Scout and Pioneer*. Birmingham, Alabama: The Frontier Classics Library, 2012.

Fehrenbach, T.R. *Comanches, The Destruction of a People*. New York: Alfred A. Knopf, 1974.

Gard, Wayne. *The Great Buffalo Hunt*. New York: Alfred A. Knopf, 1959.

Gilbert, Miles, Leo Remiger, and Sharon Cunningham, compilers. *Encyclopedia of Buffalo Hunters and Skinners*, Vol. 1, A-D. Union City, Tenn: Pioneer Press, 2003.

Haley, James L. *The Buffalo War*. Garden City, NY: Doubleday & Company, Inc., 1976.

Hart, Herbert M. *Old Forts of the Southwest*. Seattle: Superior Publishing Company, 1964.

Hecht, Arthur, comp. *Postal History in the Texas Panhandle*. Canyon, Texas: Panhandle-Plains Historical Society 1960.

Hide Town In The Texas Panhandle, 100 Years In Wheeler County and Panhandle of Texas. Dallas:Taylor Publishing Company, 1985.

Hill, Joseph A. *The Panhandle-Plains Historical Society and Its Museums.* Canyon, Texas: West Texas State College Press, 1955.

History of Hutchinson County, Texas: 104 Years, 1876-1980. Hutchinson County Historical Commission, 1980.

Johnson, Virginia Weisel. *The Unregimented General: A Biography of Nelson A. Miles.* Boston: Houghton Mifflin Company, 1962.

Lynn, Alvin R. *Kit Carson and the First Battle of Adobe Walls, A Tale of Two Journeys.* Lubbock: Texas Tech University Press, 2014.

McCarty, John L. *Adobe Walls Bride, The Story of Billy and Olive King Dixon.* San Antonio: The Naylor Company, 1955.

Miles, Nelson A. *Personal Recollections and Observations of General Nelson A. Miles.* Chicago: The Warner Company. 1897.

Mooar, J. Wright, as told to James Winford Hunt. *Buffalo Days, Stories from J. Wright Mooar.* Abilene, Texas: State House Press, 2005.

Nevin, David. *The Expressmen. New York*: Time-Life Books, 1974.

Porter, Millie Jones. *Memory Cups of Panhandle Pioneers.* Clarendon, Texas: Clarendon Press, 1945.

Presenting the Texas Panhandle. Canyon, Texas: Lan-Bea Publications, 1979.

Rathjen, Frederick W. *The Texas Panhandle Frontier.* Austin: University of Texas Press, 1973.

Robertson, Pauline Durrett, and R. L. Robertson. *Cowman's County, Fifty Frontier Ranches in the Texas Panhandle, 1876-1887.* Amarillo: Paramount Publishing Company, 1981.

Robertson, Pauline Durrett, and R.L. Robertson. *Panhandle Pilgrimage.* Canyon, Texas: Staked Plains Press, Inc. 1976.

Robertson, Willie, and William Doyle. *American Hunter: How Legendary Hunters Shaped America.* New York: Simon & Schuster, 2015.

Robinson, Charles M., III. *The Buffalo Hunters.* Austin, Texas: State House Press, 1985.

Robinson, Charles M., III. *Satanta: The Life and Death of a War Chief.* Austin: State House Press, 1997.

Sandoz, Mari. *The Buffalo Hunters, The Story of the Hide Men.* Lincoln: University of Nebraska Press, 1978 (first edition, 1954).

Smith, Victor Grant, edited by Jeanette Prodgers. *The Champion Buffalo Hunter: The Frontier Memoirs of Yellowstone Vic Smith.* Helena, Montana: Globe Pequot Press, 1977.

Tise, Sammy. *Texas County Sheriffs.* Albuquerque, NM: Oakwood Printing, 1989. p. 275.

Utley, Robert M. *Frontier Regulars, The United States Army and the Indian, 1866-1891*. New York: Macmillan Publishing Co., Inc., 1973.

Williams, J.W. *The Big Ranch Country*. Wichita Falls, Texas: Terry Brothers, Printers, 1954.

Williamson, Carl, and Jan Williamson. *Caprock Country, Last Frontier of Texas*. Amarillo: Whitney Russell Printers, 2014.

Yost, Nellie Snyder. *Medicine Lodge: The Story of a Kansas Frontier Town*. Chicago: The Swallow Press, Inc., 1970.

Periodical Articles

Anderson, H. Allen. "Coburn, James M." *Handbook of Texas, Vol. 2*, 179-180.
------- "Miami, Texas." *Handbook of Texas, Vol. 4*, 702-703.
------ "Mobeetie, Texas." *Handbook of Texas, Vol. 4*, 784-785.
------ "Parnell, Texas." *Handbook of Texas, Vol. 5*, 68-69
------ "Plemons, Texas." *Handbook of Texas, Vol. 5*, 240.
------ "Quarter Circle T Ranch." *Handbook of Texas, Vol. 5*, 382.
------ "Scissors Ranch," *Handbook of Texas, Vol. 5*, 933.
------ "Turkey Track Ranch." *Handbook of Texas, Vol. 6*, 591.
------ "Willingham, Caleb Berg." *Handbook of Texas, Vol. 6*, 996-997

"Beginning of the Buffalo Slaughter." Printed article, undated. Louise Mooar Papers, Box #2, File #9.

"Billy Dixon," *Open Road for Boys and Girls*, April 1937.

"Billy Dixon, the Hero of - The Panhandle's 'Alamo', Mason, Buffalo Hunter, Indian Fighter, Scout." *Texas Grand Lodge Magazine*, November 1934, 20-25.

Dixon, Olive King. "Frontier Rescue." *Ranch Romances*. N.d., 127-130.

Dixon, Olive King. "Pioneer Woman," *Ranch Romances*. December 1938.

Flenniken, Donna. "Billy Dixon and His Lost Medal of Honor," *Accent West*. March 1990, 16-20.

Graves, Russell A. "Trouble on the High Plains." *Accent West*, n.d., 32-35, 42.

Harrison, Lowell H. "Adobe Walls, Frontier Enterprise." *West Texas Historical Association Year Book*. Vol. XLVI, 1970, 14-24.

Hunter, J. Marvin. "The Battle of Adobe Walls."

Jeter, Garrett C. "Andrew Lewis." *The West Virginia Encyclopedia*. December 7, 2015.

Knox, Bill. "The Miracle of the Ridgepole." *Southwest Heritage*. Vol. 1. No. 2, Spring 1967.

Kyvig, David E. "Fort Elliott." *Handbook of Texas*, Vol. 2, 1099-1100.

Parmelee, Deolece M. "Hamner, Laura Vernon." *Handbook of Texas*, Vol. 3, 436.

Parsons, Chuck. "Buffalo Hunters on Lincoln County Warriors?" *The Prairie Scout*. Abilene, Kansas: The Kansas Corral of the Westerners, Inc., 1985.

Peace, W.S. "Sharps Buffalo Rifle." *Handbook of Texas*, Vol. 5, 996-997.

Potts, Marisue. "Adobe Walls Revisited, An Evolving Point of View." *Motley County Tribune*. June 30, 2011.

Roberts, Cleon. "The Afterlife of Adobe Walls." *West Texas Historical Association Year Book*, Vol. 80, 2004, 137-158.

Schreier, Philip. "The Hunting Rifle in America." *American Hunter*, May 2018. 44-50.

Thornton, J.I., and J.M. Shirokawa. "A Trajectory Analysis of Billy Dixon's Long Shot." Journal of Forensic Sciences, Vol. 34, No. 4, 1989, 1037-1041.

Vigness, David M. "Buffalo Hunting." *Handbook of Texas*, Vol. 1, 814.

Newspaper Articles

"Adobe Walls Celebration on Thursday: Re-Burial of Colonel Billy Dixon to Be Feature of Historic Event." *Amarillo Daily News*, June 16, 1929.

"Adobe Walls Ceremony Plans June 27 Completed." *The Miami Chief*, June 13, 1929.

"Adobe Walls Heroes To Be Honored By Monument." *The Lubbock Morning Avalanche*, n.d.

"Battle of 'Dobe Walls, Five-Day Fight With Comanche Band, Thrilling Remembrance of John Clinton, Abilene's Pioneer Police Chief. *Fort Worth Star-Telegram*, September 24, 1916.

Berry, Mrs. C. B. "Scout's Wife." *Amarillo Sunday News-Globe*, Golden Anniversary Edition. August 14, 1938.

"Billy Dixon Remains to be Buried near Scene of Battle." *Amarillo Daily News*, May 6, 1929.

"Billy Dixon Rites to Feature Adobe Walls Celebration." *Amarillo Globe*, June 27, 1929.

"Body of Uncle Billy Dixon Rests At Scene Of Battle That Made Him Texas Hero." N.p. [1961]. Southwest Collection.

"Celebration commemorates famous fight." *Amarillo Daily News*. January 26, 1986.

"Col. Billy Dixon Gets Last Wish: Buried at Site at Adobe Walls." *Amarillo Daily News*, June 28, 1928.

"Death Comes Suddenly to Olive Dixon," *Amarillo Globe*, March 8, 1956.

"Dedication At Adobe Walls Site, Pageant Slated." N.p., [1941]. Southwest Collection.

Dixon, Olive K. "Indians Visit Adobe Walls Battle Site." N.p. [1941]. Southwest Collection.

Dixon, Olive, Obituary. *Amarillo Globe-News*. n.d. [1956].

Dixon, Olive. Photo and caption of award to Mrs. Dixon at Oldtimers Luncheon on March 8, 1947. *Borger News-Herald*, March 16, 1947.

Dixon, Olive K. "Kidnaping of Four German Sisters Led to Brilliant Charge of Baldwin." *Amarillo Sunday News-Globe Centennial Edition*, August 14, 1938.

Dixon, Olive K. "Pioneer Tells of Early Days in Hutchinson." *The Hutchinson County Herald*, Borger, n.d.

Dixon, Olive King. "Rescue of Four German Sisters Was Rom[ ] Incident Miles Expedition Against Plains Indians in 1874 and 1875. *Fort Worth Sunday Star Telegram*, March 16, 1936.

Dixon, Olive K. "'Stand Silent! Heroes Here Have Been." *Amarillo Sunday News-Globe Centennial Edition*, August 14, 1938.

"Gala Ceremonies At Borger Today." N.p., [1941]. Southwest Collection.

Golden Anniversary Edition, 1938. *Amarillo Sunday News-Globe*, August 14, 1938. 264 pp.

Hough, Thomas. "Monument Is Tribute to Bravery Of 28 Men Who Beat Off Band Of 700 Indians." N.p., n.d. Southwest Collection.

"The Indians Are Coming." N.p., [1941]. Southwest Collection.

"Indians Arrive At 'Dobe Walls.'" N.p. [1941]. Southwest Collection.

Keith, Elmer. "The Big Fifty' Sharps Rifle." *The American Rifleman*, June 1940.

Lawrence, Fred. "Widow Of Indian Scout Tells Of Famous Battle." Haley Memorial Library, JEH II, B. Dixon, Olive.

Montgomery, Harry. "Billy Dixon's Medal to Museum; Story of Battle is Recalled." *Amarillo Globe Sunday News*, March 19, 1932.

"Mrs. Dixon's Book Is Accepted On Kansas State Reading List." N.p., n.d. On file at Amarillo Public Library Downtown.

"Mrs. Olive Dixon Services Set Tuesday," *Amarillo Globe*. March 19, 1956.

"Pioneer Bride Creates Home on Rugged Prairie," *Amarillo Sunday News*, October 2, 1955.

"Pioneer's Widow Dies; Husband Fought Indians." *Amarillo Globe-News*. N.d. [1956].

"The Recent Re-burial in Texas of 'Billy' Dixon Recalls the Indian Fight at 'Dobe Walls." *Kansas City Star*, July 7, 1929.

"Remove Body of Col. Billy Dixon from Texline: Remains of Famed Indian Fighter to be Reburied at Adobe Walls Today." *Amarillo Daily News*, June 27, 1929.

Riddle, Roy. "Indian Survivors of Adobe Walls Visit Site 65 Years After Fight." *Amarillo Globe News*, April 28, 1939.

Sargent, Joe. "War-Paint Off, Comanches Return to Scene of Second Battle of Adobe Walls." N.p., [1941], Southwest Collection.

"Story of Adobe Walls Told By Man Who Claims Is Only Living Survivor of The Battle." N.p. [1941]. Southwest Collection.

"'Tough Indian' of 1874, 'Tahan' Spreads Gospel Now But Danced to Dixon's Lead." N.p., June 30, 1941. Southwest Collection.

"Wife of Adobe Walls Hero Pays Visit to Spot Where Great Battle Was Fought." N.p. [1941]. Southwest Collection.

"Tribute to a Lady." *Amarillo Daily News*. n.d. [1956].

Interviews and Private Papers

Dixon, Olive King. "Adobe Walls." Paper presented by Mrs. Dixon for Dr. Sheffy's History Class at West Texas State Teachers College in Canyon, Texas, January 14, 1942.

Dixon, Olive King, "Reminiscences of a Pioneer." Interview by Wilda Taylor, Amarillo, on July 6, 10,11, 1938.

Dixon, Olive King. "Thanksgiving on the Panhandle Plains 1893." Paper read by Mrs. Dixon to Dr. Sheffy's history class at West Texas State Teachers College in Canyon, January 14, 1942.

[McCarty, John L.] Interview with Mrs. Olive Kng Dixon at our home, July 10, 1946.

Maynard, Olive Virginia Irwin. Interview by Bill O'Neal in Amarillo, September 7, 2018.

Mooar, John Wesley. Papers, 1871 - 1917 and undated. Financial Documents, Bills and Receipts. File, Southwest Collection.

Mooar, John Wesley, Papers, 1871-1917, Correspondence, Notes, etc. 1871-1875. File, Southwest Collection.

Mooar, Louise. "The Mooar Brothers and Adobe Walls," Typescript, 74 pp., Marietta, Georgia.

Louise Mooar Papers. 1876-1971. File, Southwest Collection. Box #2, File #6.

Mooar, Lydia Louise. Papers, 1876-1971 and undated Financial and Legal Documents, 1885-1906. File, Southwest Collection.

Mooar, Margaret McCollum (Mrs. John W.). Papers, 1870-1920. File, Southwest Collection.

Genealogical Records

Dixon, Archie King. Find A Grave.

Dixon, Olive K. 1910 United States Federal Census. Ancestry.com.

Dixon, Olive K. 1940 United States Federal Census. Ancestry.com.

Dixon, Olive K., in the Potter County, Texas, Probate Index, 1901-2013. Ancestry.com.

Dixon, Olive King. Find A Grave.

Dixon, Olive King. Texas Death Certificates, 1903-1982. Ancestry.com.

Dixon, William "Billy." Find A Grave.

Dixon, William "Billy." Wiki Article. Ancestry.com.

Dixon, William R., 1850-1913. Ancestry.com.

Dixon, William R. (senior), 1820-1880. Ancestry.com.

Irwin, Edna "Mimi" Dixon. Find A Grave.

King, John Archie, 1868-1945. Find A Grave.

King, Olive D., 1873-1956. Ancestry.com.

Privett, Nancy, 1820-unknown. Ancestry.com

Ragan, Olive Virginia Dixon. Find A Grave.

Recordings

Hutchinson County Historical Museum. Clash of Cultures, Remembering Adobe Walls, The Battle of 1874. DVD. 1941 Film.

Olive Dixon, interview by KHUZ Radio in 1947. CD, Hutchinson County Museum.

Miscellaneous

Amarillo Public Library Downtown, Reference Files:
    Biography: Dixon, Billy
    Biography: Dixon Family
    Biography: Dixon, Mrs. Olive King

Crain, Newford, U.S. Consul to Gen. N.A. Miles, Fort Leavenworth, Kansas. March 1, 1875.

Dixon, Olive King. "Death Takes One of the Four Sisters Held by Indians." Galleys for *Amarillo Globe*, June 6, 1949.

Dixon, Olive King. "Quanah Parker - Fearless and Effective Foe, He Spared Women and Children Always." *History of Armstrong County*, Vol. 1.

McCarty, John L. Box: Manuscript, Adobe Walls Bride. Panhandle-Plains Museum Research Center.

Sargent, Joe. "War Paint Off, Comanches Return to Scene of Second Battle of Adobe Walls." N.p. [1941].

The Second Battle of Adobe Walls, Pamphlet. Hutchinson County Historical Museum.

"Semi-Centennial of the Battle of Adobe Walls." *Chronicles of Oklahoma*, Vol. 2, No. 4, December 1924, pp. 402-404.

Wilson, Linda D. "Barde, Frederick Samuel." *The Encyclopedia of Oklahoma History and Culture*. www.okhistory.org.

Index

Author Bio

Bill O'Neal recently concluded six years of service (2012-2018) as State Historian of Texas, traveling tens of thousands of miles across the Lone Star State as an ambassador for Texas history. He is a past president and fellow of both the West Texas Historical Association and the East Texas Historical Association.

Bill is the author of more than forty books, as well as 300 articles and book reviews. His most recent writing award, the A.C. Greene Literary Award, was presented at the 2015 West Texas Book Festival in Abilene. In 2012 Bill received the Lifetime Achievement Award of the Wild West Historical Association, and in 2007 he was named *True West Magazine's* Best Living Non-Fiction Writer.

Bill has appeared on TV documentaries on TBS, The History Channel, The Learning Channel, CMT, A&E, and the American Heroes Channel Series, *Gunslingers*. During a long career at Panola College in Carthage, Texas, his most prestigious teaching award was a Piper Professorship, presented in 2000.

In 2013 Panola's new dormitory was named Bill O'Neal Hall, and in that same year he received an honorary Doctor of Letters degree from his alma mater, Texas A&M University-Commerce. Bill's four daughters all have entered the field of education, and he is the proud grandfather of seven grandchildren.

www.ingramcontent.com/pod-product-compliance
Lightning Source LLC
Chambersburg PA
CBHW060043100426

42742CB00014B/2687